ELEMENTS OF BOTANY
FOR BEGINNERS AND FOR
SCHOOLS
BY ASA GRAY

PREFACE.

This volume takes the place of the author's LESSONS IN BOTANY AND VEGETABLE PHYSIOLOGY, published over a quarter of a century ago. It is constructed on the same lines, and is a kind of new and much revised edition of that successful work. While in some respects more extended, it is also more concise and terse than its predecessor. This should the better fit it for its purpose now that competent teachers are common. They may in many cases develop paragraphs into lectures, and fully illustrate points which are barely, but it is hoped clearly, stated. Indeed, even for those without a teacher, it may be that a condensed is better than a diffuse exposition.

The book is adapted to the higher schools, "How Plants Grow and Behave" being the "Botany for Young People and Common Schools." It is intended to ground beginners in Structural Botany and the principles of vegetable life, mainly as concerns Flowering or Phanerogamous plants, with which botanical instruction should always begin; also to be a companion and interpreter to the Manuals and Floras by which the student threads his flowery way to a clear knowledge of the surrounding vegetable creation. Such a book, like a grammar, must needs abound in technical words, which thus arrayed may seem formidable; nevertheless, if rightly apprehended, this treatise should teach that the study of botany is not the learning of names and terms, but the acquisition of knowledge and ideas. No effort should be made to commit technical terms to memory. Any term used in describing a plant or explaining its structure can be looked up when it is wanted, and that should suffice. On the other hand, plans of [Pg iv]structure, types, adaptations, and modifications, once understood, are not readily forgotten; and they give meaning and interest to the technical terms used in explaining them.

In these "Elements" naturally no mention has been made of certain terms and names which recent cryptogamically-minded botanists, with lack of proportion and just perspective, are endeavoring to introduce into phanerogamous botany, and which are not needed nor appropriate, even in more advanced works, for the adequate recognition of the ascertained analogies and homologies.

As this volume will be the grammar and dictionary to more than one or two Manuals, Floras, etc., the particular directions for procedure which were given in the "First Lessons" are now relegated to those works themselves, which in their new editions will provide the requisite explanations. On the other hand, in view of such extended use, the Glossary at the end of this book has been considerably enlarged. It will be found to include not merely the common terms of botanical description but also many which are unusual or obsolete; yet any of them may now and then be encountered. Moreover, no small number of the Latin and Greek words which form the whole or part of the commoner specific names are added to this Glossary, some in an Anglicized, others in their Latin form. This may be helpful to students with small Latin and less Greek, in catching the meaning of a botanical name or term.

The illustrations in this volume are largely increased in number. They are mostly from the hand of Isaac Sprague.

It happens that the title chosen for this book is that of the author's earliest publication, in the year 1836, of which copies are rarely seen; so that no inconvenience is likely to arise from the present use of the name.

ASA   GRAY.

CAMBRIDGE,   MASSACHUSETTS,
March, 1887.

ELEMENTS OF BOTANY.

SECTION I. INTRODUCTORY.

1. BOTANY is the name of the science of the vegetable kingdom in general; that is, of plants.

2. Plants may be studied as to their kinds and relationships. This study is SYSTEMATIC BOTANY. An enumeration of the kinds of vegetables, as far as known, classified according to their various degrees of resemblance or difference, constitutes a general *System of plants*. A similar account of the vegetables of any particular country or district is called a *Flora*.

3. Plants may be studied as to their structure and parts. This is STRUCTURAL BOTANY, or ORGANOGRAPHY. The study of the organs or parts of plants in regard to the different forms and different uses which the same kind of organ may assume,—the comparison, for instance, of a flower-leaf or a bud-scale with a common leaf,—is VEGETABLE MORPHOLOGY, or MORPHOLOGICAL BOTANY. The study of the minute structure of the parts, to learn by the microscope what they themselves are formed of, is VEGETABLE ANATOMY, or HISTOLOGY; in other words, it is Microscopical Structural Botany. The study of the actions of plants or of their parts, of the ways in which a plant lives, grows, and acts, is the province of PHYSIOLOGICAL BOTANY, or VEGETABLE PHYSIOLOGY.

4. This book is to teach the outlines of Structural Botany and of the simpler parts of the physiology of plants, that it may be known how plants are constructed and adapted to their surroundings, and how they live, move, propagate, and have their being in an existence no less real, although more simple, than that of the animal creation which they support. Particularly, this book is to teach the principles of the structure and relationships of plants, the nature and names of their parts and their modifications, and so to prepare for the study of Systematic Botany; in which the learner may ascertain the name and the place in the system of any or all of the ordinary plants within reach, whether wild or cultivated. And in ascertaining the name of any plant, the student, if rightly taught, will come to know all about its general or particular structure, rank, and relationship to other plants.

[Pg 10]

5. The vegetable kingdom is so vast and various, and the difference is so wide between ordinary trees, shrubs, and herbs on the one hand, and mosses, moulds, and such like on the other, that it is hardly possible to frame an intelligible account of plants as a whole without contradictions or misstatements, or endless and troublesome qualifications. If we say that plants come from seeds, bear flowers, and have roots, stems, and leaves, this is not true of the lower orders. It is best for the beginner, therefore, to treat of the higher orders of plants by themselves, without particular reference to the lower.

6. Let it be understood, accordingly, that there is a higher and a lower series of plants; namely:—

PHANEROGAMOUS PLANTS, which come from seed and bear *flowers*, essentially stamens and pistils, through the co-operation of which seed is produced. For shortness, these are commonly called PHANEROGAMS, or *Phænogams*, or by the equivalent English name of FLOWERING PLANTS.[1]

CRYPTOGAMOUS PLANTS, or CRYPTOGAMS, come from minute bodies, which answer to seeds, but are of much simpler structure, and such plants have not stamens and pistils. Therefore they are called in English FLOWERLESS PLANTS. Such are Ferns, Mosses, Algæ or Seaweeds, Fungi, etc. These sorts have each to be studied separately, for each class or order has a plan of its own.

7. But Phanerogamous, or Flowering, Plants are all constructed on one plan, or *type*. That is, taking almost any ordinary herb, shrub, or tree for a pattern, it will exemplify the whole series: the parts of one plant answer to the parts of any other, with only certain differences in particulars. And the occupation and the delight of the scientific botanist is in tracing out this common plan, in detecting the likenesses under all the diversities, and in noting the meaning of these manifold diversities. So the attentive study of any one plant, from its growth out of the seed to the flowering and fruiting state and the production of seed like to that from which the plant grew, would not only give a correct general idea of the structure, growth, and characteristics of Flowering Plants in general, but also serve as a pattern or standard of comparison. Some plants will serve this purpose of a pattern much better than others. A proper pattern will be one that is perfect in the sense of having all the principal parts of a phanerogamous plant, and simple and regular in having these parts free from complications or disguises. The common Flax-plant may very well serve this purpose. Being an annual, it has the advantage of being easily raised and carried in a short time through its circle of existence, from seedling to fruit and seed.

FOOTNOTES:

[1]The name is sometimes *Phanerogamous*, sometimes *Phænogamous* (*Phanerogams*, or *Phænogams*), terms of the same meaning etymologically; the former of preferable form, but the latter shorter. The meaning of such terms is explained in the Glossary.

[Pg 11]

SECTION II. FLAX AS A PATTERN PLANT.

8. **Growth from the Seed.** Phanerogamous plants grow from seed, and their flowers are destined to the production of seeds. A seed has a rudimentary plant ready formed in it,— sometimes with the two most essential parts, i. e. stem and leaf, plainly discernible; sometimes with no obvious distinction of organs until germination begins. This incipient plant is called an EMBRYO.

9. In this section the Flax-plant is taken as a specimen, or type, and the development and history of common plants in general is illustrated by it. In flax-seed the embryo nearly fills the coats, but not quite. There is a small deposit of nourishment between the seed-coat and the embryo: this may for the present be left out of the account. This embryo consists of a pair of leaves, pressed together face to face, and attached to an extremely short stem. (Fig. 2-4.) In this rudimentary condition the real nature of the parts is not at once apparent; but when the seed grows they promptly reveal their character,—as the accompanying figures (Fig. 5-7) show.

2

FIG. 1. Pod of Flax. 2. Section lengthwise, showing two of the seeds; one whole, the other cut half away, bringing contained embryo into view. 3. Similar section of a flax-seed more magnified and divided flatwise; turned round, so that the stem-end (caulicle) of the embryo is below: the whole broad upper part is the inner face of one of the cotyledons; the minute nick at its base is the plumule. 4. Similar section through a seed turned edgewise, showing the thickness of the cotyledons, and the minute plumule between them, i. e. the minute bud on the upper end of the caulicle.

10. Before the nature of these parts in the seed was altogether understood, technical names were given to them, which are still in use. These initial leaves were named COTYLEDONS. The initial stem on which they stand was called the RADICLE. That was because it gives rise to the first root; but, as it is really the beginning of the stem, and because it is the stem that produces the root and not the root that produces the stem, it is better to name it the CAULICLE. Recently it has been named *Hypocotyle*; which signifies something below the cotyledons, without pronouncing what its nature is.

[Pg 12]

FIG. 5. Early Flax seedling; stem (caulicle), root at lower end, expanded seed-leaves (cotyledons) at the other: minute bud (plumule) between these. 6. Same later; the bud developed into second pair of leaves, with hardly any stem-part below them; then into a third pair of leaves, raised on a short joint of stem; and a fifth leaf also showing. 7. Same still older, with more leaves developed, but these singly (one after another), and with joints of stem between them.

11. On committing these seeds to moist and warm soil they soon sprout, i. e. *germinate*. The very short stem-part of the embryo is the first to grow. It lengthens, protrudes its root-end; this turns downward, if not already pointing in that direction, and while it is lengthening a root forms at its point and grows downward into the ground. This root continues to grow on from its lower end, and thus insinuates itself and penetrates into the soil. The stem meanwhile is adding to its length throughout; it erects itself, and, seeking the light, brings the seed up out of the ground. The materials for this growth have been supplied by the cotyledons or seed-leaves, still in the seed: it was the store of nourishing material they held which gave them their thickish shape, so unlike that of ordinary leaves. Now, relieved of a part of this store of food, which has formed the growth by which they have been raised into the air and light, they appropriate the remainder to their own growth. In enlarging they open and throw off the seed-husk; they expand, diverge into a horizontal position, turn green, and thus become a pair of evident leaves, the first foliage of a tiny plant. This seedling, although diminutive and most simple, possesses and puts into use, all the ORGANS of VEGETATION, namely, root, stem, and leaves, each in its proper element,—the root in the soil, the stem rising out of it, the leaves in the light and open air. It now draws in moisture and some food-materials from the soil by its root, conveys this through the stem into the leaves, where these materials, along with other crude food which these imbibe from the air, are assimilated into vegetable matter, i. e. into the material for further growth.

12. **Further Growth** soon proceeds to the formation of new parts,—downward in the production of more root, or of branches of the main root, upward in the development of more stem and leaves. That from which a stem with its leaves is continued, or a new stem (i. e. branch) originated, is a BUD. The most conspicuous and familiar buds are those of most shrubs and trees, bearing buds formed in summer or autumn, to grow the following [Pg 13]spring. But every such point for new growth may equally bear the name. When there is such a bud between the cotyledons in the seed or seedling it is called the PLUMULE. This is conspicuous enough in a bean (Fig. 29.), where the young leaf of the new growth looks like a little plume, whence the name, *plumule*. In flax-seed this is very minute indeed, but is discernible with a magnifier, and in the seedling it shows itself distinctly (Fig. 5, 6, 7).

13. As it grows it shapes itself into a second pair of leaves, which of course rests on a second joint of stem, although in this instance that remains too short to be well seen. Upon its summit appears the third pair of leaves, soon to be raised upon its proper joint of stem; the next leaf is single, and is carried up still further upon its supporting joint of stem; and so on. The root, meanwhile, continues to grow underground, not joint after joint, but continuously, from its lower end; and commonly it before long multiplies itself by branches, which lengthen by the same continuous growth. But stems are built up by a succession of leaf-bearing growths, such as are strongly marked in a reed or corn-stalk, and less so in such an herb as Flax. The word "joint" is ambiguous: it may mean either the portion between successive leaves, or their junction, where the leaves are attached. For precision, therefore, the place where the leaf or leaves are borne is called a NODE, and the naked interval between two nodes, an INTERNODE.

3

FIG. 8. Upper part of Flax-plant in blossom.

14. In this way a simple stem with its garniture of leaves is developed from the seed. But besides this direct continuation, buds may form and develop into lateral stems, that is, *into branches*, from any node. The proper origin of branches is from the AXIL of a leaf, i. e. the angle between leaf and stem on the upper side; and branches may again branch, so building up the herb, shrub, or tree. But sooner or later, and without long delay in an annual like Flax, instead of this continuance of mere vegetation, reproduction is prepared for by

[Pg 14]

15. **Blossoming.** In Flax the flowers make their appearance at the end of the stem and branches. The growth, which otherwise might continue them farther or indefinitely, now takes the form of blossom, and is subservient to the production of seed.

FIG. 9. Flax-flowers about natural size. 10. Section of a flower moderately enlarged, showing a part of the petals and stamens, all five styles, and a section of ovary with two ovules or rudimentary seeds.

16. **The Flower** of Flax consists, first, of five small green leaves, crowded into a circle: this is the CALYX, or flower-cup. When its separate leaves are referred to they are called SEPALS, a name which distinguishes them from foliage-leaves on the one hand, and from petals on the other. Then come five delicate and *colored* leaves (in the Flax, blue), which form the COROLLA, and its leaves are PETALS; then a circle of organs, in which all likeness to leaves is lost, consisting of slender stalks with a knob at summit, the STAMENS; and lastly, in the centre, the rounded body, which becomes a pod, surmounted by five slender or stalk-like bodies. This, all together, is the PISTIL. The lower part of it, which is to contain the seeds, is the OVARY; the slender organs surmounting this are STYLES; the knob borne on the apex of each style is a STIGMA. Going back to the stamens, these are of two parts, viz. the stalk, called FILAMENT, and the body it bears, the ANTHER. Anthers are filled with POLLEN, a powdery substance made up of minute grains.

17. The pollen shed from the anthers when they open falls upon or is conveyed to the stigmas; then the pollen-grains set up a kind of growth (to be discerned only by aid of a good microscope), which penetrates the style: this growth takes the form of a thread more delicate than the finest spider's web, and reaches the bodies which are to become seeds (OVULES they are called until this change occurs); these, touched by this influence, are incited to a new growth within, which becomes an embryo. So, as the ovary ripens into the seed-pod or capsule (Fig. 1, etc.) containing seeds, each seed enclosing a rudimentary new plantlet, the round of this vegetable existence is completed.

[Pg 15]

SECTION III. MORPHOLOGY OF SEEDLINGS.

18. Having obtained a general idea of the growth and parts of a phanerogamous plant from the common Flax of the field, the seeds and seedlings of other familiar plants may be taken up, and their variations from the assumed pattern examined.

19. **Germinating Maples** are excellent to begin with, the parts being so much larger than in Flax that a common magnifying glass, although convenient, is hardly necessary. The only disadvantage is that fresh seeds are not readily to be had at all seasons.

FIG. 11. Embryo of Sugar Maple, cut through lengthwise and taken out of the seed. 12, 13. Whole embryo of same just beginning to grow; *a*, the stemlet or caulicle, which in 13 has considerably lengthened.

20. The seeds of Sugar Maple ripen at the end of summer, and germinate in early spring. The embryo fills the whole seed, in which it is nicely packed; and the nature of the parts is obvious even before growth begins. There is a stemlet (caulicle) and a pair of long and narrow seed-leaves (cotyledons), doubled up and coiled, green even in the seed, and in germination at once unfolding into the first pair of foliage-leaves, though of shape quite unlike those that follow.

21. Red Maple seeds are ripe and ready to germinate at the beginning of summer, and are therefore more convenient for study. The cotyledons are crumpled in the seed, and not easy to straighten out until they unfold themselves in germination. The story of their development into the seedling is told by the accompanying Fig. 14-20; and that of Sugar Maple is closely similar. No plumule or bud appears in the embryo of these two Maples until the seed-leaves have nearly attained their full growth and are acting as foliage-leaves, and until a root is formed below. There is no great store of nourishment in these thin cotyledons; so further growth has to wait until the root and seed-leaves have collected and elaborated sufficient material for the formation of the

4

second internode and its pair of leaves, which lending their help the third pair is more promptly produced, and so on.

22. Some change in the plan comes with the Silver or Soft White Maple. (Fig. 21-25). This blossoms in earliest spring, and it drops its large and ripened keys only a few weeks later. Its cotyledons have not at all the appearance of leaves; they are short and broad, and (as there is no room to be saved by folding) they are straight, except a small fold at the top,—a vestige of the habit of Maples in general. Their unusual thickness is due [Pg 16]to the large store of nutritive matter they contain, and this prevents their developing into actual leaves. Correspondingly, their caulicle does not lengthen to elevate them above the surface of the soil; the growth below the cotyledons is nearly all of root. It is the little plumule or bud between them which makes the upward growth, and which, being well fed by the cotyledons, rapidly develops the next pair of leaves and raises them upon a long internode, and so on. The cotyledons all the while remain below, in the husk of the fruit and seed, and perish when they have yielded up the store of food which they contained.

FIG. 14. One of the pair of keys or winged fruits of Red Maple; the seed-bearing portion cut open to show the seed. 15. Seed enlarged, and divided to show the crumpled embryo which fills it. 16. Embryo taken out and partly opened. 17. Embryo which has unfolded in early stage of germination and begun to grow. 18. Seedling with next joint of stem and leaves apparent; and 19 with these parts full-grown, and bud at apex for further growth. 20. Seedling with another joint of stem and pair of leaves.

23. So, even in plants so much alike as Maples, there is considerable difference in the amount of food stored up in the cotyledons by which the growth is to be made; and there are corresponding differences in the germination. [Pg 17]The larger the supply to draw upon, the stronger the growth, and the quicker the formation of root below and of stem and leaves above. This deposit of food thickens the cotyledons, and renders them less and less leaf-like in proportion to its amount.

FIG. 21. Fruit (one key) of Silver Maple, Acer dasycarpum, of natural size, the seed-bearing portion divided to show the seed. 22. Embryo of the seed taken out. 23. Same opened out, to show the thick cotyledons and the little plumule or bud between them. 24. Germination of Silver Maple, natural size; merely the base of the fruit, containing the seed, is shown. 25. Embryo of same, taken out of the husk; upper part of growing stem cut off, for want of room.

24. **Examples of Embryos with thickened Cotyledons.** In the Pumpkin and Squash (Fig. 26, 27), the cotyledons are well supplied with nourishing matter, as their sweet taste demonstrates. Still, they are flat and not very thick. In germination this store is promptly utilized in the development of the caulicle to twenty or thirty times its length in the seed, and to corresponding thickness, in the formation of a cluster of roots at its lower end, and the early production of the incipient plumule; also in their own growth into efficient green leaves. The case of our common Bean (Phaseolus vulgaris, Fig. 28-30) is nearly the same, except that the cotyledons are much more gorged; so that, although carried up into the air and light upon the lengthening caulicle, and there acquiring a green color, they never expand into useful leaves. Instead of this, they nourish into rapid growth the plumule, which is plainly visible in the seed, as a pair of incipient leaves; and these form the first actual foliage.

25. Very similar is the germination of the Beech (Fig. 31-33), except that the caulicle lengthens less, hardly raising the cotyledons out of the ground. Nothing would be gained by elevating them, as they never grow out into efficient leaves; but the joint of stem belonging to the plumule lengthens well, carrying up its pair of real foliage-leaves.

26. It is nearly the same in the Bean of the Old World (Vicia Faba, here called Horse Bean and Windsor Bean): the caulicle lengthens very little, does not undertake to elevate the heavy seed, which is left below or [Pg 18]upon the surface of the soil, the flat but thick cotyledons remaining in it, and supplying food for the growth of the root below and the plumule above. In its near relative, the Pea (Fig. 34, 35), this use of cotyledons for storage only is most completely carried out. For they are thickened to the utmost, even into hemispheres; the caulicle does not lengthen at all; merely sends out roots from the lower end, and develops its strong plumule from the upper, the seed remaining unmoved underground. That is, in technical language, the germination is *hypogæous*.

FIG. 26. Embryo of Pumpkin-seed, partly opened. 27. Young seedling of same.

FIG. 28. Embryo of Common Bean (Phaseolus vulgaris): caulicle bent down over edge of cotyledons. 29. Same germinating: caulicle well lengthened and root beginning; thick cotyledons partly spreading; and plumule (pair of leaves) growing between them. 30. Same, older, with plumule developed into internode and pair of leaves.

27. There is sufficient nourishment in the cotyledons of a pea to make a very considerable growth before any actual foliage is required. So it is the stem-portion of the plumule which is at first conspicuous and strong-growing. Here, as seen in Fig. 35, its lower nodes bear each a useless leaf-scale instead of an efficient leaf, and only the later ones bear leaves fitted for foliage.

[Pg 19]

FIG. 31. A Beech-nut, cut across. 32. Beginning germination of the Beech, showing the plumule growing before the cotyledons have opened or the root has scarcely formed. 33. The same, a little later, with the plumule-leaves developing, and elevated on a long internode.

FIG. 34. Embryo of Pea, i. e. a pea with the coats removed; the short and thick caulicle presented to view. 35. Same in advanced germination: the plumule has developed four or five internodes, bearing single leaves; but the first and second leaves are mere scales, the third begins to serve as foliage; the next more so.

28. This *hypogæous* germination is exemplified on a larger scale by the Oak (Fig. 36, 37) and Horse-chestnut (Fig. 38, 39); but in these the downward growth is wholly a stout tap-root. It is not the caulicle; for this lengthens hardly any. Indeed, the earliest growth which carries the very short caulicle out of the shell comes from the formation of foot-stalks to the cotyledons; above these develops the strong plumule, below grows the stout root. The growth is at first entirely, for a long time [Pg 20]mainly, at the expense of the great store of food in the cotyledons. These, after serving their purpose, decay and fall away.

FIG. 36. Half of an acorn, cut lengthwise, filled by the very thick cotyledons, the base of which encloses the minute caulicle. 37. Oak-seedling.

FIG. 38. Half of a horse-chestnut, similarly cut; the caulicle is curved down on the side of one of the thick cotyledons. 39. Horse-chestnut in germination; foot-stalks are formed to the cotyledons, pushing out in their lengthening the growing parts.

29. Such thick cotyledons never separate; indeed, they sometimes grow together by some part of their contiguous faces; so that the germination seems to proceed from a solid bulb-like mass. This is the case in a horse-chestnut.

30. **Germinating Embryo supplied by its own Store of Nourishment**, i. e. the store in the cotyledons. This is so in all the illustrations thus far, essentially so even in the Flax. This nourishment was supplied by the mother plant to the ovule and seed, and thence taken into the embryo during its growth. Such embryos, filling the whole seed, are comparatively large and strong, and vigorous in germination in proportion to the amount of their growth while connected with the parent plant.

31. **Germinating Embryo supplied from a Deposit outside of Itself.** This is as common as the other mode; and it occurs in all degrees. [Pg 21]Some seeds have very little of this deposit, but a comparatively large embryo, with its parts more or less developed and recognizable. In others this deposit forms the main bulk of the seed, and the embryo is small or minute, and comparatively rudimentary. The following illustrations exemplify these various grades. When an embryo in a seed is thus surrounded by a white substance, it was natural to liken the latter to the white of an egg, and the embryo or germ to the yolk. So the matter around or by the side of the embryo was called the *Albumen*, i. e. the white of the seed. The analogy is not very good; and to avoid ambiguity some botanists call it the ENDOSPERM. As that means in English merely the inwards of a seed, the new name is little better than the old one; and, since we do not change names in botany except when it cannot be avoided, this name of *albumen* is generally kept up. A seed with such a deposit is *albuminous*, one with none is *exalbuminous*.

32. The ALBUMEN forms the main bulk of the seed in wheat, maize, rice, buckwheat, and the like. It is the floury part of the seed. Also of the cocoa-nut, of coffee (where it is dense and hard), etc.; while in peas, beans, almonds, and in most edible nuts, the store of food, although essentially the same in nature and in use, is in the embryo itself, and therefore is not counted as anything to be separately named. In both forms this concentrated food for the germinating plant is food also for man and for animals.

FIG. 40. Seed of Morning Glory divided, moderately magnified; shows a longitudinal section through the centre of the embryo as it lies crumpled in the albumen. 41. Embryo taken out whole and unfolded; the broad and very thin cotyledons notched at summit; the caulicle below. 42. Early state of germination. 43. Same, more advanced; caulicle or primary stem, cotyledons or seed-leaves, and below, the root, well developed.

6

33. For an albuminous seed with a well-developed embryo, the common Morning Glory (Ipomœa purpurea, Fig. 40-43) is a convenient example, being easy and prompt to grow, and having all the parts well apparent. The seeds (duly soaked for examination) and the germination should be compared with those of Sugar and Red Maple (19-21). The only essential difference is that here the embryo is surrounded by and crumpled up in the albumen. This substance, which is pulpy or mucilaginous in fresh and young seeds, hardens as the seed ripens, but becomes again pulpy in germination; and, as it liquefies, the thin cotyledons absorb it by their [Pg 22]whole surface. It supplements the nutritive matter contained in the embryo. Both together form no large store, but sufficient for establishing the seedling, with tiny root, stem, and pair of leaves for initiating its independent growth; which in due time proceeds as in Fig. 44, 45.

FIG. 44. Seedling of Morning Glory more advanced (root cut away); cotyledons well developed into foliage-leaves: succeeding internode and leaf well developed, and the next forming. 45. Seedling more advanced; reduced to much below natural size.

34. Smaller embryos, less developed in the seed, are more dependent upon the extraneous supply of food. The figures 46-53 illustrate four grades in this respect. The smallest, that of the Peony, is still large enough to be seen with a hand magnifying glass, and even its cotyledons may be discerned by the aid of a simple stage microscope.

35. The broad cotyledons of Mirabilis, or Four-o'clock (Fig. 52, 53), with the slender caulicle almost encircle and enclose the floury albumen, instead of being enclosed in it, as in the other illustrations. Evidently here the germinating embryo is principally fed by one of the leaf-like cotyledons, the other being out of contact with the supply. In the embryo of Abronia (Fig. 54, 55), a near relative of Mirabilis, there is a singular modification; one cotyledon is almost wanting, being reduced to a rudiment, leaving it for the other to do the work. This leads to the question of the

36. **Number of Cotyledons.** In all the preceding illustrations, the embryo, however different in shape and degree of development, is evidently [Pg 23]constructed upon one and the same plan, namely, that of two leaves on a caulicle or initial stem,—a plan which is obvious even when one cotyledon becomes very much smaller than the other, as in the rare instance of Abronia (Fig. 54, 55). In other words, the embryos so far examined are all

37. **Dicotyledonous**, that is, two-cotyledoned. Plants which are thus similar in the plan of the embryo agree likewise in the general structure of their stems, leaves, and blossoms; and thus form a class, named from their embryo DICOTYLEDONES, or in English, DICOTYLEDONOUS PLANTS. So long a name being inconvenient, it may be shortened into DICOTYLS.

FIG. 46. Section of a seed of a Peony, showing a very small embryo in the albumen, near one end. 47. This embryo detached, and more magnified.

FIG. 48. Section of a seed of Barberry, showing the straight embryo in the middle of the albumen. 49. Its embryo detached.

FIG. 50. Section of a Potato seed, showing the embryo coiled in the albumen. 51. Its embryo detached.

FIG. 52. Section of the seed of Mirabilis or Four-o'clock, showing the embryo coiled round the outside of the albumen. 53. Embryo detached; showing the very broad and leaf-like cotyledons, applied face to face, and the pair incurved.

FIG. 54. Embryo of Abronia umbellata; one of the cotyledons very small. 55. Same straightened out.

38. **Polycotyledonous** is a name employed for the less usual case in which there are more than two cotyledons. The Pine is the most familiar case. This occurs in all Pines, the number of cotyledons varying from three to twelve; in Fig. 56, 57 they are six. Note that they are all on the same level, that is, belong to the same node, so as to form a circle or *whorl* at the summit of the caulicle. When there are only three cotyledons, they divide the space equally, are one third of the circle apart. When only two they are 180° apart, that is, *opposite*.

39. The case of three or more cotyledons, which is constant in Pines and in some of their relatives (but not in all of them), is occasional among Dicotyls. And the polycotyledonous is only a variation of the dicotyledonous type,—a difference in the number of leaves in the whorl; for a pair is a whorl reduced to two members. Some suppose that there are really only [Pg 24]two cotyledons even in a Pine embryo, but these divided or split up congenitally so as to imitate a greater number. But as leaves are often in whorls on ordinary stems, they may be so at the very beginning.

FIG. 56. Section of a Pine-seed, showing its polycotyledonous embryo in the centre of the albumen, moderately magnified. 57. Seedling of same, showing the freshly expanded six cotyledons in a whorl, and the plumule just appearing.

40. **Monocotyledonous** (meaning with single cotyledon) is the name of the one-cotyledoned sort of embryo. This goes along with peculiarities in stem, leaves, and flowers, which all together associate such plants into a great class, called MONOCOTYLEDONOUS PLANTS, or, for shortness, MONOCOTYLS. It means merely that the leaves are alternate from the very first.

41. In Iris (Fig. 58, 59) the embryo in the seed is a small cylinder at one end of the mass of the albumen, with no apparent distinction of parts. The end which almost touches the seed coat is caulicle, the other end belongs to the solitary cotyledon. In germination the whole lengthens (but mainly the cotyledon) only enough to push the proximate end fairly out of the seed; from this end the root is formed, and from a little higher the plumule later emerges. It would appear therefore that the cotyledon answers to a minute leaf rolled up, and that a chink through which the plumule grows out is a part of the inrolled edges. The embryo of Indian Corn shows these parts on a larger scale and in a more open state (Fig. 66-68). There, in the seed, the cotyledon remains, imbibing nourishment from the softened albumen, and transmitting it to the growing root below and new-forming leaves above.

FIG. 58. Section of a seed of the Iris, or Flower-de-Luce, enlarged, showing its small embryo in the albumen, near the bottom. 59. A germinating seedling of the same, its plumule developed into the first four leaves (alternate), the first one rudimentary, the cotyledon remains in the seed.

FIG. 60. Section of an Onion seed showing the slender and coiled embryo in the albumen, moderately magnified. 61. Seed of same in early germination.

FIG. 62. Germinating Onion, more advanced, the chink at base of cotyledon opening for the protrusion of the plumule, consisting of a thread-shaped leaf. 63. Section of base of Fig. 62, showing plumule enclosed. 64. Section of same later, plumule emerging. 65. Later stage of 62, upper part cut off. 66. A grain of Indian Corn, flatwise, cut away a little, so as to show the embryo, lying on the albumen which makes the principal bulk of the seed. 67. A grain cut through the middle in the opposite direction, dividing the embryo through its thick cotyledon and its plumule, the latter consisting of two leaves, one enclosing the other. 68. The embryo taken out whole; the thick mass is the cotyledon, the narrow body partly enclosed by it is the plumule, the little projection at its base is the very short radicle enclosed in the sheathing base of the first leaf of the plumule.

FIG. 69. Grain of Indian Corn in germination, the ascending sprout is the first leaf of the plumule, enclosing the younger leaves within, at its base the primary root has broken through. 70. The same, advanced; the second and third leaves developing, while the sheathing first leaf does not further develop.

42. The general plan is the same in the Onion (Fig. 60-65), but with a striking difference. The embryo is long, and coiled in the albumen of the seed. To ordinary examination it shows no distinction of parts. But germination plainly shows that all except the lower end of it is cotyledon. For after it has lengthened into a long thread, the chink from which the [Pg 25]plumule in time emerges is seen at the base, or near it, so the caulicle is extremely short, and does not elongate, but sends out from its base a simple root, and afterwards others in a cluster. Not only does the cotyledon lengthen enormously in the seedling, but (unlike that of Iris, Indian Corn, and all [Pg 26]the cereal grains) it raises the comparatively light seed into the air, the tip still remaining in the seed and feeding upon the albumen. When this food is exhausted and the seedling is well established in the soil, the upper end decays and the emptied husk of the seed falls away.

43. In Maize or Indian Corn (Fig. 66-70), the embryo is more developed in the seed, and its parts can be made out. It lies against the starchy albumen, but is not enclosed therein. The larger part of it is the cotyledon, thickish, its edges involute, and its back in contact with the albumen; partly enclosed by it is the well-developed plumule or bud which is to grow. For the cotyledon remains in the seed to fulfil its office of imbibing nourishment from the softened albumen, which it conveys to the growing sprout; the part of this sprout which is visible is the first leaf of the plumule rolled up into a sheath and enclosing the rudiments of the succeeding leaves, at the base enclosing even the minute caulicle. In germination the first leaf of the plumule develops only as a sort of sheath, protecting the tender parts within; the second and the third form the first foliage. The caulicle never lengthens: the first root, which is formed at its lower end, or from any part of it, has to break through the enclosing sheath; and succeeding roots soon spring from all or any of the nodes of the plumule.

8

44. **Simple-stemmed Plants** are thus built up, by the continuous production of one leaf-bearing portion of stem from the summit of the preceding one, beginning with the initial stem (or caulicle) in the embryo. Some Dicotyls and many Monocotyls develop only in this single line of growth (as to parts above ground) until the flowering state is approached. For some examples, see Cycas (Fig. 71, front, at the left); a tall Yucca or Spanish Bayonet, and two Cocoa-nut Palms behind; at the right, a group of Sugar-canes, and a Banana behind.

FIG. 71. Simple-stemmed vegetation.

[Pg 27]

SECTION IV. GROWTH FROM BUDS: BRANCHING.

45. Most plants increase the amount of their vegetation by branching, that is, by producing lateral shoots.

46. Roots branch from any part and usually without definite order. Stems normally give rise to branches only at definite points, namely, at the nodes, and there only from the axils of leaves.

47. **Buds** (Fig. 72, 73). Every incipient shoot is a *Bud* (12). A stem continues its growth by its *terminal bud*; it branches by the formation and development of *lateral buds*. As normal lateral buds occupy the axils of leaves, they are called *axillary buds*. As leaves are symmetrically arranged on the stem, the buds in their axils and the branches into which axillary buds grow partake of this symmetry. The most conspicuous buds are the scaly winter-buds of most shrubs and trees of temperate and cold climates; but the name belongs as well to the forming shoot or branch of any herb.

FIG. 72. Shoot of Horse-chestnut, of one year's growth, taken in autumn after the leaves have fallen; showing the large terminal bud and smaller axillary buds.

FIG. 73. Similar shoot of Shagbark Hickory, Carya alba.

48. **The Terminal Bud**, in the most general sense, may be said to exist in the embryo,—as cotyledons, or the cotyledons and plumule,—and to crown each successive growth of the simple stem so long as the summit is capable of growth. The whole ascending growth of the Palm, Cycas, and the like (such as in Fig.71) is from a terminal bud. Branches, being repetitions of the main stem and growing in the same way, are also lengthened by terminal buds. Those of Horse-chestnut, Hickory, Maples, and such trees, being the resting buds of winter, are conspicuous by their protective covering of scales. These bud-scales, as will hereafter be shown, are themselves a kind of leaves.

49. **Axillary Buds** were formed on these annual shoots early in the summer. Occasionally they grow the same season into branches; at least, some of them are pretty sure to do so whenever the growing terminal bud at the end of the shoot is injured or destroyed. Otherwise they may lie dormant until the following spring. In many trees or shrubs these axillary buds do not show themselves until spring; but if searched for, they may be detected, though of small size, hidden under the bark. Sometimes, although early [Pg 28]formed, they are concealed all summer long under the base of the leaf-stalk, which is then hollowed out into a sort of inverted cup, like a candle-extinguisher, to cover them; as in the Locust, the Yellow-wood, or more strikingly in the Button-wood or Plane-tree (Fig. 74).

FIG. 74. An axillary bud, concealed under the hollowed base of the leaf-stalk, in Buttonwood or Plane-tree.

50. The *leaf-scars*, so conspicuous in Fig. 72, 73, under each axillary bud, mark the place where the stalk of the subtending leaf was attached until it fell in autumn.

51. **Scaly Buds**, which are well represented in Fig. 72, 73, commonly belong to trees and shrubs of countries in which growth is suspended during winter. The scaly coverings protect the tender young parts beneath, not so much by keeping out the cold, which of course would penetrate the bud in time, as by shielding the interior from the effects of sudden changes. There are all gradations between these and

52. **Naked Buds**, in which these scales are inconspicuous or wanting, as in most herbs, at least above ground, and most tropical trees and shrubs. But nearly related plants of the same climate may differ widely in this respect. Rhododendrons have strong and scaly winter-buds; while in Kalmia they are naked. One species of Viburnum, the Hobble-bush, has completely naked buds, what would be a pair of scales developing into the first leaves in spring; while another (the Snowball) has conspicuous scaly buds.

53. **Vigor of Vegetation from strong buds.** Large and strong buds, like those of the Horse-chestnut, Hickory, and the like, contain several leaves, or pairs of leaves, ready formed,

9

folded and packed away in small compass, just as the seed-leaves of a strong embryo are packed away in the seed: they may even contain all the blossoms of the ensuing season, plainly visible as small buds. And the stems upon which these buds rest are filled with abundant nourishment, which was deposited the summer before in the [Pg 29]wood or in the bark. Under the surface of the soil, or on it covered with the fallen leaves of autumn, similar strong buds of our perennial herbs may be found; while beneath are thick roots, rootstocks, or tubers, charged with a great store of nourishment for their use. This explains how it is that vegetation from such buds shoots forth so vigorously in the spring of the year, and clothes the bare and lately frozen surface of the soil, as well as the naked boughs of trees, very promptly with a covering of fresh green, and often with brilliant blossoms. Everything was prepared, and even formed, beforehand: the short joints of stem in the bud have only to lengthen, and to separate the leaves from each other so that they may unfold and grow. Only a small part of the vegetation of the season comes directly from the seed, and none of the earliest vernal vegetation. This is all from buds which have lived through the winter.

54. **The Arrangement of Branches**, being that of axillary buds, answers to that of the leaves. Now leaves principally are either *opposite* or *alternate*. Leaves are *opposite* when there are two from the same joint of stem, as in Maples (Fig. 20), the two being on opposite sides of the stem; and so the axillary buds and branches are opposite, as in Fig. 75. Leaves are *alternate* when there is only one from each joint of stem, as in the Oak, Lime-tree, Poplar, Button-wood (Fig. 74), Morning-Glory (Fig. 45,—not counting the seed-leaves, which of course are opposite, there being a pair of them); also in Indian Corn (Fig. 70), and Iris (Fig. 59). Consequently the axillary buds are also alternate, as in Hickory (Fig. 73); and the branches they form alternate,—making a different kind of spray from the other mode, one branch shooting on one side of the stem and the next on some other. For in the alternate arrangement no leaf is on the same side of the stem as the one next above or next below it.

55. But the symmetry of branches (unlike that of the leaves) is rarely complete. This is due to several causes, and most commonly to the

56. **Non-development of buds.** It never happens that all the buds grow. If they did, there might be as many branches in any year as there were leaves the year before. And of those which do begin to grow, a large portion perish, sooner or later, for want of nourishment, or for want of light, or because those which first begin to grow have an advantage, which they are apt to keep, taking to themselves the nourishment of the stem, and starving the weaker buds. In the Horse-chestnut (Fig. 72), Hickory (Fig. 73), Magnolia, and most other trees with large scaly buds, the terminal bud is the strongest, and has the advantage in growth; and next in strength are the upper axillary buds: while the former continues the shoot of the last year, some of the latter give rise to branches, and the rest fail to grow. In the Lilac also (Fig. 75), the uppermost axillary buds are stronger than the lower; but the terminal bud rarely appears at all; in its place the uppermost pair of axillary buds grow, and so each stem branches every year into two,—making a repeatedly two-forked ramification, as in Fig. 76.

[Pg 30]

FIG. 75. Shoot of Lilac, with winter buds; the two uppermost axillary ones strong; the terminal not developed. 76. Forking ramification of Lilac; reduced in size.

57. **Latent Buds.** Axillary buds that do not grow at the proper season, and especially those which make no appearance externally, may long remain latent, and at length upon a favorable occasion start into growth, so forming branches apparently out of place as they are out of time. The new shoots seen springing directly out of large stems may sometimes originate from such latent buds, which have preserved their life for years. But commonly these arise from

58. **Adventitious Buds.** These are buds which certain shrubs and trees produce anywhere on the surface of the wood, especially where it has been injured. They give rise to the slender twigs which often feather the sides of great branches of our American Elms. They sometimes form on the root, which naturally is destitute of buds; they are even found upon some leaves; and they are sure to appear on the trunks and roots of Willows, Poplars, and Chestnuts, when these are wounded or mutilated. Indeed Osier-Willows are *pollarded*, or cut off, from time to time, by the cultivator, for the purpose of producing a crop of slender adventitious twigs, suitable for basket-work. Such branches, being altogether irregular, of course interfere with the natural symmetry of the tree. Another cause of irregularity, in certain trees and shrubs, is the formation of what are called

FIG. 77. Tartarean Honeysuckle, with three accessory buds in each axil.

59. **Accessory or Supernumerary Buds.** There are cases where two, three, or more buds spring from the axil of a leaf, instead of the single one which is ordinarily found there. Sometimes

10

they are placed one over the other, as in the Aristolochia or Pipe-Vine, and in the Tartarean Honeysuckle (Fig. 77); also in the Honey-Locust, and in the Walnut and Butternut (Fig. 78), where [Pg 31]the upper supernumerary bud is a good way out of the axil and above the others. And this is here stronger than the others, and grows into a branch which is considerably out of the axil, while the lower and smaller ones commonly do not grow at all. In other cases three buds stand side by side in the axil, as in the Hawthorn, and the Red Maple (Fig. 79.) If these were all to grow into branches, they would stifle each other. But some of them are commonly flower-buds: in the Red Maple, only the middle one is a leaf-bud, and it does not grow until after those on each side of it have expanded the blossoms they contain.

FIG. 78. Butternut branch, with accessory buds, the uppermost above the axil.

FIG. 79. Red-Maple branch, with accessory buds placed side by side. The annular lines toward the base in this and in Fig. 72 are scars of the bud-scales, and indicate the place of the winter-bud of the preceding year.

60. **Sorts of Buds.** It may be useful to enumerate the kinds of buds which have been described or mentioned. They are

Terminal, when they occupy the summit of (or terminate) a stem,

Lateral, when they are borne on the side of a stem; of which the regular kind is the

Axillary, situated in the axil of a leaf. These are

Accessory or *Supernumerary*, when they are in addition to the normal solitary bud; and these are *Collateral*, when side by side; *Superposed*, when one above another;

Extra-axillary, when they appear above the axil, as some do when superposed, and as occasionally is the case when single.

Naked buds, those which have no protecting scales.

Scaly buds, those which have protecting scales, which are altered leaves or bases of leaves.

Leaf-buds, contain or give rise to leaves, and develop into a leafy shoot.

Flower-buds, contain or consist of blossoms, and no leaves.

Mixed buds, contain both leaves and blossoms.

61. **Definite annual Growth** from winter buds is marked in most of the shoots from strong buds, such as those of the Horse-chestnut and Hickory (Fig. 72, 73). Such a bud generally contains, already formed in miniature, all or a great part of the leaves and joints of stem it is to produce, makes its whole growth in length in the course of a few weeks, or sometimes even in a few days, and then forms and ripens its buds for the next year's similar growth.

62. **Indefinite annual Growth**, on the other hand, is well marked in such trees or shrubs as the Honey-Locust, Sumac, and in sterile shoots of [Pg 32]the Rose, Blackberry, and Raspberry. That is, these shoots are apt to grow all summer long, until stopped by the frosts of autumn or some other cause. Consequently they form and ripen no terminal bud protected by scales, and the upper axillary buds are produced so late in the season that they have no time to mature, nor has their wood time to solidify and ripen. Such stems therefore commonly die back from the top in winter, or at least all their upper buds are small and feeble; so the growth of the succeeding year takes place mainly from the lower axillary buds, which are more mature.

63. **Deliquescent and Excurrent Growth.** In the former case, and wherever axillary buds take the lead, there is, of course, no single main stem, continued year after year in a direct line, but the trunk is soon lost in the branches. Trees so formed commonly have rounded or spreading tops. Of such trees with *deliquescent* stems,—that is, with the trunk dissolved, as it were, into the successively divided branches,—the common American Elm (Fig. 80) is a good illustration.

FIG. 80. An American Elm, with Spruce-trees, and on the left Arbor Vitæ.

64. On the other hand, the main stem of Firs and Spruces, unless destroyed by some injury, is carried on in a direct line throughout the whole growth of the tree, by the development year after year of a terminal bud: this forms a single, uninterrupted shaft,—an *excurrent* trunk, which cannot be confounded with the branches that proceed from it. Of such *spiry* or *spire-shaped* trees, the Firs or Spruces are characteristic and familiar examples. There are all gradations between the two modes.

[Pg 33]

SECTION V. ROOTS.

65. It is a property of stems to produce roots. Stems do not spring from roots in ordinary cases, as is generally thought, but roots from stems. When perennial herbs arise from the ground, as they do at spring-time, they rise from subterranean stems.

11

66. **The Primary Root** is a downward growth from the root-end of the caulicle, that is, of the initial stem of the embryo (Fig. 5-7, 81). If it goes on to grow it makes a *main* or *tap-root*, as in Fig. 37, etc. Some plants keep this main root throughout their whole life, and send off only small side branches; as in the Carrot and Radish: and in various trees, like the Oak, it takes the lead of the side-branches for several years, unless accidentally injured, as a strong tap-root. But commonly the main root divides off very soon, and is lost in the branches. *Multiple primary roots* now and then occur, as in the seedling of Pumpkin (Fig. 27), where a cluster is formed even at the first, from the root-end of the caulicle.

FIG. 81. Seedling Maple, of the natural size; the root well supplied with root hairs, here large enough to be seen by the naked eye. 82. Lower end of this root, magnified, the root seen just as root-hairs are beginning to form a little behind the tip.

67. **Secondary Roots** are those which arise from other parts of the stem. Any part of the stem may produce them, but they most readily come from the nodes. As a general rule they naturally spring, or may be made to spring, from almost any young stem, when placed in favorable circumstances,—that is, when placed in the soil, or otherwise supplied with moisture and screened from the light. For the special tendency of the root is to avoid the light, seek moisture, and therefore to bury itself in the soil. *Propagation by division*, which is so common and so very important in cultivation, depends upon the proclivity of stems to strike root. Stems or branches which remain under ground give out roots as freely as roots themselves give off branches. Stems which creep on the ground most commonly root at the joints; so will most branches when bent to the ground, as in propagation by *layering*; and propagation by *cuttings* equally depends upon the tendency of the cut end of a shoot to produce roots. Thus, a piece of a plant which has stem and leaves, either developed or in the bud, may be made to produce roots, and so become an independent plant.

[Pg 34]

68. **Contrast between Stem and Root.** Stems are ascending axes; roots are descending axes. Stems grow by the successive development of internodes (13), one after another, each leaf-bearing at its summit (or node); so that it is of the essential nature of a stem to bear leaves. Roots bear no leaves, are not distinguishable into nodes and internodes, but grow on continuously from the lower end. They commonly branch freely, but not from any fixed points nor in definite order.

69. Although roots generally do not give rise to stems, and therefore do not propagate the plant, exceptions are not uncommon. For as stems may produce adventitious buds, so also may roots. The roots of the Sweet Potato among herbs, and of the Osage Orange among trees freely produce adventitious buds, developing into leafy shoots; and so these plants are propagated by *root-cuttings*. But most growths of subterranean origin which pass for roots are forms of stems, the common Potato for example.

70. Roots of ordinary kinds and uses may be roughly classed into *fibrous* and *fleshy*.

71. **Fibrous Roots**, such as those of Indian Corn (Fig. 70), of most annuals, and of many perennials, serve only for absorption: these are slender or thread-like. Fine roots of this kind, and the fine branches which most roots send out are called ROOTLETS.

72. The whole surface of a root absorbs moisture from the soil while fresh and new; and the newer roots and rootlets are, the more freely do they imbibe. Accordingly, as long as the plant grows above ground, and expands fresh foliage, from which moisture largely escapes into the air, so long it continues to extend and multiply its roots in the soil beneath, renewing and increasing the fresh surface for absorbing moisture, in proportion to the demand from above. And when growth ceases above ground, and the leaves die and fall, or no longer act, then the roots generally stop growing, [Pg 35]and their soft and tender tips harden. From this period, therefore, until growth begins anew the next spring, is the best time for transplanting; especially for trees and shrubs.

73. The absorbing surface of young roots is much increased by the formation, near their tips, of ROOT-HAIRS (Fig. 81, 82), which are delicate tubular outgrowths from the surface, through the delicate walls of which moisture is promptly imbibed.

FIG. 83-85. Forms of tap-root.

74. **Fleshy Roots** are those in which the root becomes a storehouse of nourishment. Typical roots of this kind are those of such biennials as the turnip and carrot; in which the food created in the first season's vegetation is accumulated, to be expended the next season in a vigorous growth and a rapid development of flowers, fruit, and seed. By the time the seed is matured the exhausted root dies, and with it the whole plant.

75. Fleshy roots may be single or multiple. The single root of the commoner biennials is the primary root, or tap-root, which begins to thicken in the seedling. Names are given to its shapes, such as

Conical, when it thickens most at the crown, or where it joins the stem, and tapers regularly downwards to a point, as in the Parsnip and Carrot (Fig. 84);

Turnip-shaped or *napiform,* when greatly thickened above, but abruptly becoming slender below; as the Turnip (Fig. 83); and

[Pg 36]

Spindle-shaped, or *Fusiform,* when thickest in the middle and tapering to both ends; as the common Radish (Fig. 85).

76. These examples are of primary roots. It will be seen that turnips, carrots, and the like, are not pure root throughout; for the caulicle, from the lower end of which the root grew, partakes of the thickening, perhaps also some joints of stem above: so the bud-bearing and growing top is stem.

FIG. 86. Sweet-Potato plant forming thickened roots. Some in the middle are just beginning to thicken; one at the left has grown more; one at the right is still larger.

FIG. 87. Fascicled fusiform roots of a Dahlia: *a, a,* buds on base of stem.

77. A fine example of secondary roots (67), some of which remain fibrous for absorption, while a few thicken and store up food for the next season's growth, is furnished by the Sweet Potato (Fig. 86). As stated above, these are used for propagation by cuttings; for any part will produce adventitious buds and shoots. The Dahlia produces *fascicled* (i. e. clustered) fusiform roots of the same kind, at the base of the stem (Fig. 87): but these, like most roots, do not produce adventitious buds. The buds by which Dahlias are propagated belong to the surviving base of the stem above.

78. **Anomalous Roots,** as they may be called, are those which subserve other uses than absorption, food-storing, and fixing the plant to the soil.

Aerial Roots, i. e. those that strike from stems in the open air, are common in moist and warm climates, as in the Mangrove which reaches the coast of Florida, the Banyan, and, less strikingly, in some herbaceous plants, such as Sugar Cane, and even in Indian Corn. Such roots reach the ground at length, or tend to do so.

Aerial Rootlets are abundantly produced by many climbing plants, such as the Ivy, Poison Ivy, Trumpet Creeper, etc., springing from the side of stems, which they fasten to trunks of trees, walls, or other supports. These are used by the plant for climbing.

FIG. 88. Epiphytes of Florida and Georgia, viz., Epidendrum conopseum, a small Orchid, and Tillandsia usneoides, the so-called Long Moss or Black Moss, which is no moss, but a flowering plant, also *T. recurvata;* on a bough of Live Oak.

79. **Epiphytes, or Air-Plants** (Fig. 88), are called by the former name because commonly growing [Pg 37]upon the trunks or limbs of other plants; by the latter because, having no connection with the soil, they must derive their sustenance from the air only. They have aerial roots, which do not reach the ground, but are used to fix the plant to the surface upon which the plant grows: they also take a part in absorbing moisture from the air.

80. **Parasitic Plants,** of which there are various kinds, strike their roots, or what answer to roots, into the tissue of foster plants, or form attachments with their surface, so as to prey upon their juices. Of this sort is the Mistletoe, the seed of which germinates on the bough where it falls or is left by birds; and the forming root penetrates the bark and engrafts itself into the wood, to which it becomes united as firmly as a natural branch to its parent stem; and indeed the parasite lives just as if it were a branch of the tree it grows and feeds on. A most common parasitic herb is the Dodder; which abounds in low grounds in summer, and coils its long and slender, leafless, yellowish stems—resembling tangled threads of yarn—round and round the stalks of other plants; wherever they touch piercing the bark with minute and very short rootlets in the form of suckers, which draw out the nourishing juices of the plants laid hold of. Other parasitic plants, like the Beech-drops and Pine-sap, fasten their roots under ground upon the roots of neighboring plants, and rob them of their juices.

81. Some plants are partly parasitic; while most of their roots act in the ordinary way, others make suckers at their tips which grow fast to the roots of other plants and rob them of nourishment. Some of our species of Gerardia do this (Fig. 89).

FIG. 89. Roots of Yellow Gerardia, some attached to and feeding on the root of a Blueberry-bush.

13

82. There are phanerogamous plants, like Monotropa or Indian Pipe, the roots of which feed mainly on decaying vegetable matter in the soil. These are SAPROPHYTES, and they imitate Mushrooms and other Fungi in their mode of life.

83. **Duration of Roots, etc.** Roots are said to be either *annual, biennial,* or *perennial.* As respects the first and second, these terms may be applied either to the root or to the plant.

84. **Annuals,** as the name denotes, live for only one year, generally for [Pg 38]only a part of the year. They are of course herbs; they spring from the seed, blossom, mature their fruit and seed, and then die, root and all. Annuals of our temperate climates with severe winters start from the seed in spring, and perish at or before autumn. Where the winter is a moist and growing season and the summer is dry, *winter annuals* prevail; their seeds germinate under autumn or winter rains, grow more or less during winter, blossom, fructify, and perish in the following spring or summer. Annuals are fibrous-rooted.

85. **Biennials,** of which the Turnip, Beet, and Carrot are familiar examples, grow the first season without blossoming, usually thicken their roots, laying up in them a stock of nourishment, are quiescent during the winter, but shoot vigorously, blossom, and seed the next spring or summer, mainly at the expense of the food stored up, and then die completely. Annuals and biennials flower only once; hence they have been called *Monocarpic* (that is, once-fruiting) plants.

86. **Perennials** live and blossom year after year. A perennial herb, in a temperate or cooler climate, usually dies down to the ground at the end of the season's growth. But subterranean portions of stem, charged with buds, survive to renew the development. Shrubs and trees are of course perennial; even the stems and branches above ground live on and grow year after year.

87. There are all gradations between annuals and biennials, and between these and perennials, as also between herbs and shrubs; and the distinction between shrubs and trees is quite arbitrary. There are perennial herbs and even shrubs of warm climates which are annuals when raised in a climate which has a winter,—being destroyed by frost. The Castor-oil plant is an example. There are perennial herbs of which only small portions survive, as off-shoots, or, in the Potato, as tubers, etc.

SECTION VI. STEMS.

88. **The Stem** is the axis of the plant, the part which bears all the other organs. Branches are secondary stems, that is, stems growing out of stems. The stem at the very beginning produces roots, in most plants a single root from the base of the embryo-stem, or caulicle. As this root becomes a *descending axis,* so the stem, which grows in the opposite direction is called the *ascending axis.* Rising out of the soil, the stem bears leaves; and leaf-bearing is the particular characteristic of the stem. But there are forms of stems that remain underground, or make a part of their growth there. These do not bear leaves, in the common sense; yet they bear rudiments of leaves, or what answers to leaves, although not in the form of foliage. The so-called stemless or *acaulescent* plants are those which bear no obvious stem (*caulis*) above ground, but only flower-stalks, and the like.

[Pg 39]

89. **Stems above ground,** through differences in duration, texture, and size, form herbs, shrubs, trees, etc., or in other terms are

Herbaceous, dying down to the ground every year, or after blossoming.

Suffrutescent, slightly woody below, there surviving from year to year.

Suffruticose or *Frutescent,* when low stems are decidedly woody below, but herbaceous above.

Fruticose or *Shrubby,* woody, living from year to year, and of considerable size,—not, however, more than three or four times the height of a man.

Arborescent, when tree-like in appearance or mode of growth, or approaching a tree in size.

Arboreous, when forming a proper tree-trunk.

90. As to direction taken in growing, stems may, instead of growing upright or erect, be

Diffuse, that is, loosely spreading in all directions.

Declined, when turned or bending over to one side.

Decumbent, reclining on the ground, as if too weak to stand.

Assurgent or *Ascending,* rising obliquely upwards.

Procumbent or *Prostrate,* lying flat on the ground from the first.

Creeping or *Repent,* prostrate on or just beneath the ground, and striking root, as does the White Clover, the Partridge-berry, etc.

Climbing or *Scandent,* ascending by clinging to other objects for support, whether by *tendrils,* as do the Pea, Grape-Vine, and Passion-flower and Virginia Creeper (Fig. 92, 93); by their twisting leaf-stalks, as the Virgin's Bower; or by rootlets, like the Ivy, Poison Ivy, and Trumpet Creeper.

14

Twining or *Voluble*, when coiling spirally around other stems or supports; like the Morning-Glory (Fig. 90) and the Hop.

FIG. 90. Twining or voluble stem of Morning-Glory.

91. Certain kinds of stems or branches, appropriated to special uses, have received distinct substantive names; such as the following:

92. **A Culm**, or straw-stem, such as that of Grasses and Sedges.

93. **A Caudex** is the old name for such a peculiar trunk as a Palm-stem; it is also used for an upright and thick rootstock.

94. **A Sucker** is a branch rising from stems under ground. Such are produced abundantly by the Rose, Raspberry, and other plants said to multiply "by the root." If we uncover them, we see at once the great difference between these subterranean branches and real roots. They are only creeping branches under ground. Remarking how the upright shoots from these branches become separate [Pg 40]plants, simply by the dying off of the connecting under-ground stems, the gardener expedites the result by cutting them through with his spade. That is, he propagates the plant "by division."

95. **A Stolon** is a branch from above ground, which reclines or becomes prostrate and strikes root (usually from the nodes) wherever it rests on the soil. Thence it may send up a vigorous shoot, which has roots of its own, and becomes an independent plant when the connecting part dies, as it does after a while. The Currant and the Gooseberry naturally multiply in this way, as well as by suckers (which are the same thing, only the connecting part is concealed under ground). Stolons must have suggested the operation of *layering* by bending down and covering with soil branches which do not naturally make stolons; and after they have taken root, as they almost always will, the gardener cuts through the connecting stem, and so converts a rooting branch into a separate plant.

96. **An Offset** is a short stolon, or sucker, with a crown of leaves at the end, as in the Houseleek (Fig. 91), which propagates abundantly in this way.

FIG. 91. Houseleek (Sempervivum), with offsets.

97. **A Runner**, of which the Strawberry presents the most familiar and characteristic example, is a long and slender, tendril-like stolon, or branch from next the ground, destitute of conspicuous leaves. Each runner of the Strawberry, after having grown to its full length, strikes root from the tip, which fixes it to the ground, then forms a bud there, which develops into a tuft of leaves, and so gives rise to a new plant, which sends out new runners to act in the same way. In this manner a single Strawberry plant will spread over a large space, or produce a great number of plants, in the course of the summer, all connected at first by the slender runners; but these die in the following winter, if not before, and leave the plants as so many separate individuals.

98. **Tendrils** are branches of a very slender sort, like runners, not destined like them for propagation, and therefore always destitute of buds or leaves, being intended only for climbing. Simple tendrils are such as those of Passion-flowers (Fig. 92). Compound or branching tendrils are borne by the Cucumber and Pumpkin, by the Grape-Vine, Virginia Creeper, etc.

FIG. 92. A small Passion-flower (*Passiflora sicyoides*), showing the tendrils.

99. A tendril commonly grows straight and outstretched until it reaches some neighboring support, such as a stem, when its apex hooks around it to secure a hold; then the whole tendril shortens itself by coiling up spirally, and so draws the shoot of the growing plant nearer to the supporting object. But the tendrils of the Virginia Creeper (Ampelopsis, Fig. [Pg 41]93), as also the shorter ones of the Japanese species, effect the object differently, namely, by expanding the tips of the tendrils into a flat disk, with an adhesive face. This is applied to the supporting object, and it adheres firmly; then a shortening of the tendril and its branches by coiling brings up the growing shoot close to the support. This is an adaptation for climbing mural rocks or walls, or the trunks of trees, to which ordinary tendrils are unable to cling. The Ivy and Poison Ivy attain the same result by means of aerial rootlets (78).

FIG. 93. Piece of the stem of Virginia Creeper, bearing a leaf and a tendril. 94. Tips of a tendril, about the natural size, showing the disks by which they hold fast to walls, etc.

100. Some tendrils are leaves or parts of leaves, as those of the Pea (Fig. 35). The nature of the tendril is known by its position. A tendril from the axil of a leaf, like that of Passion-flowers (Fig. 92) is of course a stem, i. e. a branch. So is one which terminates a stem, as in the Grape-Vine.

101. **Spines** or **Thorns** (Fig. 95, 96) are commonly stunted and hardened branches or tips of stems or branches, as are those of Hawthorn, Honey-Locust, etc. In the Pear and Sloe all

gradations occur between spines and spine-like (spinescent) branches. Spines may be reduced and indurated leaves; as in the Barberry, where their nature is revealed by their situation, underneath an axillary bud. But [Pg 42]prickles, such as those of Blackberry and Roses, are only excrescences of the bark, and not branches.

FIG. 95. A branching thorn of Honey-Locust, being an indurated leafless branch developed from an accessory bud far above the axil: at the cut portion below, three other buds (a) are concealed under the petiole.

FIG. 96. Spine of Cockspur Thorn, developed from an axillary bud, as the leaf-scar below witnesses: an accessory leaf-bud is seen at its base.

102. Equally strange forms of stems are characteristic of the Cactus family (Fig. 111). These may be better understood by comparison with

103. **Subterranean Stems and Branches.** These are very numerous and various; but they are commonly overlooked, or else are confounded with roots. From their situation they are out of ordinary sight; but they will well repay examination. For the vegetation that is carried on under ground is hardly less varied or important than that above ground. All their forms may be referred to four principal kinds: namely, the *Rhizoma* (*Rhizome*) or *Rootstock*, the *Tuber*, the *Corm* or solid bulb, and the true *Bulb*.

FIG. 97. Rootstocks, or creeping subterranean branches, of the Peppermint.

104. **The Rootstock, or Rhizoma**, in its simplest form, is merely a creeping stem or branch growing beneath the surface of the soil, or partly covered by it. Of this kind are the so-called *creeping*, *running*, or *scaly roots*, such as those by which the Mint (Fig. 97), the Couch-grass, or Quick-grass, and many other plants, spread so rapidly and widely,—"by the root," as it is said. That these are really *stems*, and not roots, is evident from the way in which [Pg 43]they grow; from their consisting of a succession of joints; and from the leaves which they bear on each *node*, in the form of small scales, just like the lowest ones on the upright stem next the ground. They also produce buds in the axils of these scales, showing the scales to be leaves; whereas real roots bear neither leaves nor axillary buds. Placed as they are in the damp and dark soil, such stems naturally produce roots, just as the creeping stem does where it lies on the surface of the ground.

105. It is easy to see why plants with these running rootstocks take such rapid and wide possession of the soil, and why they are so hard to get rid of. They are always perennials; the subterranean shoots live over the first winter, if not longer, and are provided with vigorous buds at every joint. Some of these buds grow in spring into upright stems, bearing foliage, to elaborate nourishment, and at length produce blossoms for reproduction by seed; while many others, fed by nourishment supplied from above, form a new generation of subterranean shoots; and this is repeated over and over in the course of the season or in succeeding years. Meanwhile, as the subterranean shoots increase in number, the older ones, connecting the successive growths, die off year by year, liberating the already rooted side-branches as so many separate plants; and so on indefinitely. Cutting these running rootstocks into pieces, therefore, by the hoe or the plough, far from destroying the plant, only accelerates the propagation; it converts one many-branched plant into a great number of separate individuals. Cutting into pieces only multiplies the pest; for each piece (Fig. 98) is already a plantlet, with its roots and with a bud in the axil of its scale-like leaf (either latent or apparent), and with prepared nourishment enough to develop this bud into a leafy stem; and so a single plant is all the more speedily converted into a multitude. Whereas, when the subterranean parts are only roots, cutting away the stem completely destroys the plant, except in the rather rare cases where the root freely produces adventitious buds.

FIG. 98. A piece of the running rootstock of the Peppermint, with its node or joint, and an axillary bud ready to grow.

106. Rootstocks are more commonly thickened by the storing up of considerable nourishing matter in their tissue. The common species of Iris (Fig. 164) in the gardens have stout rootstocks, which are only partly covered by the soil, and which bear foliage-leaves instead of mere scales, closely covering the upper part, while the lower produces roots. As the leaves die, year by year, and decay, a scar left in the form of a ring marks the place where each leaf was attached, that is, marks so many nodes, separated by very short internodes.

107. Some rootstocks are marked with large round scars of a different [Pg 44]sort, like those of the Solomon's Seal (Fig. 99), which gave this name to the plant, from their looking somewhat like the impression of a seal upon wax. Here the rootstock sends up every spring an herbaceous stalk or stem, which bears the foliage and flowers, and dies in autumn. The *seal* is the circular scar left by the death and separation of the base of the stout stalk from the living rootstock. As but one of these is formed each year, they mark the limits of a year's growth. The

bud at the end of the rootstock in the figure (which was taken in summer) will grow the next spring into the stalk of the season, which, dying in autumn, will leave a similar scar, while another bud will be formed farther on, crowning the ever-advancing summit or growing end of the stem.

FIG. 99. Rootstock of Solomon's Seal, with the bottom of the stalk of the season, and the bud for the next year's growth.

108. As each year's growth of stem makes its own roots, it soon becomes independent of the older parts. And after a certain age, a portion annually dies off behind, about as fast as it increases at the growing end, death following life with equal and certain step, with only a narrow interval. In vigorous plants of Solomon's Seal or Iris, the living rootstock is several inches or a foot in length; while in the short rootstock of Trillium or Birthroot (Fig. 100) life is reduced to a narrower span.

FIG. 100. The very short rootstock and strong terminal bud of a Trillium or Birthroot.

109. An upright or short rootstock, like this of Trillium, is commonly called a CAUDEX (93); or when more shortened and thickened it would become a corm.

110. **A Tuber** may be understood to be a portion of a rootstock thickened, and with buds (eyes) on the sides. Of course, there are all gradations between a tuber and a rootstock. Helianthus tuberosus, the so-called Jerusalem Artichoke (Fig. 101), and the common Potato, are typical and familiar examples of the tuber. The stalks by which the tubers are attached to the parent stem are at once seen to be different from the roots, both in appearance and manner of growth. The scales on the tubers are the rudiments of leaves; the eyes are the buds in their axils. The Potato-plant [Pg 45]has three forms of branches: 1. Those that bear ordinary leaves expanded in the air, to digest what they gather from it and what the roots gather from the soil, and convert it into nourishment. 2. After a while a second set of branches at the summit of the plant bear flowers, which form fruit and seed out of a portion of the nourishment which the leaves have prepared. 3. But a larger part of this nourishment, while in a liquid state, is carried down the stem, into a third sort of branches under ground, and accumulated in the form of starch at their extremities, which become tubers, or depositories of prepared solid food,—just as in the Turnip, Carrot, and Dahlia (Fig. 83-87), it is deposited in the root. The use of the store of food is obvious enough. In the autumn the whole plant dies, except the seeds (if it formed them) and the tubers; and the latter are left disconnected in the ground. Just as that small portion of nourishing matter which is deposited in the seed feeds the embryo when it germinates, so the much larger portion deposited in the tuber nourishes its buds, or eyes, when they likewise grow, the next spring, into new plants. And the great supply enables them to shoot with a greater vigor at the beginning, and to produce a greater amount of vegetation than the seedling plant could do in the same space of time; which vegetation in turn may prepare and store up, in the course of a few weeks or months, the largest quantity of solid nourishing material, in a form most available for food. Taking advantage of this, man has transported the Potato from the cool Andes of Chili to other cool climates, and makes it yield him a copious supply of food, especially important in countries where the season is too short, or the summer's heat too little, for profitably cultivating the principal grain-plants.

FIG. 101. Tubers of Helianthus tuberosus, called "artichokes."

FIG. 102. Bulblet-like tubers, such as are occasionally formed on the stem of a Potato-plant above ground.

111. **The Corm or Solid Bulb**, like that of Cyclamen (Fig. 103), and of Indian Turnip (Fig. 104), is a very short and thick fleshy subterranean stem, often broader than high. It sends off roots from its lower end, or rather face, leaves and stalks from its upper. The corm of Cyclamen goes on to enlarge and to produce a succession of flowers and leaves year after year. [Pg 46]That of Indian Turnip is formed one year and is consumed the next. Fig. 104 represents it in early summer, having below the corm of last year, from which the roots have fallen. It is partly consumed by the growth of the stem for the season, and the corm of the year is forming at base of the stem above the line of roots.

FIG. 103. Corm of Cyclamen, much reduced in size: roots from lower face, leaf-stalks and flower-stalks from the upper.

FIG. 104. Corm of Indian Turnip (Arisæma).

112. The corm of Crocus (Fig. 105, 106), like that of its relative Gladiolus, is also reproduced annually, the new ones forming upon the summit and sides of the old. Such a corm is like a tuber in budding from the sides, i. e. from the axils of leaves; but these leaves, instead of being small scales, are the sheathing bases of foliage-leaves which covered the surface. It

resembles a true bulb in having these sheaths or broad scales; but in the corm or solid bulb, this solid part or stem makes up the principal bulk.

FIG. 105. Corm of a Crocus, the investing sheaths or dead leaf-bases stripped off. The faint cross-lines represent the scars, where the leaves were attached, i. e. the nodes: the spaces between are the internodes. The exhausted corm of the previous year is underneath; forming ones for next year on the summit and sides.

FIG. 106. Section of the same.

113. **The Bulb**, strictly so-called, is a stem like a reduced corm as to its solid part (or plate); while the main body consists of thickened scales, which are leaves or leaf-bases. These are like bud-scales; so that in fact a bulb is a bud with fleshy scales on an exceedingly short stem. Compare a White Lily bulb (Fig. 107) with the strong scaly buds of the Hickory and Horse-chestnut (Fig. 72 and 73), and the resemblance will appear. In corms, as in tubers and rootstocks, the store of food for future growth is deposited in the stem; while in the bulb, the greater part is deposited in the bases of the leaves, changing them into thick scales, which closely overlap or enclose one another.

114. **A Scaly Bulb** (like that of the Lily, Fig. 107, 108) is one in which the scales are thick but comparatively narrow.

FIG. 107. Bulb of a wild Lily. 108. The same divided lengthwise, showing two forming buds of the next generation.

FIG. 109. A ground leaf of White Lily, its base (cut across) thickened into a bulb-scale. This plainly shows that bulb-scales are leaves.

115. **A Tunicated or Coated Bulb** is one in which the scales enwrap each other, forming concentric coats or layers, as in Hyacinth and Onion.

[Pg 47]

116. **Bulblets** are very small bulbs growing out of larger ones; or small bulbs produced above ground on some plants, as in the axils of the leaves of the bulbiferous Lilies of the gardens (Fig. 110), and often in the flower-clusters of the Leek and Onion. They are plainly buds with thickened scales. They never grow into branches, but detach themselves when full grown, fall to the ground, and take root there to form new plants.

FIG. 110. Bulblets in the axils of leaves of a Tiger Lily.

117. **Consolidated Vegetation.** An ordinary herb, shrub, or tree is evidently constructed on the plan developing an extensive surface. In fleshy rootstocks, tubers, corms, and bulbs, the more enduring portion of the plant is concentrated, and reduced for the time of struggle (as against drought, heat, or cold) to a small amount of exposed surface, and this mostly sheltered in the soil. There are many similar consolidated forms which are not subterranean. Thus plants like the Houseleek (Fig. 91) imitate a bulb. Among Cactuses the columnar species of Cereus (Fig. 111, *b*), may be likened to rootstocks. A green rind serves the purpose of foliage; but the surface is as nothing compared with an ordinary leafy plant of the same bulk. Compare, for instance, the largest Cactus known, the Giant Cereus of the Gila River (Fig. 111, in the background), which rises to the height of fifty or sixty feet, with a common leafy tree of the same height, such as that in Fig. 89, and estimate how vastly greater, even without the foliage, the surface of the latter is than that of the former. Compare, in the [Pg 48]same view, an Opuntia or Prickly-Pear Cactus, its stem and branches formed of a succession of thick and flattened joints (Fig. 111, *a*), which may be likened to tubers, or an Epiphyllum (*d*), having short and flat joints, with an ordinary leafy shrub or herb of equal size. And finally, in Melon-Cactuses, Echinocactus (*c*), or other globose forms (which may be likened to permanent corms), with their globular or bulb-like shapes, we have plants in the compactest shape; their spherical figure being such as to expose the least possible amount of substance to the air. These are adaptations to climates which are very dry, either throughout or for a part of the year. Similarly, bulbous and corm-bearing plants, and the like, are examples of a form of vegetation which in the growing season may expand a large surface to the air and light, while during the period of rest the living vegetable is reduced to a globe, or solid form of the least possible surface; and this protected by its outer coats of dead and dry scales, as well as by its situation under ground. Such are also adapted to a season of drought. They largely belong to countries which have a long hot season of little or no rain, when, their stalks and foliage above and their roots beneath early perishing, the plants rest securely in their compact bulbs, filled with nourishment and retaining their moisture with great tenacity, until the rainy season comes round. Then they shoot forth leaves and flowers with

wonderful rapidity, and what was perhaps a desert of arid sand becomes green with foliage and gay with blossoms, almost in a day.

[Pg 49]
SECTION VII. LEAVES.

118. STEMS bear leaves, at definite points (nodes, 13); and these are produced in a great variety of forms, and subserve various uses. The commonest kind of leaf, which therefore may be taken as the type or pattern, is an expanded green body, by means of which the plant exposes to the air and light the matters which it imbibes, exhales certain portions, and assimilates the residue into vegetable matter for its nourishment and growth.

119. But the fact is already familiar (10-30) that leaves occur under other forms and serve for other uses,—for the storage of food already assimilated, as in thickened seed-leaves and bulb-scales; for covering, as in bud-scales; and still other uses are to be pointed out. Indeed, sometimes they are of no service to the plant, being reduced to mere scales or rudiments, such as those on the rootstocks of Peppermint (Fig. 97) or the tubers of Jerusalem Artichoke (Fig. 101). These may be said to be of service only to the botanist, in explaining to him the plan upon which a plant is constructed.

120. Accordingly, just as a rootstock, or a tuber, or a tendril is a kind of stem, so a bud-scale, or a bulb-scale, or a cotyledon, or a petal of a flower, is a kind of leaf. Even in respect to ordinary leaves, it is natural to use the word either in a wider or in a narrower sense; as when in one sense we say that a leaf consists of blade and petiole or leaf-stalk, and in another sense say that a leaf is petioled, or that the leaf of Hepatica is three-lobed. The connection should make it plain whether by leaf we mean leaf-blade only, or the blade with any other parts it may have. And the student will readily understand that by leaf in its largest or *morphological* sense, the botanist means the organ which occupies the place of a leaf, whatever be its form or its function.

§ 1. LEAVES AS FOLIAGE.

121. This is tautological; for foliage is simply leaves: but it is very convenient to speak of typical leaves, or those which serve the plant for assimilation, as foliage-leaves, or ordinary leaves. These may first be considered.

122. **The Parts of a Leaf.** The ordinary leaf, complete in its parts, consists of *blade, foot-stalk,* or *petiole,* and a pair of *stipules.*

123. First the BLADE or LAMINA, which is the essential part of ordinary leaves, that is, of such as serve the purpose of foliage. In structure it consists of a softer part, the *green pulp,* called *parenchyma,* which is traversed and supported by a fibrous frame, the parts of which are called *ribs* or *veins,* on account of a certain likeness in arrangement to the veins of animals. [Pg 50]The whole surface is covered by a transparent skin, the *Epidermis,* not unlike that which covers the surface of all fresh shoots.

124. Note that the leaf-blade expands horizontally,—that is, normally presents its faces one to the sky, the other to the ground, or when the leaf is erect the upper face looks toward the stem that bears it, the lower face away from it. Whenever this is not the case there is something to be explained.

125. The framework consists of *wood,*—a fibrous and tough material which runs from the stem through the leaf-stalk, when there is one, in the form of parallel threads or bundles of fibres; and in the blade these spread out in a horizontal direction, to form the *ribs* and *veins* of the leaf. The stout main branches of the framework are called the *Ribs.* When there is only one, as in Fig. 112, 114, or a middle one decidedly larger than the rest, it is called the *Midrib.* The smaller divisions are termed *Veins;* and their still smaller subdivisions, *Veinlets.* The latter subdivide again and again, until they become so fine that they are invisible to the naked eye. The fibres of which they are composed are hollow; forming tubes by which the sap is brought into the leaves and carried to every part.

FIG. 112. Leaf of the Quince: *b,* blade; *p,* petiole; *st,* stipules.

126. **Venation** is the name of the mode of veining, that is, of the way in which the veins are distributed in the blade. This is of two principal kinds; namely, the *parallel-veined,* and the *netted-veined.*

127. In *Netted-veined* (also called *Reticulated*) leaves, the veins branch off from the main rib or ribs, divide into finer and finer veinlets, and the branches unite with each other to form meshes of network. That is, they *anastomose,* as anatomists say of the veins and arteries of the body. The Quince-leaf, in Fig. 112, shows this kind of veining in a leaf with a single rib. The Maple, Basswood, Plane or Buttonwood (Fig. 74) show it in leaves of several ribs.

19

128. In *parallel-veined* leaves, the whole framework consists of slender ribs or veins, which run parallel with each other, or nearly so, from the base to the point of the leaf,—not dividing and subdividing, nor forming meshes, except by minute cross-veinlets. The leaf of any grass, or that of the Lily of the Valley (Fig. 113) will furnish a good illustration. Such parallel veins Linnæus called *Nerves*, and parallel-veined leaves are still commonly called *nerved* leaves, while those of the other kind are said to be [Pg 51]*veined*,—terms which it is convenient to use, although these "nerves" and "veins" are all the same thing, and have no likeness to the *nerves* and little to the veins of animals.

129. *Netted-veined* leaves belong to plants which have a pair of seed-leaves or cotyledons, such as the Maple (Fig. 20, 24), Beech (Fig. 33), and the like; while*parallel-veined* or *nerved* leaves belong to plants with one cotyledon or true seed-leaf; such as the Iris (Fig. 59), and Indian Corn (Fig. 70). So that a mere glance at the leaves generally tells what the structure of the embryo is, and refers the plant to one or the other of these two grand classes,—which is a great convenience. For when plants differ from each other in some one important respect, they usually differ correspondingly in other respects also.

FIG. 113. A (parallel-veined) leaf of the Lily of the Valley. 114. One of the Calla Lily.

130. Parallel-veined leaves are of two sorts,—one kind, and the commonest, having the ribs or nerves all running from the base to the point of the leaf, as in the examples already given; while in another kind they run from a midrib to the margin, as in the common Pickerel-weed of our ponds, in the Banana, in Calla (Fig.114), and many similar plants of warm climates.

131. Netted-veined leaves are also of two sorts, as in the examples already referred to. In one case the veins all rise from a single rib (the midrib), as in Fig. 112,116-127. Such leaves are called *Feather-veined* or *Penni-veined*, i. e. *Pinnately-veined*; both terms meaning the same thing, namely, that the veins are arranged on the sides of the rib like the plume of a feather on each side of the shaft.

[Pg 52]

132. In the other case (as in Fig. 74, 129-132), the veins branch off from three, five, seven, or nine ribs, which spread from the top of the leaf-stalk, and run through the blade like the toes of a web-footed bird. Hence these are said to be *Palmately* or *Digitately* veined, or (since the ribs diverge like rays from a centre)*Radiate-veined.*

133. Since the general outline of leaves accords with the framework or skeleton, it is plain that *feather-veined* (or *penni-veined*) leaves will incline to elongated shapes, or at least to be longer than broad; while in *radiate-veined* leaves more rounded forms are to be expected. A glance at the following figures shows this.

FIG. 115-120. A series of shapes of feather-veined leaves.

134. **Forms of Leaves as to General Outline.** It is necessary to give names to the principal shapes, and to define them rather precisely, since they afford easy marks for distinguishing species. The same terms are used for all other flattened parts as well, such as petals; so that they make up a great part of the descriptive language of Botany. It will be a good exercise for young students to look up leaves answering to these names and definitions. Beginning with the narrower and proceeding to the broadest forms, a leaf is said to be

Linear (Fig. 115), when narrow, several times longer than wide, and of the same breadth throughout.

Lanceolate, or *Lance-shaped*, when conspicuously longer than wide, and tapering upwards (Fig. 116), or both upwards and downwards.

Oblong (Fig. 117), when nearly twice or thrice as long as broad.

Elliptical (Fig. 118) is oblong with a flowing outline, the two ends alike in width.

Oval is the same as broadly elliptical, or elliptical with the breadth considerably more than half the length.

Ovate (Fig. 119), when the outline is like a section of a hen's egg lengthwise, the broader end downward.

Orbicular, or *Rotund* (Fig. 132), circular in outline, or nearly so.

FIG. 121, oblanceolate; 122, spatulate; 123, obovate; and 124, wedge-shaped, feather-veined, leaves.

135. A leaf which tapers toward the base instead of toward the apex may be

Oblanceolate (Fig. 121) when of the lance-shaped form, only more tapering toward the base than in the opposite direction.

Spatulate (Fig. 122) when more rounded above, but tapering thence to a narrow base, like an old-fashioned spatula.

Obovate (Fig. 123) or inversely ovate, that is, ovate with the narrower end down.

Cuneate or *Cuneiform*, that is, *Wedge-shaped* (Fig. 124), broad above and tapering by nearly straight lines to an acute angle at the base.

FIG. 125, sagittate; 126, auriculate; and 127, halberd-shaped or hastate leaves.

136. **As to the Base**, its shape characterizes several forms, such as

Cordate or *Heart-shaped* (Fig. 120, 129), when a leaf of an ovate form, or something like it, has the outline of its rounded base turned in (forming a notch or*sinus*) where the stalk is attached.

Reniform, or *Kidney-shaped* (Fig. 131), like the last, only rounder and broader than long.

Auriculate, or *Eared*, having a pair of small and blunt projections, or *ears*, at the base, as in one species of Magnolia (Fig. 126).

Sagittate, or *arrow-shaped*, where such ears are acute and turned downwards, while the main body of the blade tapers upwards to a point, as in the common Sagittaria or Arrow-head, and in the Arrow-leaved Polygonum (Fig. 125).

Hastate, or *Halberd-shaped*, when such lobes at the base point outwards, giving the shape of the halberd of the olden time, as in another Polygonum (Fig. 127).

FIG. 128-132. Various forms of radiate-veined leaves.

Peltate, or *Shield-shaped* (Fig. 132), is the name applied to a curious modification of the leaf, commonly of a rounded form, where the footstalk is attached to the lower surface, instead of the base, and therefore is naturally [Pg 54]likened to a shield borne by the outstretched arm. The common Watershield, the Nelumbium, and the White Water-lily, and also the Mandrake, exhibit this sort of leaf. On comparing the shield-shaped leaf of the common Marsh Pennywort (Fig. 132) with that of another common species (Fig. 130), it is at once seen that a shield-shaped leaf is like a kidney-shaped (Fig. 130, 131) or other rounded leaf, with the margins at the base brought together and united.

137. **As to the Apex**, the following terms express the principal variations:—

Acuminate, *Pointed*, or *Taper-pointed*, when the summit is more or less prolonged into a narrowed or tapering point; as in Fig. 133.

Acute, ending in an acute angle or not prolonged point; Fig. 134.

Obtuse, with a blunt or rounded apex; as in Fig. 135, etc.

Truncate, with the end as if cut off square; as in Fig. 136.

Retuse, with rounded summit slightly indented, forming a very shallow notch, as in Fig. 137.

Emarginate, or *Notched*, indented at the end more decidedly; as in Fig. 138.

Obcordate, that is, inversely heart-shaped, where an obovate leaf is more deeply notched at the end (Fig. 139), as in White Clover and Wood-sorrel; so as to resemble a cordate leaf inverted.

Cuspidate, tipped with a sharp and rigid point; as in Fig. 140.

Mucronate, abruptly tipped with a small and short point, like a mere projection of the midrib; as in Fig. 141.

Aristate, *Awn-pointed*, and *Bristle-pointed*, are terms used when this mucronate point is extended into a longer bristle-form or slender appendage.

The first six of these terms can be applied to the lower as well as to the upper end of a leaf or other organ. The others belong to the apex only.

FIG. 133-141. Forms of the apex of leaves.

138. **As to degree and nature of Division**, there is first of all the difference between

Simple Leaves, those in which the blade is of one piece, however much it may be cut up, and

Compound Leaves, those in which the blade consists of two or more separate pieces, upon a common leaf-stalk or support. Yet between these two kinds every intermediate gradation is to be met with.

FIG. 142-147. Kinds of margin of leaves.

139. **As to Particular Outlines of Simple Leaves** (and the same applies to their separate parts), they are

Entire, when their general outline is completely filled out, so that the margin is an even line, without teeth or notches.

Serrate, or *Saw-toothed*, when the margin only is cut into sharp teeth, like those of a saw, and pointing forwards; as in Fig. 142.

Dentate, or *Toothed*, when such teeth point outwards, instead of forwards; as in Fig. 143.

Crenate, or *Scalloped*, when the teeth are broad and rounded; as in Fig. 144.

Repand, *Undulate*, or *Wavy*, when the margin of the leaf forms a wavy line, bending slightly inwards and outwards in succession; as in Fig. 145.

Sinuate, when the margin is more strongly sinuous or turned inwards and outwards; as in Fig. 146.

Incised, *Cut*, or *Jagged*, when the margin is cut into sharp, deep, and irregular teeth or incisions; as in Fig. 147.

Lobed, when deeply cut. Then the pieces are in a general way called LOBES. The number of the lobes is briefly expressed by the phrase *two-lobed, three-lobed, five-lobed, many-lobed*, etc., as the case may be.

140. When the depth and character of the lobing needs to be more particularly specified, the following terms are employed, viz.:—

Lobed, in a special sense, when the incisions do not extend deeper than about half-way between the margin and the centre of the blade, if so far, and are more or less rounded; as in the leaves of the Post-Oak, Fig. 148, and the Hepatica, Fig. 152.

Cleft, when the incisions extend half way down or more, and especially when they are sharp; as in Fig. 149, 153. And the phrases *two-cleft*, or, in the Latin form, *bifid*, *three-cleft* or *trifid*, *four-cleft* or *quadrifid*, *five-cleft* or *quinquefid*, etc., or *many-cleft*, in the Latin form, *multifid*,—express the number of the *Segments*, or portions.

Parted, when the incisions are still deeper, but yet do not quite reach to the midrib or the base of the blade; as in Fig. 150, 154. And the terms *two-parted*, *three-parted*, etc., express the number of such divisions.

Divided, when the incisions extend quite to the midrib, as in the lower part of Fig. 151, or to the leaf-stalk, as in Fig. 155; which really makes the [Pg 56]leaf compound. Here, using the Latin form, the leaf is said to be *bisected*, *trisected* (Fig. 155), etc., according to the number of the divisions.

FIG. 148, pinnately lobed; 149, pinnately cleft; 150, pinnately parted; 151, pinnately divided, leaves.

FIG. 152, palmately three-lobed; 153, palmately three-cleft; 154, palmately three-parted; 155, palmately three-divided or trisected, leaves.

141. **The Mode of Lobing or Division** corresponds to that of the veining, whether *pinnately veined* or *palmately veined*. In the former the notches or incisions, or *sinuses*, coming between the principal veins or ribs are directed toward the midrib: in the latter they are directed toward the apex of the petiole; as the figures show.

142. So degree and mode of division may be tersely expressed in brief phrases. Thus, in the four upper figures of pinnately veined leaves, the first is said to be *pinnately lobed* (in the special sense), the second *pinnately cleft* (or *pinnatifid* in Latin form), the third *pinnately parted*, the fourth *pinnately divided*, or *pinnatisected*.

143. Correspondingly in the lower row, of palmately veined leaves, the first is *palmately lobed*, the second *palmately cleft*, the third *palmately parted*, the fourth *palmately divided*. Or, in other language of the same meaning (but now less commonly employed), they are said to be *digitately lobed, cleft, parted,* or *divided*.

144. The number of the divisions or lobes may come into the phrase. Thus in the four last named figures the leaves are respectively *palmately three-lobed, three-cleft* (or *trifid*), *three-parted, three-divided*, or better (in Latin form), *trisected*. And so for higher numbers, as *five-lobed, five-cleft*, [Pg 57]etc., up to *many-lobed, many-cleft* or *multifid*, etc. The same mode of expression may be used for pinnately lobed leaves, as *pinnately 7-lobed, -cleft, -parted*, etc.

145. The divisions, lobes, etc., may themselves be *entire* (without teeth or notches), or *serrate*, or otherwise toothed or incised; or lobed, cleft, parted, etc.: in the latter cases making *twice pinnatifid, twice palmately* or *pinnately lobed, parted,* or *divided* leaves, etc. From these illustrations one will perceive how the botanist, in two or three words, may describe any one of the almost endlessly diversified shapes of leaves, so as to give a clear and definite idea of it.

146. **Compound Leaves.** A compound leaf is one which has its blade in entirely separate parts, each usually with a stalklet of its own; and the stalklet is often *jointed* (or *articulated*) with the main leaf-stalk, just as this is jointed with the stem. When this is the case, there is no doubt that the leaf is compound. But when the pieces have no stalklets, and are not jointed with the main leaf-stalk, it may be considered either as a divided simple leaf, or a compound leaf, according to the circumstances. This is a matter of names where all intermediate forms may be expected.

147. While the pieces or projecting parts of a simple leaf-blade are called *Lobes*, or in deeply cut leaves, etc., *Segments*, or *Divisions*, the separate pieces or blades of a compound leaf are called LEAFLETS.

148. Compound leaves are of two principal kinds, namely, the *Pinnate* and the *Palmate*; answering to the two modes of veining in reticulated leaves, and to the two sorts of lobed or divided leaves (141).

FIG. 156-158. Pinnate leaves, the first with an odd leaflet (*odd-pinnate*); the second with a tendril in place of uppermost leaflets; the third *abruptly pinnate*, or of even pairs.

149. *Pinnate* leaves are those in which the leaflets are arranged on the sides of a main leaf-stalk; as in Fig. 156-158. They answer to the [Pg 58]*feather-veined* (i. e. *pinnately-veined*) simple leaf; as will be seen at once on comparing the forms. The *leaflets* of the former answer to the *lobes* or *divisions* of the latter; and the continuation of the petiole, along which the leaflets are arranged, answers to the midrib of the simple leaf.

150. Three sorts of pinnate leaves are here given. Fig. 156 is *pinnate with an odd* or *end leaflet*, as in the Common Locust and the Ash. Fig. 157 is *pinnate with a tendril at the end*, in place of the odd leaflet, as in the Vetches and the Pea. Fig. 158 is evenly or *abruptly pinnate*, as in the Honey-Locust.

FIG. 159. Palmate (or digitate) leaf of five leaflets, of the Sweet Buckeye.

151. *Palmate* (also named *Digitate*) leaves are those in which the leaflets are all borne on the tip of the leaf-stalk, as in the Lupine, the Common Clover, the Virginia Creeper (Fig. 93), and the Horse-chestnut and Buckeye (Fig. 159). They evidently answer to the *radiate-veined* or *palmately-veined* simple leaf. That is, the Clover-leaf of three leaflets is the same as a palmately three-ribbed leaf cut into three separate leaflets. And such a simple five-lobed leaf as that of the Sugar Maple, if more cut, so as to separate the parts, would produce a palmate leaf of five leaflets, like that of the Horse-chestnut or Buckeye.

152. Either sort of compound leaf may have any number of leaflets; yet palmate leaves cannot well have a great many, since they are all crowded together on the end of the main leaf-stalk. Some Lupines have nine or eleven; the Horse-chestnut has seven, the Sweet Buckeye more commonly five, the Clover three. A pinnate leaf often has only seven or five leaflets, or only three, as in Beans of the genus Phaseolus, etc.; in some rarer cases only two; in the Orange and Lemon and also in the common Barberry there is only one! The joint at the place where the leaflet is united with the petiole distinguishes this last case from a simple leaf. In other species of these genera the lateral leaflets also are present.

153. The leaflets of a compound leaf may be either *entire* (as in Fig. 126-128), or *serrate*, or lobed, cleft, parted, etc.; in fact, may present all the variations of simple leaves, and the same terms equally apply to them.

154. When the division is carried so far as to separate what would be one leaflet into two, three, or several, the leaf becomes *doubly* or *twice compound*, either *pinnately* or *palmately*, as the case may be. For example, while the clustered leaves of the Honey-Locust are *simply pinnate*, that is, *once pinnate*, those on new shoots are *bipinnate*, or *twice pinnate*, as in Fig. 160. When these leaflets are again divided in the same way, the leaf [Pg 59]becomes *thrice pinnate*, or *tripinnate*, as in many Acacias. The first divisions are called *Pinnæ*; the others, *Pinnules*; and the last, or little blades themselves, *Leaflets*.

FIG. 160. A twice-pinnate (abruptly) leaf of the Honey-Locust.

155. So the palmate leaf, if again compounded in the same way, becomes *twice palmate*, or, as we say when the divisions are in threes, *twice ternate* (in Latin form *biternate*); if a third time compounded, *thrice ternate* or *triternate*. But if the division goes still further, or if the degree is variable, we simply say that the leaf is *decompound*; either palmately or pinnately decompound, as the case may be. Thus, Fig. 161 represents a four times ternately compound (in other words a *ternately decompound*) leaf of a common Meadow Rue.

FIG. 161. Ternately decompound leaf of Meadow Rue.

156. When the botanist, in describing leaves, wishes to express the number of the leaflets, he may use terms like these:—

Unifoliolate, for a compound leaf of a single leaflet; from the Latin *unum*, one, and *foliolum*, leaflet.

Bifoliolate, of two leaflets, from the Latin *bis*, twice, and *foliolum*, leaflet.

Trifoliolate (or *ternate*), of three leaflets, as the Clover; and so on.

Palmately bifoliolate, trifoliolate, quadrifoliolate, plurifoliolate (of several leaflets), etc.: or else

Pinnately bi-, tri-, quadri-, or *plurifoliolate* (that is, of two, three, four, five, or several leaflets), as the case may be: these are terse ways of denoting in single phrases both the number of leaflets and the kind of compounding.

157. Of foliage-leaves having certain peculiarities in structure, the following may be noted:—

[Pg 60]

158. **Perfoliate Leaves.** In these the stem that bears them seems to run through the blade of the leaf, more or less above its base. A common Bellwort (Uvularia perfoliata, Fig. 162) is a familiar illustration. The lower and earlier leaves show it distinctly. Later, the plant is apt to produce some leaves merely clasping the stem by the sessile and heart-shaped base, and the latest may be merely sessile. So the series explains the peculiarity: in the formation of the leaf the bases, meeting around the stem, grow together there.

FIG. 162. A summer branch of Uvularia perfoliata; lower leaves perfoliate, upper cordate-clasping, uppermost simply sessile.

FIG. 163. Branch of a Honeysuckle, with connate-perfoliate leaves.

159. **Connate-perfoliate.** Such are the upper leaves of true Honeysuckles. Here (Fig. 163) of the opposite and sessile leaves, some pairs, especially the uppermost, in the course of their formation unite around the stem, which thus seems to run through the disk formed by their union.

FIG. 164. Rootstock and equitant leaves of Iris. 165. A section across the cluster of leaves at the bottom, showing the equitation.

160. **Equitant Leaves.** While ordinary leaves spread horizontally, and present one face to the sky and the other to the earth, there are some that present their tip to the sky, and their faces right and left to the horizon. Among these are the *equitant* leaves of the Iris or Flower-de-Luce. Inspection shows that each leaf was formed as if *folded together lengthwise*, [Pg 61]so that what would be the upper surface is within, and all grown together, except next the bottom, where each leaf covers the next younger one. It was from their straddling over each other, like a man on horseback (as is seen in the cross-section, Fig. 165), that Linnæus, with his lively fancy, called these *Equitant* leaves.

161. **Leaves with no distinction of Petiole and Blade.** The leaves of Iris just mentioned show one form of this. The flat but narrow leaves of Jonquils, Daffodils, and the cylindrical leaf of Onions are other instances. *Needle-shaped* leaves, like those of the Pine, Larch, and Spruce, and the *awl-shaped* as well as the *scale-shaped* leaves of Junipers, Red Cedar, and Arbor-Vitæ (Fig. 166), are examples.

FIG. 166. Branch of Arbor-Vitæ, with awl-shaped and scale-shaped leaves.

162. **Phyllodia.** Sometimes an expanded *petiole* takes the place of the blade; as in numerous New Holland Acacias, some of which are now common in greenhouses. Such counterfeit blades are called *phyllodia,*—meaning leaf-like bodies. They may be known from true blades by their standing edgewise, their margins being directed upwards and downwards; while in true blades the faces look upwards and downwards; excepting in equitant leaves, as already explained.

163. **Falsely Vertical Leaves.** These are apparent exceptions to the rule, the blade standing edgewise instead of flatwise to the stem; but this position comes by a twist of the stalk or the base of the blade. Such leaves present the two faces about equally to the light. The Compass-plant (Silphium laciniatum) is an example. So also the leaves of Boltonia, of Wild Lettuce, and of a vast number of Australian Myrtaceous shrubs and trees, which much resemble the phyllodia of the Acacias of the same country. They are familiar in Callistemon, the Bottle-brush Flower, and in Eucalyptus. But in the latter the leaves of the young tree have the normal structure and position.

FIG. 167. The ambiguous leaf? (cladophyllum) of Myrsiphyllum.

FIG. 168. Same of Ruscus, or Butcher's Broom.

164. **Cladophylla**, meaning *branch-leaves.* The foliage of Ruscus (the Butcher's Broom of Europe) and of Myrsiphyllum of South Africa (cultivated for decoration under the false [Pg 62]name of Smilax) is peculiar and puzzling. If these blades (Fig. 167, 168) are really leaves, they are most anomalous in occupying the axil of another leaf, reduced to a little scale. Yet they have an upper and lower face, as leaves should, although they soon twist, so as to stand more or less edgewise. If they are branches which have assumed exactly the form and office of leaves, they are equally extraordinary in not making any further development. But in Ruscus, flowers are borne

on one face, in the axil of a little scale: and this would seem to settle that they are branches. In Asparagus just the same things as to position are thread-shaped and branch-like.

§ 2. LEAVES OF SPECIAL CONFORMATION AND USE.

FIG. 169. A young Agave Americana, or Century-plant; fleshy-leaved.

165. **Leaves for Storage.** A leaf may at the same time serve both ordinary and special uses. Thus in those leaves of Lilies, such as the common White Lily, which spring from the bulb, the upper and green part serves for foliage and elaborates nourishment, while the thickened portion or bud-scale beneath serves for the storage of this nourishment. The thread-shaped leaf of the Onion fulfils the same office, and the nourishing matter it prepares is deposited in its sheathing base, forming one of the concentric layers of the onion. When these layers, so thick and succulent, have given up their store to the growing parts within, they are left as thin and dry husks. In a Houseleek, an Aloe or an Agave, the green color of the surface of the fleshy leaf indicates that it is doing the work of foliage; the deeper-seated white portion within is the storehouse of the nourishment which the green surface has elaborated. So, also, the seed-leaves or cotyledons are commonly used for storage. Some, as in one of the Maples, the Pea, Horse-chestnut, Oak, etc., are for nothing else. Others, as in Beech and in our common [Pg 63]Beans, give faint indications of service as foliage also, chiefly in vain. Still others, as in the Pumpkin and Flax, having served for storage, develop into the first efficient foliage. Compare 11, 22-30, and the accompanying figures.

FIG. 170. Series of bud-scales and foliage-leaves from a developing bud of the Low Sweet Buckeye (Æsculus parviflora), showing nearly complete gradation, from a scale to a compound leaf of five leaflets; and that the scales answer to reduced petioles.

166. **Leaves as Bud-Scales** serve to protect the forming parts within. Having fulfilled this purpose they commonly fall off when the shoot develops and foliage-leaves appear. Occasionally, as in Fig. 170, there is a transition of bud-scales to leaves, which reveals the nature of the former. The Lilac also shows a gradation from bud-scale to simple leaf. In Cornus florida (the Flowering Dogwood), the four bud-scales which through the winter protect the head of forming flowers remain until blossoming, and then the base of each grows out into [Pg 64]a large and very showy petal-like leaf; the original dry scale is apparent in the notch at the apex.

FIG. 171. Shoot of common Barberry, showing transition of foliage-leaves to spines.

167. **Leaves as Spines** occur in several plants. A familiar instance is that of the common Barberry (Fig. 171). In almost any summer shoot, most of the gradations may be seen between the ordinary leaves, with sharp bristly teeth, and leaves which are reduced to a branching spine or thorn. The fact that the spines of the Barberry produce a leaf-bud in their axil also proves them to be leaves.

FIG. 172. Leaves of Solanum jasminoides, the petiole adapted for climbing.
FIG. 173. Leaf of Lathyrus Aphaca, consisting of a pair of stipules and a tendril.

168. **Leaves for Climbing** are various in adaptation. True foliage-leaves serve this purpose; as in Gloriosa, where the attenuated tip of a simple leaf (otherwise like that of a Lily) hooks around a supporting object; or in Solanum jasminoides of the gardens (Fig. 172), and in Maurandia, etc., where the leaf-stalk coils round and clings to a support; or in the compound leaves of Clematis and of Adlumia, in which both the leaflets and their stalks hook or coil around the support.

169. Or in a compound leaf, as in the Pea and most Vetches, and in Cobæa, while the lower leaflets serve for foliage, some of the uppermost are developed as tendrils for climbing (Fig. 167). In the common Pea this is so with all but one or two pairs of leaflets.

170. In one European Vetch, the leaflets are wanting and the whole petiole is a tendril, while the stipules become the only foliage (Fig. 173).

171. **Leaves as Pitchers**, or hollow tubes, are familiar in the common Pitcher-plant or Side-saddle Flower (Sarracenia, Fig. 174) of our bogs. These pitchers are generally half full of water, in which flies and other insects are drowned, often in such numbers as to make a rich manure for the plant. More curious are some of the southern species of Sarracenia, which seem to be specially adapted to the capture and destruction of flies and other insects.

FIG. 174. Leaf of Sarracenia purpurea, entire, and another with the upper part cut off.
FIG. 175. Leaf of Nepenthes; foliage, tendril, and pitcher combined.
[Pg 65]

172. The leaf of Nepenthes (Fig. 175) combines three structures and uses. The expanded part below is foliage: this tapers into a tendril for climbing; and this bears a pitcher with a lid. Insects are caught, and perhaps digested, in the pitcher.

FIG. 176. Leaves of Dionæa; the trap in one of them open, in the others closed.

173. **Leaves as Fly-traps.** Insects are caught in another way, and more expertly, by the most extraordinary of all the plants of this country, the Dionæa or Venus's Fly-trap, which grows in the sandy bogs around Wilmington, North Carolina. Here (Fig. 176) each leaf bears at its summit an appendage which opens and shuts, in shape something like a steel-trap, and operating much like one. For when open, no sooner does a fly alight on its surface, and brush against any one of the two or three bristles that grow there, than the trap suddenly closes, capturing the intruder. If the fly escapes, the trap soon slowly opens, and is ready for another capture. When retained, the insect is after a time moistened by a secretion from minute glands of the inner surface, and is digested. In the various species of Drosera or Sundew, insects are caught [Pg 66]by sticking fast to very viscid glands at the tip of strong bristles, aided by adjacent gland-tipped bristles which bend slowly toward the captive. The use of such adaptations and operations may be explained in another place.

§ 3. STIPULES.

174. A leaf complete in its parts consists of blade, leaf-stalk or petiole, and a pair of stipules. But most leaves have either fugacious or minute stipules or none at all; many have no petiole (the blade being *sessile* or stalkless); some have no clear distinction of blade and petiole; and many of these, such as those of the Onion and all phyllodia (166), consist of petiole only.

175. The base of the petiole is apt to be broadened and flattened, sometimes into thin margins, sometimes into a sheath which embraces the stem at the point of attachment.

FIG. 177. Leaf of Red Clover: *st*, stipules, adhering to the base of *p*, the petiole; *b*, blade of three leaflets.

FIG. 178. Part of stem and leaf of Prince's-Feather (Polygonum orientale) with the united sheathing stipules forming a sheath or *ocrea*.

FIG. 179. Terminal winter bud of Magnolia Umbrella, natural size. 180. Outermost bud-scale (pair of stipules) detached.

176. **Stipules** are such appendages, either wholly or partly separated from the petiole. When quite separate they are said to be *free*, as in Fig. 112. When attached to the base of the petiole, as in the Rose and in [Pg 67]Clover (Fig. 177), they are *adnate*. When the two stipules unite and sheathe the stem above the insertion, as in Polygonum (Fig. 178), this sheath is called an *Ocrea* from its likeness to a greave or leggin.

177. In Grasses, when the sheathing base of the leaf may answer to petiole, the summit of the sheath commonly projects as a thin and short membrane, like an ocrea: this is called a LIGULA or LIGULE.

178. When stipules are green and leaf-like they act as so much foliage. In the Pea they make up no small part of the actual foliage. In a related plant (Lathyrus Aphaca, Fig. 173), they make the whole of it, the remainder of the leaf being tendril.

179. In many trees the stipules are the bud-scales, as in the Beech, and very conspicuously in the Fig-tree, Tulip-tree, and Magnolia (Fig. 179). These fall off as the leaves unfold.

180. The stipules are spines or prickles in Locust and several other Leguminous trees and shrubs; they are tendrils in Smilax or Greenbrier.

§ 4. THE ARRANGEMENT OF LEAVES.

181. **Phyllotaxy,** meaning leaf-arrangement, is the study of the position of leaves, or parts answering to leaves, upon the stem.

FIG. 181. Alternate leaves, in Linden, Lime-tree, or Basswood.

FIG. 182. Opposite leaves, in Red Maple.

182. The technical name for the attachment of leaves to the stem is the *insertion*. Leaves (as already noticed, 54) are *inserted* in three modes. They are

Alternate (Fig. 181), that is, one after another, or in other words, with only a single leaf to each node;

[Pg 68]

Opposite (Fig. 182), when there is a pair to each node, the two leaves in this case being always on opposite sides of the stem;

Whorled or *Verticillate* (Fig. 183) when there are more than two leaves on a node, in which case they divide the circle equally between them, forming a *Verticel* or whorl. When there are three leaves in the whorl, the leaves are one third of the circumference apart; when four, one quarter, and so on. So the plan of opposite leaves, which is very common, is merely that of whorled leaves, with the fewest leaves to the whorl, namely, two.

FIG. 183. Whorled leaves of Galium.

183. In both modes and in all their modifications, the arrangement is such as to distribute the leaves systematically and in a way to give them a good exposure to the light.

FIG. 184. A piece of stem of Larch with two clusters (fascicles) of numerous leaves.

FIG. 185. Piece of a branch of Pitch Pine, with three leaves in a fascicle or bundle, in the axil of a thin scale which answers to a primary leaf. The bundle is surrounded at the base by a short sheath, formed of the delicate scales of the axillary bud.

184. No two or more leaves ever grow from the same point. The so-called *Fascicled* or *Clustered* leaves are the leaves of a branch the nodes of which are very close, just as they are in the bud, so keeping the leaves in a cluster. This is evident in the Larch (Fig. 184), in which examination shows each cluster to be made up of numerous leaves crowded on a spur or short axis. In spring there are only such clusters; but in summer some of them lengthen into ordinary shoots with scattered alternate leaves. So, likewise, each cluster of two or three needle-shaped leaves in Pitch Pines (as in Fig. 185), or of five leaves in White Pine, answers to a similar extremely short branch, springing from the axil of a thin and slender scale, which represents a leaf of the main shoot. For Pines produce two kinds of leaves,—1. primary, the proper leaves of the shoots, not as foliage, but in the shape of delicate scales in spring, which soon fall away; and 2. secondary, the *fascicled* leaves, from buds in the axils of the former, and these form the actual foliage.

[Pg 69]

185. **Phyllotaxy of Alternate Leaves.** Alternate leaves are distributed along the stem in an order which is uniform for each species. The arrangement in all its modifications is said to be *spiral*, because, if we draw a line from the *insertion* (i. e. the point of attachment) of one leaf to that of the next, and so on, this line will wind spirally around the stem as it rises, and in the same species will always bear the same number of leaves for each turn round the stem. That is, any two successive leaves will always be separated from each other by an equal portion of the circumference of the stem. The distance in *height* between any two leaves may vary greatly, even on the same shoot, for that depends upon the length of the *internodes*, or spaces between the leaves; but the distance as measured around the circumference (in other words, the *Angular Divergence*, or angle formed by any two successive leaves) is uniformly the same.

186. **Two-ranked.** The greatest possible divergence is, of course, where the second leaf stands on exactly the opposite side of the stem from the first, the third on the side opposite the second, and therefore over the first, and the fourth over the second. This brings all the leaves into two ranks, one on one side of the stem and one on the other, and is therefore called the *Two-ranked* arrangement. It occurs in all Grasses,—in Indian Corn, for instance; also, in the Basswood (Fig. 181). This is the simplest of all arrangements, and the one which most widely distributes successive leaves, but which therefore gives the fewest vertical ranks. Next is the

187. **Three-ranked** arrangement,—that of all Sedges, and of White Hellebore. Here the second leaf is placed one third of the way round the stem, the third leaf two thirds of the way round, the fourth leaf accordingly directly over the first, the fifth over the second, and so on. That is, three leaves occur in each turn round the stem, and they are separated from each other by one third of the circumference. (Fig. 186, 187.)

FIG. 186. Two-ranked arrangement, shown in a piece of the stalk of a Sedge, with the leaves cut off above their bases; the leaves are numbered in order, from 1 to 6. 187. Diagram or cross-section of the same, in one plane; the leaves similarly numbered; showing two cycles of three.

188. **Five-ranked** is the next in the series, and the most common. It is seen in the Apple (Fig. 188), Cherry, Poplar, and the greater number of trees and shrubs. In this case the line traced from leaf to leaf will pass twice round the stem before it reaches a leaf [Pg 70]situated directly over any below (Fig. 189). Here the sixth leaf is over the first; the leaves stand in five perpendicular ranks, with equal angular distance from each other; and this distance between any two successive leaves is just two fifths of the circumference of the stem.

FIG. 188. Shoot with its leaves 5-ranked, the sixth leaf over the first; as in the Apple-tree.

FIG. 189. Diagram of this arrangement, with a spiral line drawn from the attachment of one leaf to the next, and so on; the parts on the side turned from the eye are fainter.

27

FIG. 190. A ground-plan of the same; the section of the leaves similarly numbered; a dotted line drawn from the edge of one leaf to that of the next marks out the spiral.

189. The five-ranked arrangement is expressed by the fraction 2/5. This fraction denotes the divergence of the successive leaves, i. e. the angle they form with each other: the numerator also expresses the number of turns made round the stem by the spiral line in completing one cycle or set of leaves, namely, two; and the denominator gives the number of leaves in each cycle, or the number of perpendicular ranks, namely, five. In the same way the fraction 1/2 stands for the two-ranked mode, and 1/3 for the three-ranked: and so these different sorts are expressed by the series of fractions 1/2, 1/3, 2/5. Other cases follow in the same numerical progression, the next being the

190. **Eight-ranked** arrangement. In this the ninth leaf stands over the first, and three turns are made around the stem to reach it; so it is expressed by the fraction 3/8. This is seen in the Holly, and in the common Plantain. Then comes the

191. **Thirteen-ranked** arrangement, in which the fourteenth leaf is over the first, after five turns around the stem. The common Houseleek (Fig. 191) is a good example.

192. The series so far, then, is 1/2, 1/3, 2/5, 3/8, 5/13; the numerator and the denominator of each fraction being those of the two next preceding ones added together. At this rate the next higher should be 8/21, then 13/34, and so on; and in fact just such cases are met with, and (commonly) no others. These higher sorts are found in the Pine Family, both in the leaves and the cones and in many other plants with small and crowded leaves. But in those the number of the ranks, or of leaves in each cycle, can only rarely [Pg 71]be made out by direct inspection. They may be indirectly ascertained, however, by studying the *secondary* spirals, as they are called, which usually become conspicuous, at least two series of them, one turning to the right and one to the left, as shown in Fig. 191. For an account of the way in which the character of the phyllotaxy may be deduced from the secondary spirals, see Structural Botany, Chapter IV.

FIG. 191. A young plant of the Houseleek, with the leaves (not yet expanded) numbered, and exhibiting the 13-ranked arrangement; and showing secondary spirals.

FIG. 192. Opposite leaves of Euonymus, or Spindle-tree, showing the successive pairs crossing each other at right angles.

193. **Phyllotaxy of Opposite and whorled Leaves.** This is simple and comparatively uniform. The leaves of each pair or whorl are placed over the intervals between those of the preceding, and therefore under the intervals of the pair or whorl next above. The whorls or pairs alternate or cross each other, usually at right angles, that is, they *decussate*. Opposite leaves, that is, whorls of two leaves only, are far commoner than whorls of three or four or more members. This arrangement in successive decussating pairs gives an advantageous distribution on the stem in four vertical ranks. Whorls of three give six vertical ranks, and so on. Note that in descriptive botany leaves in whorls of two are simply called *opposite* leaves; and that the term *verticillate* or *whorled*, is employed only for cases of more than two, unless the latter number is specified.

194. **Vernation or Præfoliation**, the disposition of the leaf-blades in the bud, comprises two things; 1st, the way in which each separate leaf is folded, coiled, or packed up in the bud; and 2d, the arrangement of the leaves in the bud with respect to one another. The latter of course depends very much upon the phyllotaxy, i. e. the position and order of the leaves upon the stem. The same terms are used for it as for the arrangement of the leaves of the flower in the flower-bud. See, therefore, "Æstivation, or Præfloration."

195. As to each leaf separately, it is sometimes *straight* and open in vernation, but more commonly it is either *bent*, *folded*, or *rolled up*. When the upper part is bent down upon the lower, as the young blade in the Tulip-tree is bent upon the leaf-stalk, it is said to be *Inflexed* or *Reclined* in vernation. When folded by the midrib so that its two halves are placed face to face, it is *Conduplicate* (Fig. 193), as in the Magnolia, the Cherry, and the Oak. When folded back and forth like the plaits of a fan, it is [Pg 72]*Plicate* or *Plaited* (Fig. 194), as in the Maple and Currant. If rolled, it may be so either from the tip downwards, as in Ferns and the Sundew (Fig. 197), when in unrolling it resembles the head of a crosier, and is said to be *Circinate*; or it may be rolled up parallel with the axis, either from one edge into a coil, when it is *Convolute* (Fig. 195), as in the Apricot and Plum; or rolled from both edges towards the midrib,—sometimes inwards, when it is *Involute* (Fig.198), as in the Violet and Water-Lily; sometimes outwards, when it is *Revolute* (Fig. 196), in the Rosemary and Azalea. The figures are diagrams, representing sections through the leaf, in the way they were represented by Linnæus.

196. Flowers are for the production of seed (16). Stems and branches, which for a time put forth leaves for vegetation, may at length put forth flowers for reproduction.

§ 1. POSITION AND ARRANGEMENT OF FLOWERS, OR INFLORESCENCE.

197. Flower-buds appear just where leaf-buds appear; that is, they are either *terminal* or *axillary* (47-49). Morphologically, flowers answer to shoots or branches, and their parts to leaves.

198. In the same species the flowers are usually from axillary buds only, or from terminal buds only; but in some they are both axillary and terminal.

199. **Inflorescence**, which is the name used by Linnæus to signify mode of flower-arrangement, is accordingly of three classes: namely, *Indeterminate*, when the flowers are in the axils of leaves, that is, are from axillary buds; *Determinate*, when they are from terminal buds, and so *terminate* a stem or branch; and *Mixed*, when these two are combined.

200. **Indeterminate Inflorescence** (likewise, and for the same reason, called *indefinite inflorescence*) is so named because, as the flowers all come from axillary buds, the terminal bud may keep on growing and prolong the stem indefinitely. This is so in Moneywort (Fig. 199).

FIG. 199. Piece of a flowering-stem of Moneywort (Lysimachia nummularia,) with single flowers successively produced in the axils of the leaves, from below upwards, as the stem grows on.

[Pg 73]

201. When flowers thus arise singly from the axils of ordinary leaves, they are *axillary* and *solitary*, not collected into flower-clusters.

202. But when several or many flowers are produced near each other, the accompanying leaves are apt to be of smaller size, or of different shape or character: then they are called BRACTS, and the flowers thus brought together form a cluster. The kinds of flower-clusters of the indeterminate class have received distinct names, according to their form and disposition. They are principally *Raceme, Corymb, Umbel, Spike, Head, Spadix, Catkin,* and *Panicle.*

203. In defining these it will be necessary to use some of the following terms of descriptive botany which relate to inflorescence. If a flower is stalkless, i. e. sits directly in the axil or other support, it is said to be *sessile*. If raised on a naked stalk of its own (as in Fig. 199) it is *pedunculate*, and the stalk is a PEDUNCLE.

204. A peduncle on which a flower-cluster is raised is a *Common peduncle*. That which supports each separate flower of the cluster is a *Partial peduncle*, and is generally called a PEDICEL. The portion of the general stalk along which flowers are disposed is called the *Axis of inflorescence*, or, when covered with sessile flowers, the *Rhachis* (back-bone), and sometimes the *Receptacle*. The leaves of a flower-cluster generally are termed BRACTS. But when bracts of different orders are to be distinguished, those on the common peduncle or axis, and which have a flower in their axil, keep the name of *bracts*; and those on the pedicels or partial flower-stalks, if any, that of BRACTLETS or *Bracteoles*. The former is the preferable English name.

FIG. 200. A raceme, with a general peduncle (*p*), pedicels (*p′*), bracts (*b*), and bractlets (*b′*). Plainly the bracts here answer to the leaves in Fig.199.

205. **A Raceme** (Fig. 200) is that form of flower-cluster in which the flowers, each on their own foot-stalk or pedicel, are arranged along the sides of a common stalk or axis of inflorescence; as in the Lily of the Valley, Currant, Barberry, one section of Cherry, etc. Each flower comes from the axil of a small leaf, or bract, which, however, is often so small that it might escape notice, and even sometimes (as in the Mustard Family) disappears altogether. The lowest blossoms of a[Pg 74]raceme are of course the oldest, and therefore open first, and the order of blossoming is *ascending* from the bottom to the top. The summit, never being stopped by a terminal flower, may go on to grow, and often does so (as in the common Shepherd's Purse), producing lateral flowers one after another for many weeks.

FIG. 201. A raceme. 202. A corymb. 203. An umbel.

206. **A Corymb** (Fig. 202) is the same as a raceme, except that it is flat and broad, either convex, or level-topped. That is, a raceme becomes a corymb by lengthening the lower pedicels while the uppermost remain shorter. The axis of a corymb is short in proportion to the lower pedicels. By extreme shortening of the axis the corymb may be converted into

207. **An Umbel** (Fig. 203) as in the Milkweed, a sort of flower-cluster where the pedicels all spring apparently from the same point, from the top of the peduncle, so as to resemble, when spreading, the rays of an umbrella; whence the name. Here the pedicels are sometimes called

29

the *Rays* of the umbel. And the bracts, when brought in this way into a cluster or circle, form what is called an INVOLUCRE.

208. The corymb and the umbel being more or less level-topped, bringing the flowers into a horizontal plane or a convex form, the ascending order of development appears as *Centripetal*. That is, the flowering proceeds from the margin or circumference regularly towards the centre; the lower flowers of the former answering to the outer ones of the latter.

209. In these three kinds of flower-clusters, the flowers are raised on conspicuous *pedicels* (204) or stalks of their own. The shortening of these pedicels, so as to render the flowers *sessile* or nearly so, converts a raceme into a *Spike*, and a corymb or an umbel into a *Head*.

210. **A Spike** is a flower cluster with a more or less lengthened axis, along which the flowers are sessile or nearly so; as in the Plantain (Fig. 204).

FIG. 204. Spike of the common Plantain or Ribwort.

211. **A Head** (*Capitulum*) is a round or roundish cluster of flowers, [Pg 75]which are sessile on a very short axis or receptacle, as in the Button-ball, Button-bush (Fig.205), and Red Clover. It is just what a spike would become if its axis were shortened; or an umbel, if its pedicels were all shortened until the flowers became sessile. The head of the Button-bush is naked; but that of the Thistle, of the Dandelion, and the like, is surrounded by empty bracts, which form an *Involucre*. Two particular forms of the spike and the head have received particular names, namely, the *Spadix* and the *Catkin*.

FIG. 205. Head of the Button-bush (Cephalanthus).

FIG. 206. Spadix and spathe of the Indian Turnip; the latter cut through below.

212. **A Spadix** is a fleshy spike or head, with small and often imperfect flowers, as in the Calla, Indian Turnip, (Fig. 206), Sweet Flag, etc. It is commonly surrounded or embraced by a peculiar enveloping leaf, called a SPATHE.

213. **A Catkin, or Ament,** is the name given to the scaly sort of spike of the Birch (Fig. 207) and Alder, the Willow and Poplar, and one sort of flower-clusters of the Oak, Hickory, and the like,—the so-called *Amentaceous* trees.

FIG. 207. Catkin, or Ament, of Birch.

214. *Compound* flower-clusters of these kinds are not uncommon. When the stalks which in the simple umbel are the pedicels of single flowers themselves branch into an umbel, a *Compound Umbel* is formed. [Pg 76]This is the inflorescence of Caraway (Fig. 208), Parsnip, and almost all of the great family of Umbelliferous (umbel-bearing) plants.

FIG. 208. Compound Umbel of Caraway.

215. The secondary or partial umbels of a compound umbel are UMBELLETS. When the umbellets are subtended by an involucre, this secondary involucre is called an INVOLUCEL.

216. A *Compound raceme* is a cluster of racemes racemosely arranged, as in Smilacina racemosa. A *compound corymb* is a corymb some branches of which branch again in the same way, as in Mountain Ash. A *compound spike* is a spicately disposed cluster of spikes.

FIG. 209. Diagram of a simple panicle.

217. **A Panicle,** such as that of Oats and many Grasses, is a compound flower-cluster of a more or less open sort which branches with apparent irregularity, neither into corymbs nor racemes. Fig. 209 represents the simplest panicle. It is, as it were, a raceme of which some of the pedicels have branched so as to bear a few flowers on pedicels of their own, while others remain simple. A *compound panicle* is one that branches in this way again and again.

FIG. 210. Diagram of an opposite-leaved plant, with a single terminal flower. 211. Same, with a cyme of three flowers; *a*, the first flower, of the main axis; *b b*, those of branches. 212. Same, with flowers also of the third order, *c c*.

218. **Determinate Inflorescence** is that in which the flowers are from terminal buds. The simplest case is that of a solitary terminal flower, as in Fig. 210. This stops the growth of the stem; for its terminal bud, becoming a blossom, can no more lengthen in the manner of a leaf-bud. Any [Pg 77]further growth must be from axillary buds developing into branches. If such branches are leafy shoots, at length terminated by single blossoms, the inflorescence still consists of solitary flowers at the summit of stem and branches. But if the flowering branches bear only bracts in place of ordinary leaves, the result is the kind of flower-cluster called

219. **A Cyme.** This is commonly a flat-topped or convex flower-cluster, like a corymb, only the blossoms are from terminal buds. Fig. 211 illustrates the simplest cyme in a plant with opposite leaves, namely, with three flowers. The middle flower, *a*, terminates the stem; the two others, *b b*, terminate branches, one from the axil of each of the uppermost leaves; and being later than the middle one, the flowering proceeds from the centre outwards, or is *Centrifugal.* This is the opposite of the indeterminate mode, or that where all the flower-buds are axillary. If flowering branches appear from the axils below, the lower ones are the later, so that the order of blossoming continues *centrifugal* or, which is the same thing, *descending,* as in Fig. 213, making a sort of reversed raceme or *false raceme,*—a kind of cluster which is to the true raceme just what the flat cyme is to the corymb.

FIG. 213. Diagram of a simple cyme in which the axis lengthens, so as to take the form of a raceme.

220. Wherever there are bracts or leaves, buds may be produced from their axils and appear as flowers. Fig. 212 represents the case where the branches, *b b*, of Fig. 211, each with a pair of small leaves or bracts about their middle, have branched again, and produced the branchlets and flowers *c c*, on each side. It is the continued repetition of this which forms the full or compound cyme, such as that of the Laurestinus, Hobble-bush, Dogwood, and Hydrangea (Fig. 214).

FIG. 214. Compound cyme of Hydrangea arborescens, with neutral enlarged flowers round the circumference.

221. **A Fascicle** (meaning a bundle), like that of the Sweet William and Lychnis of the gardens, is only a cyme with the flowers much crowded.

222. **A Glomerule** is a cyme still more compacted, so as to imitate a head. It may be known from a true head by the flowers not expanding centripetally, that is, not from the circumference towards the centre.

223. The illustrations of determinate or *cymose* inflorescence have been taken from plants with opposite leaves, which give rise to the most regular cymes. But the Rose, Cinquefoil, Buttercup, etc., with alternate leaves, furnish also good examples of cymose inflorescence.

224. **A Cymule** (or diminutive cyme) is either a reduced small cyme of few flowers, or a branch of a compound cyme, i. e. a partial cyme.

225. **Scorpioid** or **Helicoid Cymes**, of various sorts, are forms of determinate inflorescence (often puzzling to the student) in which one half of the ramification fails to appear. So that they may be called *incomplete cymes.* The commoner forms may be understood by comparing a complete [Pg 78]cyme, like that of Fig. 215 with Fig. 216, the diagram of a cyme of an opposite-leaved plant, having a series of terminal flowers and the axis continued by the development of a branch in the axil of only one of the leaves at each node. The dotted lines on the left indicate the place of the wanting branches, which if present would convert this *scorpioid cyme* into the complete one of Fig. 215. Fig. 217 is a diagram of similar inflorescence with alternate leaves. Both are kinds of *false racemes* (219). When the bracts are also wanting in such cases, as in many Borragineous plants, the true nature of the inflorescence is very much disguised.

FIG. 215. A complete forking cyme of an Arenaria, or Chickweed.

FIG. 216. Diagram of a scorpioid cyme, with opposite leaves or bracts.
FIG. 217. Diagram of analogous scorpioid cyme, with alternate leaves or bracts.
[Pg 79]
226. These distinctions between determinate and indeterminate inflorescence, between corymbs and cymes, and between the true and the false raceme and spike, were not recognized by botanists much more than half a century ago, and even now are not always attended to in descriptions. It is still usual and convenient to describe rounded or flat-topped and open ramification as *corymbose,* even when essentially cymose; also to call the reversed or false racemes or spikes by these (strictly incorrect) names.

227. **Mixed Inflorescence** is that in which the two plans are mixed or combined in compound clusters. A *mixed panicle* is one in which, while the primary ramification is of the indeterminate order, the secondary or ultimate is wholly or partly of the determinate order. A contracted or elongated inflorescence of this sort is called a THYRSUS. Lilac and Horse-chestnut afford common examples of mixed inflorescence of this sort. When loose and open such flower-clusters are called by the general name of *Panicles.* The heads of Compositæ are centripetal; but the branches or peduncles which bear the heads are usually of centrifugal order.

§ 2. PARTS OR ORGANS OF THE FLOWER.

228. These were simply indicated in Section II. 16. Some parts are necessary to seed-bearing; these are *Essential Organs*, namely, the *Stamens* and *Pistils*. Others serve for protection or for attraction, often for both. Such are the leaves of the Flower, or the *Floral Envelopes*.

229. **The Floral Envelopes**, taken together, are sometimes called the PERIANTH, also *Perigone*, in Latin form *Perigonium*. In a flower which possesses its full number of organs, the floral envelopes are of two kinds, namely, an outer circle, the CALYX, and an inner, the COROLLA.

230. **The Calyx** is commonly a circle of green or greenish leaves, but not always. It may be the most brightly colored part of the blossom. Each calyx-leaf or piece is called a SEPAL.

231. **The Corolla** is the inner circle of floral envelopes or flower-leaves, usually of delicate texture and *colored*, that is, of some other color than green. Each corolla-leaf is called a PETAL.

232. There are flowers in abundance which consist wholly of floral envelopes. Such are the so-called full *double flowers*, of which the choicer roses and camellias of the cultivator are familiar examples. In them, under the gardener's care and selection, petals have taken the place of both stamens and pistils. These are monstrous or unnatural flowers, incapable of producing seed, and subservient only to human gratification. Their common name of *double* flowers is not a sensible one: except that it is fixed by custom, it were better to translate their Latin name, *flores pleni*, and call them *full flowers*, meaning full of leaves.

233. Moreover, certain plants regularly produce *neutral flowers*, consisting of floral envelopes only. In Fig. 214, some are seen around the margin [Pg 80]of the cyme in Hydrangea. They are likewise familiar in the Hobble-bush and in Wild-Cranberry tree, Viburnum Oxycoccus; where they form an attractive setting to the cluster of small and comparatively inconspicuous perfect flowers which they adorn. In the Guelder Rose, or Snow-ball of ornamental cultivation, all or most of the blossoms of this same shrub are transformed into neutral flowers.

FIG. 218. A *flos plenus*, namely, a full double flower of Rose.

234. **The Essential Organs** are likewise of two kinds, placed one above or within the other; namely, first, the STAMENS or fertilizing organs, and second, thePISTILS, which are to be fertilized and bear the seeds.

FIG. 219. A stamen: *a*, filament; *b*, anther, discharging pollen.

FIG. 220. A pistil; with ovary, *a*, half cut away, to show the contained ovules; *b*, style; *c*, stigma.

235. **A Stamen** consists of two parts, namely, the FILAMENT or stalk (Fig. 219 *a*), and the ANTHER (*b*). The latter is the only essential part. It is a case, commonly with two lobes or cells, each opening lengthwise by a slit, at the proper time, and discharging a powder or dust-like substance, usually of a yellow color. This powder is the POLLEN, or fertilizing matter, to produce which is the office of the stamen.

236. **A Pistil** (Fig. 220, 221) when complete, has three parts; OVARY, STYLE, and STIGMA. The *Ovary*, at base, is the hollow portion, which contains one or moreOVULES or rudimentary seeds. The *Style* is the tapering [Pg 81]portion above: the *Stigma* is a portion of the style, usually its tip, with moist naked surface, upon which grains of pollen may lodge and adhere, and thence make a growth which extends down to the ovules. When there is no style then the stigma occupies the tip of the ovary.

FIG. 221. Model of a simple pistil, with ovary cut across and slightly opened ventrally, to show the ovules and their attachment.

237. **The Torus** or **Receptacle** is the end of the flower-stalk, or the portion of axis or stem out of which the several organs of the flower grow, upon which they are borne (Fig. 223).

FIG. 222. Flower of Sedum ternatum, a Stonecrop.

FIG. 223. Parts of same, two of each kind, separated and displayed; the torus or receptacle in the centre; *a*, a sepal; *b*, a petal; *c*, a stamen; *d*, a pistil.

238. The parts of the flower are thus disposed on the receptacle or axis essentially as are leaves upon a very short stem; first the sepals, or outer floral leaves; then the petals or inner floral leaves; then the stamens; lastly, at summit or centre, the pistils, when there are two or more of them, or the single pistil, when only one. Fig. 223 shows the organs displayed, two of each kind, of such a simple and symmetrical flower as that of a Sedum or Stonecrop, Fig. 222.

§ 3. PLAN OF FLOWER.

239. All flowers are formed upon one general plan, but with almost infinite variations, and many disguises. This common plan is best understood by taking for a type, or standard for

comparison, some *perfect, complete, regular,* and *symmetrical* blossom, and one as simple as such a blossom could well be. Flowers are said to be

Perfect (hermaphrodite), when provided with both kinds of essential organs, i. e. with both stamens and pistils.

Complete, when, besides, they have the two sets of floral envelopes, namely, [Pg 82]calyx and corolla. Such are completely furnished with all that belongs to a flower.

Regular, when all the parts of each set are alike in shape and size.

Symmetrical, when there is an equal number of parts in each set or circle of organs.

240. Flax-flowers were taken for a pattern in Section II. 16. But in them the five pistils have their ovaries as it were consolidated into one body. Sedum, Fig. 222, has the pistils and all the other parts free from such combination. The flower is perfect, complete, regular, and symmetrical, but is not quite as simple as it might be; for there are twice as many stamens as there are of the other organs. Crassula, a relative of Sedum, cultivated in the conservatories for winter blossoming (Fig. 224) is simpler, being *isostemonous,* or with just as many stamens as petals or sepals, while Sedum is *diplostemonous,* having double that number: it has, indeed, two sets of stamens.

FIG. 224. Flower of a Crassula. 225. Diagram or ground-plan of same.

241. **Numerical Plan.** A certain number either runs through the flower or is discernible in some of its parts. This number is most commonly either five or three, not very rarely four, occasionally two. Thus the *ground-plan* of the flowers thus far used for illustration is five. That of Trillium (Fig. 226, 227) is three, as it likewise is as really, if not as plainly, in Tulips and Lilies, Crocus, Iris, and all that class of blossoms. In some Sedums all the flowers are in fours. In others the first flowers are on the plan of five, the rest mostly on the plan of four, that is, with four sepals, four petals, eight stamens (i. e. twice four), and four pistils. Whatever the ground number may be, it runs through the whole in symmetrical blossoms.

FIG. 226. Flower of a Trillium; its parts in threes.

FIG. 227. Diagram of flower of Trillium. In this, as in all such diagrams of cross-section of blossoms, the parts of the outer circle represent the calyx; the next, corolla; within, stamens (here in two circles of three each, and the cross-section is through the anthers); in the centre, section of three ovaries joined into a compound one of three cells.

242. **Alternation of the successive Circles.** In these flowers the parts of the successive circles *alternate;* and such is the rule. That is, [Pg 83]the petals stand over the intervals between the sepals; the stamens, when of the same number, stand over the intervals between the petals; or when twice as many, as in the Trillium, the outer set alternates with the petals, and the inner set, alternating with the other, of course stands before the petals; and the pistils alternate with these. This is just as it should be on the theory that the circles of the blossom answer to whorls of leaves, which alternate in this way. While in such flowers the circles are to be regarded as whorls, in others they are rather to be regarded as condensed spirals of alternate leaves. But, however this may be, in the mind of a morphological botanist,

243. **Flowers are altered Branches,** and their parts, therefore, altered leaves. That is, certain buds, which might have grown and lengthened into a leafy branch, do, under other circumstances and to accomplish other purposes, develop into blossoms. In these the axis remains short, nearly as it is in the bud; the leaves therefore remain close together in sets or circles; the outer ones, those of the calyx, generally partake more or less of the character of foliage; the next set are more delicate, and form the corolla, while the rest, the stamens and pistils, appear under forms very different from those of ordinary leaves, and are concerned in the production of seed. This view gives to Botany an interest which one who merely notices the shape and counts the parts of blossoms, without understanding their plan, has no conception of.

244. That flowers answer to branches may be shown, first, from their position. As explained in the section on Inflorescence, flowers arise from the same places as branches, and from no other; flower-buds, like leaf-buds, appear either on the summit of a stem, that is, as a terminal bud, or in the axil of a leaf, as an axillary bud. And, as the plan of a symmetrical flower shows, the arrangement of the parts on their axis or receptacle is that of leaves upon the stem.

245. That the sepals and petals are of the nature of leaves is evident from their appearance; they are commonly called the leaves of the flower. The calyx is most generally green in color, and foliaceous (leaf-like) in texture. And though the corolla is rarely green, yet neither are proper leaves always green. In our wild Painted-cup, and in some scarlet Sages, common in gardens, the leaves just under the flowers are of the brightest red or scarlet, often much brighter-colored than the corolla itself. And sometimes (as in many Cactuses, and in Carolina Allspice) there is such a regular gradation from the last leaves of the plant (bracts or bractlets) into the leaves of the calyx,

33

that it is impossible to say where the one ends and the other begins. If sepals are leaves, so also are petals; for there is no clearly fixed limit between them. Not only in the Carolina Allspice and Cactus (Fig. 229), but in the Water-Lily (Fig. 228) and in a variety of flowers with more than one row of petals, there is such a complete transition between calyx and corolla that no one can surely tell how many of the leaves belong to the one and how many to the other.

[Pg 84]

FIG. 228. Series of sepals, petals, and stamens of White Water-Lily, showing the transitions.

FIG. 229. A Cactus blossom.

246. That stamens are of the same general nature as petals, and therefore a modification of leaves, is shown by the gradual transitions that occur between the one and the other in many blossoms; especially in cultivated flowers, such as Roses and Camellias, when they begin to *double*, that is, to change their stamens into petals. Some wild and natural flowers show the same interesting transitions. The Carolina Allspice and the White Water-Lily exhibit complete gradations not only between sepals and petals, but between petals and stamens. The sepals of our Water-Lily are green outside, but white and petal-like on the inside; the petals, in many rows, gradually grow narrower towards the centre of the flower; some of these are tipped with a trace of a yellow anther, but still are petals; the next are more contracted and stamen-like, but with a flat petal-like filament; and a further narrowing of this completes the genuine stamen.

247. Pistils and stamens now and then change into each other in some Willows; pistils often turn into petals in cultivated flowers; and in the Double Cherry they are occasionally replaced by small green leaves. Sometimes a whole blossom changes into a cluster of green leaves, as in the "green roses" occasionally noticed in gardens, and sometimes it degenerates into a leafy branch. So the botanist regards pistils also as answering to leaves; that is, to single leaves when simple and separate, to a whorl of leaves when conjoined.

[Pg 85]

§ 4. MODIFICATIONS OF THE TYPE.

248. **The Deviations**, as they may be called, from the assumed type or pattern of flower are most various and extensive. The differences between one species and another of the same genus are comparatively insignificant; those between different genera are more striking; those between different families and classes of plants more and more profound. They represent different adaptations to conditions or modes of life, some of which have obvious or probable utilities, although others are beyond particular explanation. The principal modifications may be conveniently classified. First those which in place of perfect (otherwise called *hermaphrodite* or bisexual) flowers, give origin to

249. **Unisexual, or Separated, or Diclinous Flowers**, *imperfect* flowers, as they have been called in contradistinction to perfect flowers; but that term is too ambiguous. In these some flowers want the stamens, while others want the pistils. Taking hermaphrodite flowers as the pattern, it is natural to say that the missing organs are *suppressed*. This expression is justified by the very numerous cases in which the missing parts are *abortive*, that is, are represented by rudiments or vestiges, which serve to exemplify the plan, although useless as to office. Unisexual flowers are

Monœcious (or *Monoicous*, i. e. of one household), when flowers of both sorts or sexes are produced by the same individual plant, as in the Ricinus or Castor-oil Plant, Fig. 230.

Diœcious (or *Dioicous*, i. e. of separate households), when the two kinds are borne on different plants; as in Willows, Poplars, Hemp, and Moonseed, Fig. 231, 232.

Polygamous, when the flowers are some of them perfect, and some staminate or pistillate only.

FIG. 230. Unisexual flowers of Castor-oil plant: *s*, staminate flower; *p*, pistillate flower.

FIG. 231, staminate, and 232, pistillate flower of Moonseed.

[Pg 86]

250. A blossom having stamens and no pistil is a *Staminate* or *Male* flower. Sometimes it is called a *Sterile* flower, not appropriately, for other flowers may equally be sterile. One having pistil but no stamens is a *Pistillate* or *Female* flower.

FIG. 233. Flower of Anemone Pennsylvanica; apetalous, hermaphrodite.

FIG. 234. Flower of Saururus or Lizard's-tail; naked, but hermaphrodite.

251. **Incomplete Flowers** are so named in contradistinction to complete: they want either one or both of the floral envelopes. Those of Fig. 230 are incomplete, having calyx but no corolla. So is the flower of Anemone (Fig. 233), although its calyx is colored like a corolla. The flowers of Saururus or Lizard's-tail, although perfect, have neither calyx nor corolla (Fig. 234). Incomplete flowers, accordingly, are

Naked or *Achlamydeous*, destitute of both floral envelopes, as in Fig. 234, or

Apetalous, when wanting only the corolla. The case of corolla present and calyx wholly wanting is extremely rare, although there are seeming instances. In fact, a single or simple perianth is taken to be a calyx, unless the absence or abortion of a calyx can be made evident.

FIG. 235. Flower of Mustard. 236. Its stamens and pistil separate and enlarged.

FIG. 237. Flower of a Violet. 238. Its calyx and corolla displayed: the five smaller parts are the sepals; the five intervening larger ones are the petals.

252. In contradistinction to regular and symmetrical, very many flowers are

Irregular, that is, with the members of some or all of the floral circles unequal or dissimilar, and

Unsymmetrical, that is, when the circles of the flower or some of them differ in the number of their members. (Symmetrical and unsymmetrical are used in a different sense in some recent books, but the older use should be adhered to). Want of numerical symmetry and irregularity commonly go together; and both are common. Indeed, few flowers are entirely [Pg 87]symmetrical beyond calyx, corolla, and perhaps stamens; and probably no irregular blossoms are quite symmetrical.

253. **Irregular and Unsymmetrical Flowers** may therefore be illustrated together, beginning with cases which are comparatively free from other complications. The blossom of Mustard, and of all the very natural family which it represents (Fig. 235, 236), is regular but unsymmetrical in the stamens. There are four equal sepals, four equal petals; but six stamens, and only two members in the pistil, which for the present may [Pg 88]be left out of view. The want of symmetry is in the stamens. These are in two circles, an outer and an inner. The outer circle consists of two stamens only; the inner has its proper number of four. The flower of Violet, which is on the plan of five, is symmetrical in calyx, corolla, and stamens, inasmuch as each of these circles consists of five members; but it is conspicuously irregular in the corolla, one of the petals being very different from the rest.

FIG. 239. Flower of a Larkspur. 240. Its calyx and corolla displayed; the five larger parts are the sepals; the four smaller, of two shapes, are the petals; the place of the fifth petal is vacant. 241. Diagram of the same; the place for the missing petal marked by a dotted line.

FIG. 242. Flower of a Monkshood. 243. Its parts displayed; five sepals, the upper forming the hood; the two lateral alike, broad and flat; the two lower small. The two pieces under the hood represent the corolla, reduced to two odd-shaped petals; in centre the numerous stamens and three pistils. 244. Diagram of the calyx and corolla; the three dotted lines in the place of missing petals.

254. The flowers of Larkspur, and of Monkshood or Aconite, which are nearly related, are both strikingly irregular in calyx and corolla, and considerably unsymmetrical. In Larkspur (Fig. 239-241) the irregular calyx consists of five sepals, one of which, larger than the rest, is prolonged behind into a large sac or spur; but the corolla is of only four petals (of two shapes),— the fifth, needed to complete the symmetry, being left out. And the Monkshood (Fig. 242-244) has five very dissimilar sepals, and a corolla of only two very small and curiously-shaped petals,— the three needed to make up the symmetry being left out. The stamens in both are out of symmetry with the ground-plan, being numerous. So are the pistils, which are usually diminished to three, sometimes to two or to one.

255. **Flowers with Multiplication of Parts** are very common. The stamens are indefinitely numerous in Larkspur and in Monkshood (Fig. 242, 243), while the pistils are fewer than the ground-plan suggests. Most Cactus-flowers have all the organs much increased in number (Fig. 229), and so of the Water-Lily. In Anemone (Fig. 233) the stamens and pistils are multiplied while the petals are left out. In Buttercups or Crowfoot, while the sepals and petals conform to the ground-plan of five, both stamens and pistils are indefinitely multiplied (Fig. 245).

FIG. 245. Flower of Ranunculus bulbosus, or Buttercup, in section.

256. **Flowers modified by Union of Parts**, so that these parts more or less lose the appearance of separate leaves or other organs growing out of the end of the stem or receptacle, are extremely common. There are two kinds of such union, namely:—

Coalescence of parts of the same circle by their contiguous margins; and

Adnation, or the union of adjacent circles or unlike parts.

257. **Coalescence** is not rare in leaves, as in the upper pairs of Honeysuckles, Fig. 163. It may all the more be expected in the crowded circles or whorls of flower-leaves. Datura or Stramonium (Fig. 246) shows this coalescence both in calyx and corolla, the five sepals and the five petals being thus united to near their tips, each into a tube or long and narrow cup. These unions make needful the following terms:—

[Pg 89]

Gamopetalous, said of a corolla the petals of which are thus coalescent into one body, whether only at base or higher. The union may extend to the very summit, as in Morning Glory and the like (Fig. 247), so that the number of petals in it may not be apparent. The old name for this was *Monopetalous*, but that means "one-petalled;" while gamopetalous means "petals united," and therefore is the proper term.

FIG. 246. Flower of Datura Stramonium; gamosepalous and gamopetalous.

FIG. 247. Funnelform corolla of a common Morning Glory, detached from its polysepalous calyx.

Polypetalous is the counterpart term, to denote a corolla of *distinct*, that is, separate petals. As it means "many petalled," it is not the best possible name, but it is the old one and in almost universal use.

Gamosepalous applies to the calyx when the sepals are in this way united.

Polysepalous, to the calyx when of separate sepals or calyx-leaves.

258. Degree of union or of separation in descriptive botany is expressed in the same way as is the lobing of leaves (139). See Fig. 249-253, and the explanations.

259. A corolla when gamopetalous commonly shows a distinction (well marked in Fig. 249-251) between a contracted tubular portion below, the TUBE, and the spreading part above, the BORDER or LIMB. The junction between tube and limb, or a more or less enlarged upper portion of the tube between the two, is the THROAT. The same is true of the calyx.

260. Some names are given to particular forms of the gamopetalous corolla, applicable also to a gamosepalous calyx, such as

Wheel-shaped, or *Rotate*; when spreading out at once, without a tube or with a very short one, something in the shape of a wheel or of its diverging spokes, Fig. 252, 253.

Salver-shaped, or *Salver-form*; when a flat-spreading border is raised on [Pg 90]a narrow tube, from which it diverges at right angles, like the salver represented in old pictures, with a slender handle beneath, Fig. 249-251, 255.

FIG. 248. Polypetalous corolla of Soapwort, of five petals with long claws or stalk-like bases.

FIG. 249. Flower of Standing Cypress (Gilia coronopifolia); gamopetalous: the tube answering to the long claws in 248, except that they are coalescent: the limb or border (the spreading part above) is *five-parted*, that is, the petals not there united except at very base.

FIG. 250. Flower of Cypress-vine (Ipomœa Quamoclit); like preceding, but limb *five-lobed*.

FIG. 251. Flower of Ipomœa coccinea; limb almost *entire*.

FIG. 252. Wheel-shaped or rotate and five-parted corolla of Bittersweet, Solanum Dulcamara. 253. Wheel-shaped and five-lobed corolla of Potato.

Bell-shaped, or *Campanulate*; where a short and broad tube widens upward, in the shape of a bell, as in Fig. 254.

FIG. 254. Flower of a Campanula or Harebell, with a campanulate or bell-shaped corolla; 255, of a Phlox, with salver-shaped corolla; 256, of Dead Nettle (Lamium), with labiate *ringent* (or gaping) corolla; 257, of Snapdragon, with labiate *personate* corolla; 258, of Toad-Flax, with a similar corolla spurred at the base.

Funnel-shaped, or *Funnelform*; gradually spreading at the summit of a tube which is narrow below, in the shape of a funnel or tunnel, as in the corolla of the common Morning Glory (Fig. 247) and of the Stramonium (Fig. 246).

[Pg 91]

Tubular; when prolonged into a tube, with little or no spreading at the border, as in the corolla of the Trumpet Honeysuckle, the calyx of Stramonium (Fig. 246), etc.

261. Although sepals and petals are usually all blade or lamina (123), like a sessile leaf, yet they may have a contracted and stalk-like base, answering to petiole. This is called its CLAW, in

Latin *Unguis*. *Unguiculate* petals are universal and strongly marked in the Pink tribe, as in Soapwort (Fig. 248).

FIG. 259. Unguiculate (clawed) petal of a Silene; with a two-parted crown.

FIG. 260. A small Passion-flower, with crown of slender threads.

262. Such petals, and various others, may have an outgrowth of the inner face into an appendage or fringe, as in Soapwort, and in Silene (Fig. 259), where it is at the junction of claw and blade. This is called a CROWN, or *Corona*. In Passion-flowers (Fig. 260) the crown consists of numerous threads on the base of each petal.

FIG. 261. Front view of a papilionaceous corolla. 262. The parts of the same, displayed: *s*, Standard, or Vexillum; *w*, Wings, or Alæ; *k*, Keel, or Carina.

263. **Irregular Flowers** may be polypetalous, or nearly so, as in the papilionaceous corolla; but most of them are irregular through coalescence, which often much disguises the numerical symmetry also. As affecting the corolla the following forms have received particular names:

264. **Papilionaceous Corolla**, Fig. 261, 262. This is polypetalous, except that two of the petals cohere, usually but slightly. It belongs only to the Leguminous or Pulse family. The name means butterfly-like; but the likeness is hardly obvious. The names of the five petals of the *papilionaceous* corolla are curiously incongruous. They are,

[Pg 92]

The STANDARD or *Banner* (*Vexillum*), the large upper petal which is external in the bud and wrapped around the others.

The WINGS (*Alæ*), the pair of side petals, of quite different shape from the standard.

The KEEL (*Carina*), the two lower and usually smallest petals; these are lightly coalescent into a body which bears some likeness, not to the keel, but to the prow of a boat; and this encloses the stamens and pistil. A Pea-blossom is a typical example; the present illustration is from a species of Locust, Robinia hispida.

265. **Labiate Corolla** (Fig. 256-258), which would more properly have been called *Bilabiate*, that is, two-lipped. This is a common form of gamopetalous corolla; and the calyx is often bilabiate also. These flowers are all on the plan of five; and the irregularity in the corolla is owing to unequal union of the petals as well as to diversity of form. The two petals of the upper or posterior side of the flower unite with each other higher up than with the lateral petals (in Fig. 256, quite to the top), forming the *Upper lip*: the lateral and the lower similarly unite to form the *Lower lip*. The single notch which is generally found at the summit of the upper lip, and the two notches of the lower lip, or in other words the two lobes of the upper and the three of the lower lip, reveal the real composition. So also does the alternation of these five parts with those of the calyx outside. When the calyx is also bilabiate, as in the Sage, this alternation gives three lobes or sepals to the upper and two to the lower lip. Two forms of the labiate corolla have been designated, viz.:—

Ringent or *Gaping*, when the orifice is wide open, as in Fig. 256.

Personate or *Masked*, when a protuberance or intrusion of the base of the lower lip (called a *Palate*) projects over or closes the orifice, as in Snapdragon and Toad-Flax, Fig. 257, 258.

FIG. 263. Corolla of a purple Gerardia laid open, showing the four stamens; the cross shows where the fifth stamen would be, if present.

FIG. 264. Corolla, laid open, and stamens of Pentstemon grandiflorus, with a sterile filament in the place of the fifth stamen, and representing it.

FIG. 265. Corolla of Catalpa laid open, displaying two good stamens and three abortive ones or vestiges.

[Pg 93]

266. There are all gradations between labiate and regular corollas. In those of Gerardia, of some species of Pentstemon, and of Catalpa (Fig. 263-265), the labiate character is slight, but is manifest on close inspection. In almost all such flowers the plan of five, which is obvious or ascertainable in the calyx and corolla, is obscured in the stamens by the abortion or suppression of one or three of their number.

FIG. 266. Two flower-heads of Chiccory.

FIG. 267. One of them half cut away, better showing some of the flowers.

267. **Ligulate Corolla.** The ligulate or *Strap-shaped* corolla mainly belongs to the family of Compositæ, in which numerous small flowers are gathered into a head, within an involucre that imitates a calyx. It is best exemplified in the Dandelion and in Chiccory (Fig. 266). Each one of these straps or *Ligules*, looking like so many petals, is the corolla of a distinct flower: the base is a short tube, which opens out into the ligule: the five minute teeth at the end indicate the number of constituent petals. So this is a kind of gamopetalous corolla, which is open along one side nearly [Pg 94]to the base, and outspread. The nature of such a corolla (and of the stamens also, to be explained in the next section) is illustrated by the flower of a Lobelia, Fig. 285.

FIG. 268. Head of flowers of a Coreopsis, divided lengthwise.

268. In Asters, Daisies, Sunflower, Coreopsis (Fig. 268), and the like, only the marginal (or *Ray*) corollas are ligulate; the rest (those of the *Disk*) are regularly gamopetalous, tubular, and five-lobed at summit; but they are small and individually inconspicuous, only the *ray-flowers* making a show. In fact, those of Coreopsis and of Sunflower are simply for show, these ray-flowers being not only sterile, but *neutral*, that is, having neither stamens nor pistil. But in Asters, Daisies, Golden-rods, and the like, these ray-flowers are pistillate and fertile, serving therefore for seed-bearing as well as for show. Let it not be supposed that the show is useless. See Section XIII.

FIG. 269. A slice of the preceding more enlarged, with one tubular perfect flower (*a*) left standing on the receptacle, with its bractlet or chaff (*b*), one ligulate and neutral ray-flower (*cc*) and part of another; *dd*, section of bracts or leaves of the involucre.

269. **Adnation, or Consolidation**, is the union of the members of parts belonging to different circles of the flower (256). It is of course understood that in this (as likewise in coalescence) the parts are not formed and then conjoined, but are produced in union. They are born united, as the term *adnate* implies. To illustrate this kind of union, take the accompanying series of flowers (Fig. 270-274), shown in vertical section. In the first, Fig. 270, Flax-flower, there is no adnation; sepals, petals, and stamens, are *free* as well as distinct, being separately borne on the receptacle, one circle within or above the next; only the five pistils have their ovaries coalescent. In Fig. 271, a Cherry-flower, the petals and stamens are borne on the throat of the calyx-tube; that is, the sepals are coalescent into a cup, and the petals and stamens are adnate to the inner face of this; in other [Pg 95]words, the sepals, petals, and stamens are all consolidated up to a certain height. In Fig. 272, a Purslane-flower, the same parts are adnate to or consolidated with the ovary up to its middle. In Fig. 273, a Hawthorn-flower, the consolidation has extended over the whole ovary; and petals and stamens are adnate to the calyx still further. In Fig. 274, a Cranberry-blossom, it is the same except that all the parts are free at the same height; all seem to arise from the top of the ovary.

270. In botanical description, to express tersely such differences in the relation of these organs to the pistil, they are said to be

Hypogynous (i. e. under the pistil) when they are all *free*, that is, not adnate to pistil nor connate with each other, as in Fig. 270.

FIG. 270. Flax-flower in section; the parts all free,—hypogynous.

FIG. 271. Cherry-flower in section; petals and stamens adnate to tube of calyx,—perigynous.

FIG. 272. Purslane-flower in section; calyx, petals, stamens, all adnate to lower half of ovary,—perigynous.

Perigynous (around the pistil) when connate with each other, that is, when petals and stamens are *inserted* or borne on the calyx, whether as in Cherry-flowers (Fig. 271) they are free from the pistil, or as in Purslane and Hawthorn (Fig. 272, 273) they are also adnate below to the ovary.

Epigynous (on the ovary) when so adnate that all these parts appear to arise from the very summit of the ovary, as in Fig. 274. The last two terms are not very definitely distinguished.

271. Another and a simpler form of expression is to describe parts of the flower as being

Free, when not united with or *inserted* upon other parts.

Distinct, when parts of the same kind are not united. This term is the counterpart of coalescent, as free is the counterpart of adnate. Many writers use the term "free" indiscriminately for both; but it is better to distinguish them.

[Pg 96]

Connate is a term common for either not free or not distinct, that is, for parts united congenitally, whether of same or of different kinds.

Adnate, as properly used, relates to the union of dissimilar parts.

38

272. In still another form of expression, the terms superior and inferior have been much used in the sense of above and below.

Superior is said of the ovary of Flax-flower, Cherry, etc., because above the other parts; it is equivalent to "ovary free." Or it is said of the calyx, etc., when above the ovary, as in Fig. 273-275.

Inferior, when applied to the ovary, means the same as "calyx adnate;" when applied to the floral envelopes, it means that they are free.

FIG. 273. Hawthorn-blossom in section; parts adnate to whole face of ovary, and with each other beyond; another grade of perigynous.

FIG. 274. Cranberry-blossom in section; parts epigynous.

273. **Position of Flower or of its Parts.** The terms superior and inferior, or upper and lower, are also used to indicate the relative position of the parts of a flower in reference to the axis of inflorescence. An axillary flower stands between the bract or leaf which subtends it and the axis or stem which bears this bract or leaf. This is represented in sectional diagrams (as in Fig. 275, 276) by a transverse line for the bract, and a small circle for the axis of inflorescence. Now the side of the blossom which faces the bract is the

Anterior, or *Inferior*, or *Lower* side; while the side next the axis is the

Posterior, or *Superior*, or *Upper* side of the flower.

FIG. 275. Diagram of papilionaceous flower (Robinia, Fig. 261), with bract below; axis of inflorescence above.

FIG. 276. Diagram of Violet-flower; showing the relation of parts to bract and axis.

274. So, in the labiate corolla (Fig. 256-258), the lip which is composed of three of the five petals is the *anterior*, or *inferior*, or *lower* lip; the other is the *posterior*, or *superior*, or *upper* lip.

[Pg 97]

275. In Violets (Fig. 238, 276), the odd sepal is posterior (next the axis); the odd petal is therefore anterior, or next the subtending leaf. In the papilionaceous flower (Fig. 261, and diagram, Fig. 275), the odd sepal is anterior, and so two sepals are posterior; consequently, by the alternation, the odd petal (the standard) is posterior or upper, and the two petals forming the keel are anterior or lower.

§ 5. ARRANGEMENT OF PARTS IN THE BUD.

276. **Æstivation** was the fanciful name given by Linnæus to denote the disposition of the parts, especially the leaves of the flower, before *Anthesis*, i. e. before the blossom opens. *Præfloration*, a better term, is sometimes used. This is of importance in distinguishing different families or genera of plants, being generally uniform in each. The æstivation is best seen by making a slice across the flower-bud; and it may be expressed in diagrams, as in the accompanying figures.

277. The pieces of the calyx or the corolla either overlap each other in the bud, or they do not. When they do not overlap, the æstivation is

Valvate, when the pieces meet each other by their abrupt edges, without any infolding or overlapping; as the calyx of the Linden or Basswood (Fig. 277).

FIG. 277. Diagram of a flower of Linden, showing the calyx valvate and corolla imbricate in the bud, etc.

Induplicate, which is valvate with the margins of each piece projecting inwards, as in the calyx of a common Virgin's-bower, Fig. 278, or

FIG. 278. Valvate-induplicate æstivation of calyx of common Virgin's-bower.

FIG. 279. Valvate-involute æstivation of same in Vine-bower, Clematis Vitialla.

Involute, which is the same but the margins rolled inward, as in most of the large-flowered species of Clematis, Fig. 279.

Reduplicate, a rarer modification of valvate, is similar but with margins projecting outward.

Open, the parts not touching in the bud, as the calyx of Mignonette.

278. When the pieces overlap in the bud, it is in one of two ways; either every piece has one edge in and one edge out, or some pieces are wholly outside and others wholly inside. In the first case the æstivation is

Convolute, also named *Contorted* or *Twisted*, as in Fig. 280, a cross-section of a corolla very strongly thus convolute or rolled up together, and in the corolla of a Flax-flower (Fig. 281), where the petals only moderately overlap in this way. Here one edge of every petal covers the next before [Pg 98]it, while its other edge is covered by the next behind it. The other mode is the

FIG. 280. Convolute æstivation, as in the corolla-lobes of Oleander.

FIG. 281. Diagram of a Flax-flower; calyx imbricated and corolla convolute in the bud.

Imbricate or *Imbricated*, in which the outer parts cover or overlap the inner so as to "break joints," like tiles or shingles on a roof; whence the name. When the parts are three, the first or outermost is wholly external, the third wholly internal, the second has one margin covered by the first while the other overlaps the third or innermost piece: this is the arrangement of alternate three-ranked leaves (187). When there are five pieces, as in the corolla of Fig. 225, and calyx of Fig. 281, as also of Fig. 241, 276, two are external, two are internal, and one (the third in the spiral) has one edge covered by the outermost, while its other edge covers the innermost; which is just the five-ranked arrangement of alternate leaves (188). When the pieces are four, two are outer and two are inner; which answers to the arrangement of opposite leaves.

279. The imbricate and the convolute modes sometimes vary one into the other, especially in the corolla.

280. In a gamopetalous corolla or gamosepalous calyx, the shape of the tube in the bud may sometimes be noticeable. It may be

Plicate or *Plaited*, that is, folded lengthwise; and the plaits may either be turned outwards, forming projecting ridges, as in the corolla of Campanula; or turned inwards, as in that of Gentian Belladonna; or

Supervolute, when the plaits are convolutely wrapped round each other, as in the corolla of Morning Glory and of Stramonium, Fig. 282.

FIG. 282. Upper part of corolla of Datura Stramonium in the bud; and below a section showing the convolution of the plaits.

SECTION IX. STAMENS IN PARTICULAR.

281. **Andrœcium** is a technical name for the staminate system of a flower (that is, for the stamens taken together), which it is sometimes convenient to use. The preceding section has dealt with modifications of the flower pertaining mainly to calyx and corolla. Those relating to the stamens are now to be indicated. First as to

[Pg 99]

282. Insertion, or place of attachment. The stamens usually go with the petals. Not rarely they are at base

Epipetalous, that is, inserted on (or adnate to) the corolla, as in Fig. 283. When free from the corolla, they may be

FIG. 283. Corolla of Morning Glory laid open, to show the five stamens inserted on it, near the base.

Hypogynous, inserted on the receptacle under the pistil or gynœcium.

Perigynous, inserted on the calyx, that is, with the lower part of filament adnate to the calyx-tube.

Epigynous, borne apparently on the top of the ovary; all which is explained in Fig. 270-274.

FIG. 284. Style of a Lady's Slipper (Cypripedium), and stamens united with it; *a, a,* the anthers of the two good stamens; *st*, an abortive stamen, what should be its anther changed into a petal-like body; *stig*, the stigma.

Gynandrous is another term relating to insertion of rarer occurrence, that is, where the stamens are inserted on (in other words, adnate to) the style, as in Lady's Slipper (Fig. 284), and in the Orchis family generally.

283. **In Relation to each Other,** stamens are more commonly

Distinct, that is, without any union with each other. But when united, the following technical terms of long use indicate their modes of mutual connection:—

Monadelphous (from two Greek words, meaning "in one brotherhood"), when united by their filaments into one set, usually into a ring or cup below, or into a tube, as in the Mallow Family (Fig. 286), the Passion-flower (Fig. 260), the Lupine (Fig. 287), and in Lobelia (Fig. 285).

FIG. 285. Flower of Lobelia cardinalis, Cardinal flower; corolla making approach to the ligulate form; filaments (*st*) monadelphous, and anthers (*a*) syngenesious.

FIG. 286. Flower of a Mallow, with calyx and corolla cut away; showing monadelphous stamens.

FIG. 287. Monadelphous stamens of Lupine. 288. Diadelphous stamens (9 and 1) of a Pea-blossom.

Diadelphous (meaning in two brotherhoods), when united by the filaments into two sets, as in the Pea and most of its near relatives (Fig. 288), usually nine in one set, and one in the other.

Triadelphous (three brotherhoods), when the filaments are united in three sets or clusters, as in most species of Hypericum.

[Pg 100]

Pentadelphous (five brotherhoods), when in five sets, as in some species of Hypericum and in American Linden (Fig. 277, 289).

Polyadelphous (many or several brotherhoods) is the term generally employed when these sets are several, or even more than two, and the particular number is left unspecified. These terms all relate to the filaments.

Syngenesious is the term to denote that stamens have their anthers united, coalescent into a ring or tube; as in Lobelia (Fig. 285), in Violets, and in all of the great family of Compositæ.

284. **Their Number** in a flower is commonly expressed directly, but sometimes adjectively, by a series of terms which were the name of classes in the Linnæan artificial system, of which the following names, as also the preceding, are a survival:—

Monandrous, i. e. solitary-stamened, when the flower has only one stamen,

Diandrous, when it has two stamens only,

Triandrous, when it has three stamens,

Tetrandrous, when it has four stamens,

Pentandrous, when it has five stamens,

Hexandrous, when with six stamens, and so on to

Polyandrous, when it has many stamens, or more than a dozen.

FIG. 289. One of the five stamen-clusters of the flower of American Linden, with accompanying scale. The five clusters are shown in section in the diagram of this flower, Fig. 277.

FIG. 290. Five syngenesious stamens of a Coreopsis. 291. Same, with tube laid open and displayed.

285. For which terms, see the Glossary. They are all Greek numerals prefixed to -*andria* (from the Greek), which Linnæus used for *andrœcium*, and are made into an English adjective, -*androus*. Two other terms, of same origin, designate particular cases of number (four or six) in connection with unequal length. Namely, the stamens are

Didynamous, when, being only four, they form two pairs, one pair longer than the other, as in the Trumpet Creeper, in Gerardia (Fig. 263), etc.

[Pg 101]

Tetradynamous, when, being only six, four of them surpass the other two, as in the Mustard-flower and all the Cruciferous family, Fig. 235.

286. **The Filament** is a kind of stalk to the anther, commonly slender or thread-like: it is to the anther nearly what the petiole is to the blade of a leaf. Therefore it is not an essential part. As a leaf may be without a stalk, so the anther may be *Sessile*, or without a filament.

FIG. 292. Stamen of Isopyrum, with innate anther. 293. Of Tulip-tree, with adnate (and extrorse) anther. 294. Of Evening Primrose, with versatile anther.

287. **The Anther** is the essential part of the stamen. It is a sort of case, filled with a fine powder, *the Pollen*, which serves to fertilize the pistil, so that it may perfect seeds. The anther is said to be

Innate (as in Fig. 292), when it is attached by its base to the very apex of the filament, turning neither inward nor outward;

Adnate (as in Fig. 293), when attached as it were by one face, usually for its whole length, to the side of a continuation of the filament; and

Versatile (as in Fig. 294), when fixed by or near its middle only to the very point of the filament, so as to swing loosely, as in the Lily, in Grasses, etc. Versatile or adnate anthers are

Introrse, or *Incumbent*, when facing inward, that is, toward the centre of the flower, as in Magnolia, Water-Lily, etc.

Extrorse, when facing outwardly, as in the Tulip-tree.

288. Rarely does a stamen bear any resemblance to a leaf, or even to a petal or flower-leaf. Nevertheless, the botanist's idea of a stamen is that it answers to a leaf developed in a peculiar form and for a special purpose. In the filament he sees the stalk of the leaf; in the anther, the blade. The blade of a leaf consists of two similar sides; so the anther consists of two LOBES or CELLS, one answering to the left, the other to the right, side of the blade. The two lobes are often connected by a prolongation of the filament, which answers to the midrib of a

leaf; this is called the CONNECTIVE. This is conspicuous in Fig. 292, where the connective is so broad that it separates the two cells of the anther to some distance.

FIG. 295. Diagram of the lower part of an anther, cut across above, and the upper part of a leaf, to show how the one answers to the other; the filament to petiole, the connective to midrib; the two cells to the right and left halves of the blade.

289. A simple conception of the morphological relation of an anther to a leaf is given in Fig. 295, an ideal figure, the lower part representing a stamen with the top of its anther cut away; the upper, the corresponding upper part of a leaf.

[Pg 102]

290. So anthers are generally *two-celled*. But as the pollen begins to form in two parts of each cell (the anterior and the posterior), sometimes these two strata are not confluent, and the anther even at maturity may be *four-celled*, as in Moonseed (Fig. 296); or rather, in that case (the word *cell* being used for each lateral half of the organ), it is *two-celled*, but the cells *bilocellate*.

FIG. 296. Stamen of Moonseed, with anther cut across; this 4-celled, or rather 4-locellate.

FIG. 297. Stamen of Pentstemon pubescens; the two anther-cells diverging, and almost confluent.

FIG. 298. Stamen of Mallow; the anther supposed to answer to that of Fig. 297, but the cells completely confluent into one.

FIG. 299. Stamen of Globe Amaranth; very short filament bearing a single anther-cell; it is open from top to bottom, showing the pollen within.

FIG. 300-305. Stamens of several plants of the Labiate or Mint Family. FIG. 300. Of a Monarda: the two anther-cells with bases divergent so that they are transverse to the filament, and their contiguous tips confluent, so as to form one cell opening by a continuous line. FIG. 301. Of a Calamintha: the broad connective separating the two cells. FIG. 302. Of a Sage (Salvia Texana); with long and slender connective resembling forks of the filament, one bearing a good anther-cell; the other an abortive or poor one. FIG. 303. Another Sage (S. coccinea), with connective longer and more thread-shaped, the lower fork having its anther-cell wholly wanting. FIG. 304. Of a White Sage, Audibertia grandiflora; the lower fork of connective a mere vestige. FIG. 305. Of another White Sage (A. stachyoides), the lower fork of connective suppressed.

291. But anthers may become *one-celled*, and that either by confluence or by suppression.

292. By confluence, when the two cells run together into one, as they nearly do in most species of Pentstemon (Fig. 297), more so in Monarda (Fig. 300), and completely in the Mallow (Fig. 298) and all the Mallow family.

[Pg 103]

293. By suppression in certain cases the anther may be reduced to one cell or halved. In Globe Amaranth (Fig. 299) there is a single cell without vestige of any other. Different species of Sage and of the White Sages of California show various grades of abortion of one of the anther-cells, along with a singular lengthening of the connective (Fig. 302-305).

294. The splitting open of an anther for the discharge of its pollen is termed its *Dehiscence*.

FIG. 306. Stamen with the usual dehiscence of anther down the side of each cell.

FIG. 307. Stamen of Pyrola; cells opening by a terminal hole.

FIG. 308. Stamen of Barberry; cells of anther each opening by an uplifted valve.

295. As the figures show, this is commonly by a line along the whole length of each cell, either lateral or, when the anthers are extrorse, often along the outer face, and when introrse, along the inner face of each cell. Sometimes the opening is only by a chink, hole, or pore at the top, as in the Azalea, Pyrola (Fig. 307), etc.; sometimes a part of the face separates as a sort of trap-door (or valve), hinged at the top, and opening to allow the escape of the pollen, as in the Sassafras, Spice-bush, and Barberry (Fig. 308).

296. **Pollen.** This is the powdery matter, commonly of a yellow color, which fills the cells of the anther, and is discharged during blossoming, after which the stamens generally fall or wither away. Under the microscope it is found to consist of grains, usually round or oval, and all alike in the same species, but very different in different plants. So that the plant may sometimes be recognized from the pollen alone. Several forms are shown in the accompanying figures.

FIG. 309. Magnified pollen of a Lily, smooth and oval; 310, of Echinocystis, grooved lengthwise; 311, of Sicyos, with bristly points and smooth bands; 312, of Musk Plant (Mimulus), with spiral grooves; 313, of Succory, twelve-sided and dotted.

42

297. An ordinary pollen-grain has two coats; the outer coat thickish, but weak, and frequently adorned with lines or bands, or studded with points; the inner coat is extremely thin and delicate, but extensible, and its cavity when fresh contains a thickish protoplasmic fluid, often rendered turbid by an immense number of minute particles that float in it. As the pollen matures this fluid usually dries up, but the protoplasm does not lose its vitality. When the grain is wetted it absorbs water, swells up, and is apt to burst, discharging the contents. But when weak syrup is used it absorbs this slowly, and the tough inner coat will sometimes break through the outer and begin a kind of growth, like that which takes place when the pollen is placed upon the stigma.

FIG. 314. Magnified pollen of Hibiscus and other Mallow-plants, beset with prickly projections; 315, of Circæa, with angles bearing little lobes; 316, of Evening Primrose, the three lobes as large as the central body; 317, of Kalmia, four grains united, as in most of the Heath family; 318, of Pine, as it were of three grains or cells united; the lateral empty and light.

298. Some pollen-grains are, as it were, lobed (as in Fig. 315, 316), or formed of four grains united (as in the Heath family, Fig. 317): that of Pine (Fig. 318) has a large rounded and empty bladder-like expansion upon each side. This renders such pollen very buoyant, and capable of being transported to a great distance by the wind.

299. In species of Acacia simple grains lightly cohere into globular pellets. In Milkweeds and in most Orchids all the pollen of an anther-cell is compacted or coherent into one mass, called a *Pollen-mass*, or POLLINIUM, plural POLLINIA. (Fig. 319-322.)

FIG. 319. Pollen, a pair of pollinia of a Milkweed, Asclepias, attached by stalks to a gland; moderately magnified.

FIG. 320. Pollinium of an Orchis (Habenaria), with its stalk attached to a sticky gland; magnified. 321. Some of the packets or partial pollinia, of which Fig. 320 is made up, more magnified.

FIG. 322. One of the partial pollinia, torn up at top to show the grains (which are each composed of four), and highly magnified.

SECTION X. PISTILS IN PARTICULAR.
§ 1. ANGIOSPERMOUS OR ORDINARY GYNŒCIUM.

300. **Gynœcium** is the technical name for the pistil or pistils of a flower taken collectively, or for whatever stands in place of these. The various modifications of the gynœcium and the terms which relate to them require particular attention.

301. The PISTIL, when only one, occupies the centre of the flower; when there are two pistils, they stand facing each other in the centre of the flower; when several, they commonly form a ring or circle; and when very numerous, they are generally crowded in rows or spirals on the surface of a more or less enlarged or elongated receptacle. Their number gives rise to certain terms, the counterpart of those used for stamens (284), which are survivals of the names of orders in the Linnæan artificial system. The names were coined by prefixing Greek numerals to -*gynia* used for gynœcium, and changed into adjectives in the form of -*gynous*. That is, a flower is

Monogynous, when it has a single pistil, whether that be simple or compound;

Digynous, when it has only two pistils; *Trigynous*, when with three; *Tetragynous*, with four; *Pentagynous*, with five; *Hexagynous*, with six; and so on to *Polygynous*, with many pistils.

302. **The Parts of a Complete Pistil**, as already twice explained (16, 236), are the OVARY, the STYLE, and the STIGMA. The ovary is one essential part: it contains the rudiments of seeds, called OVULES. The stigma at the summit is also essential: it receives the pollen, which fertilizes the ovules in order that they may become seeds. But the style, commonly a tapering or slender column borne on the summit of the ovary, and bearing the stigma on its apex or its side, is no more necessary to a pistil than the filament is to the stamen. Accordingly, there is no style in many pistils: in these the stigma is *sessile*, that is, rests directly on the ovary (as in Fig.326). The stigma is very various in shape and appearance, being sometimes a little knob (as in the Cherry, Fig. 271), sometimes a point or small surface of bare tissue (as in Fig. 327-330), and sometimes a longitudinal crest or line (as in Fig. 324, 341-343), or it may occupy the whole length of the style, as in Fig. 331.

303. The word Pistil (Latin, *Pistillum*) means a pestle. It came into use in the first place for such flowers as those of Crown Imperial, or Lily, in which the pistil in the centre was likened to the pestle, and the perianth around it to the mortar, of the apothecary.

304. A pistil is either *simple* or *compound*. It is simple when it answers to a single flower-leaf, compound when it answers to two or three, or a fuller circle of such leaves conjoined.

[Pg 106]

305. **Carpels.** It is convenient to have a name for each flower-leaf of the gynœcium; so it is called a *Carpel*, in Latin *Carpellum* or *Carpidium*. A simple pistil is a carpel. Each component flower-leaf of a compound pistil is likewise a carpel. When a flower has two or more pistils, these of course are simple pistils, that is, separate carpels or pistil-leaves. There may be only a single simple pistil to the flower, as in a Pea or Cherry blossom (Fig. 271); there may be two such, as in many Saxifrages; or many, as in the Strawberry. More commonly the single pistil in the centre of a blossom is a compound one. Then there is seldom much difficulty in ascertaining the number of carpels or pistil-leaves that compose it.

306. **The Simple Pistil**, viewed morphologically, answers to a leaf-blade with margins incurved and united where they meet, so forming a closed case or pod (the ovary), and bearing ovules at the suture or junction of these margins: a tapering upper portion with margins similarly inrolled, is supposed to form the style; and these same margins, exposed at the tip or for a portion of the length, become the stigma. Compare, under this view, the three accompanying figures.

FIG. 323. An inrolled small leaf, such as in double-flowered Cherry blossoms is often seen to occupy the place of a pistil.

FIG. 324. A simple pistil (of Isopyrum), with ovary cut across; the inner (ventral) face turned toward the eye: the ovules seem to be borne on the ventral suture, answering to leaf-margins: the stigma above seen also to answer to leaf-margins.

FIG. 325. Pod or simple pistil of Caltha or Marsh-Marigold, which has opened, and shed its seeds.

307. So a simple pistil should have a one-celled ovary, only one line of attachment for the ovules, a single style, and a single stigma. Certain variations from this normal condition which sometimes occur do not invalidate this morphological conception. For instance, the stigma may become two-lobed or two-ridged, because it consists of two leaf-margins, as Fig. 324 shows; it may become 2-locellate by the turning or growing inward of one of the sutures, so as to divide the cavity.

308. There are two or three terms which primarily relate to the parts of a simple pistil or carpel, and are thence carried on to the compound pistil, viz.:—

VENTRAL SUTURE, the line which answers to the united margins of the carpel-leaf, therefore naturally called a suture or seam, and the ventral or inner one, because in the circle of carpel-leaves it looks inward or to the centre of the flower.

DORSAL SUTURE is the line down the back of the carpel, answering to [Pg 107]the midrib of the leaf,—not a seam therefore; but at maturity many fruits, such as pea-pods, open by this dorsal as well as by the ventral line.

PLACENTA, a name given to the surface, whatever it be, which bears the ovules and seeds. The name may be needless when the ovules grow directly on the ventral suture, or from its top or bottom; but when there are many ovules there is usually some expansion of an ovule-bearing or seed-bearing surface; as is seen in our Mandrake or Podophyllum, Fig. 326.

FIG. 326. Simple pistil of Podophyllum, cut across, showing ovules borne on placenta.

FIG. 327. Pistil of a Saxifrage, of two simple carpels or pistil-leaves, united at the base only, cut across both above and below.

FIG. 328. Compound 3-carpellary pistil of common St. John's-wort, cut across: the three styles separate.

FIG. 329. The same of shrubby St. John's-wort; the three styles as well as ovaries here united into one.

FIG. 330. Compound 3-carpellary pistil of Tradescantia or Spiderwort; the three stigmas as well as styles and ovary completely coalescent into one.

309. **A Compound Pistil** is a combination of two, three, or a greater number of pistil-leaves or carpels in a circle, united into one body, at least by their ovaries. The annexed figures should make it clear. A series of Saxifrages might be selected the gynœcium of which would show every gradation between two simple pistils, or separate carpels, and their complete coalescence into one compound and two-celled ovary. Even when the constituent styles and stigmas are completely coalescent into one, the nature of the combination is usually revealed by some external lines or grooves, or (as in Fig. 328-330) by the internal partitions, or the number of the placentæ. The simplest case of compound pistil is that

310. **With two or more Cells and Axile Placentæ**, namely, with as many cells as there are carpels, that have united to compose the organ. [Pg 108]Such a pistil is just what would be formed if the simple pistils (two, three, or five in a circle, as the case may be), like those of a Pæony or Stonecrop (Fig. 224, 225), pressed together in the centre of the flower, were to cohere by their contiguous parts. In such a case the placentæ are naturally *axile*, or all brought together in the axis or centre; and the ovary has as many DISSEPIMENTS, or internal *Partitions*, as there are carpels in its composition. For these are the contiguous and coalescent walls or sides of the component carpels. When such pistils ripen into pods, they often separate along these lines into their elementary carpels.

FIG. 331, 332. Pistil of a Sandwort, with vertical and transverse section of the ovary: free central placenta.

311. **One-celled, with free Central Placenta.** The commoner case is that of Purslane (Fig. 272) and of the Pink and Chickweed families (Fig. 331, 332). This is explained by supposing that the partitions (such as those of Fig. 329) have early vanished or have been suppressed. Indeed, traces of them may often be detected in Pinks. On the other hand, it is equally supposable that in the Primula family the free central is derived from parietal placentation by the carpels bearing ovules only at base, and forming a consolidated common placenta in the axis. Mitella and Dionæa help out this conception.

FIG. 333. Plan of a one-celled ovary of three carpel-leaves, with parietal placentæ, cut across below, where it is complete; the upper part showing the top of the three leaves it is composed of, approaching, but not united.

FIG. 334. Cross section of the ovary of Frost weed (Helianthemum), with three parietal placentæ, bearing ovules.

FIG. 335. Cross section of an ovary of Hypericum graveolens, the three large placentæ meeting in the centre, so as to form a three-celled ovary. 336. Same in fruit, the placentæ now separate and rounded.

312. **One-celled, with Parietal Placentæ.** In this not uncommon case it is conceived that the two or three or more carpel-leaves of such a compound pistil coalesce by their adjacent edges, just as sepal-leaves do to form a gamosepalous calyx, or petals to form a gamopetalous corolla, and as is shown in the diagram, Fig. 333, and in an actual cross-section, Fig. 334. Here each carpel is an open leaf, or with some introflexion, bearing ovules along its margins; and each placenta consists of the contiguous [Pg 109]margins of two pistil-leaves grown together. There is every gradation between this and the three-celled ovary with the placentæ in the axis, even in the same genus, sometimes even in different stages in the same pistil (Fig. 335, 336).

§ 2. GYMNOSPERMOUS GYNŒCIUM.

313. The ordinary pistil has a closed ovary, and accordingly the pollen can act upon the contained ovules only indirectly, through the stigma. This is expressed in a term of Greek derivation, viz.:—

Angiospermous, meaning that the seeds are borne in a sac or closed vessel. The counterpart term is

Gymnospermous, meaning naked-seeded. This kind of pistil, or gynœcium, the simplest of all, yet the most peculiar, characterizes the Pine family and its relatives.

FIG. 337. A pistil, that is, a scale of the cone, of a Larch, at the time of flowering; inside view, showing its pair of naked ovules.

FIG. 338. Branchlet of the American Arbor-Vitæ, considerably larger than in nature, terminated by its pistillate flowers, each consisting of a single scale (an open pistil), together forming a small cone.

FIG. 339. One of the scales or carpels of the last, removed and more enlarged, the inside exposed to view, showing a pair of ovules on its base.

314. While the ordinary simple pistil is conceived by the botanist to be a leaf rolled together into a closed pod (306), those of the Pine, Larch (Fig. 337), Cedar, and Arbor-Vitæ (Fig. 338, 339) are open leaves, in the form of scales, each bearing two or more ovules on the inner face, next the base. At the time of blossoming, these pistil-leaves of the young cone diverge, and the pollen, so abundantly shed from the staminate blossoms, falls directly upon the exposed ovules. Afterward the scales close over each other until the seeds are ripe. Then they separate that the seeds may be shed. As the pollen acts directly on the ovules, such pistil (or organ acting as pistil) has no stigma.

315. In the Yew, and in Torreya and Gingko, the gynœcium is reduced to extremest simplicity, that is, to a naked ovule, without any visible carpel.

316. In Cycas the large naked ovules are borne on the margins or lobes of an obvious open leaf. All GYMNOSPERMOUS plants have other peculiarities, also distinguishing them, as a class, from ANGIOSPERMOUS plants.

[Pg 110]

SECTION XI. OVULES.

317. **Ovule** (from the Latin, meaning a little egg) is the technical name of that which in the flower answers to and becomes the seed.

FIG. 340. A cluster of ovules, pendulous on their funicles.

318. Ovules are *naked* in gymnospermous plants (as just described), in all others they are enclosed in the ovary. They may be produced along the whole length of the cell or cells of the ovary, and then they are apt to be numerous, or only from some part of it, generally the top or the bottom. In this case they are usually few or single (*solitary*, as in Fig. 341-343). They may be *sessile*, i. e. without stalk, or they may be attached by a distinct stalk, the FUNICLE or FUNICULUS (Fig. 340).

FIG. 341. Section of the ovary of a Buttercup, lengthwise, showing its ascending ovule.

FIG. 342. Section of the ovary of Buckwheat, showing the erect ovule.

FIG. 343. Section of the ovary of Anemone, showing its suspended ovule.

319. Considered as to then position and direction in the ovary, they are

Horizontal, when they are neither turned upward nor downward, as in Podophyllum (Fig. 326),

Ascending, when rising obliquely upwards, usually from the side of the cell, not from its very base, as in the Buttercup (Fig. 341), and the Purslane (Fig. 272),

Erect, when rising upright from the very base of the cell, as in the Buckwheat (Fig. 342),

Pendulous, when hanging from the side or from near the top, as in the Flax (Fig. 270), and

Suspended, when hanging perpendicularly from the very summit of the cell, as in the Anemone (Fig. 343). All these terms equally apply to seeds.

320. In structure an ovule is a pulpy mass of tissue, usually with one or two coats or coverings. The following parts are to be noted, viz.—

KERNEL or NUCLEUS, the body of the ovule. In the Mistletoe and some related plants, there is only this nucleus, the coats being wanting.

TEGUMENTS, or coats, sometimes only one, more commonly two. When two, one has been called PRIMINE, the other SECUNDINE. It will serve all purposes to call them simply outer and inner ovule coats.

ORIFICE, or FORAMEN, an opening through the coats at the organic apex of the ovule. In the seed it is *Micropyle*.

CHALAZA, the place where the coats and the kernel of the ovule blend.

HILUM, the place of junction of the funiculus with the body of the ovule.

[Pg 111]

FIG. 344. Orthotropous ovule of Buckwheat: *c*, hilum and chalaza; *f*, orifice.

FIG. 345. Campylotropous ovule of a Chickweed: *c*, hilum and chalaza; *f*, orifice.

FIG. 346. Amphitropous ovule of Mallow: *f*, orifice; *h*, hilum; *r*, rhaphe; *c*, chalaza.

FIG. 347. Anatropous ovule of a Violet, the parts lettered as in the last.

321. **The Kinds of Ovules.** The ovules in their growth develop in three or four different ways and thereby are distinguished into

Orthotropous or *Straight*, those which develop without curving or turning, as in Fig. 344. The chalaza is at the insertion or base, the foramen or orifice is at the apex. This is the simplest, but the least common kind of ovule.

Campylotropous or *Incurved*, in which, by the greater growth of one side, the ovule curves into a kidney-shaped outline, so bringing the orifice down close to the base or chalaza; as in Fig. 345.

Amphitropous or *Half Inverted*, Fig. 346. Here the forming ovule, instead of curving perceptibly, keeps its axis nearly straight, and, as it grows, turns round upon its base so far as to become transverse to its funiculus, and adnate to its upper part for some distance. Therefore in this case the attachment of the funiculus or stalk is about the middle, the chalaza is at one end, the orifice at the other.

FIG. 348-350. Three early stages in the growth of ovule of a Magnolia, showing the forming outer and inner coats which even in the later figure have not yet completely enclosed the nucleus; 351, further advanced, and 352, completely anatropous ovule.

FIG. 353. Longitudinal section, and 354, transverse section of 352.

FIG. 355. Same as 353, enlarged showing the parts in section: a, outer coat; b, inner coat; c, nucleus; d, rhaphe.

Anatropous or *Inverted*, as in Fig. 347, the commonest kind, so called because in its growth it has as it were turned over upon its stalk, to which it has continued adnate. The organic base, or chalaza, thus becomes the apparent summit, and the [Pg 112]orifice is at the base, by the side of the hilum or place of attachment. The adnate portion of the funiculus, which appears as a ridge or cord extending from the hilum to the chalaza, and which distinguishes this kind of ovule, is called the RHAPHE. The amphitropous ovule (Fig. 346) has a short or incomplete rhaphe.

322. Fig. 348-352 show the stages through which an ovule becomes anatropous in the course of its growth. The annexed two figures are sections of such an ovule at maturity; and Fig. 355 is Fig. 353 enlarged, with the parts lettered.

SECTION XII. MODIFICATIONS OF THE RECEPTACLE.

FIG. 356. Longitudinal section of flower of Silene Pennsylvanica, showing stipe between calyx and corolla.

FIG. 357. Flower of a Cleome of the section Gynandropsis, showing broadened receptacle to bear petals, lengthened stipe below the stamens, and another between these and pistil.

FIG. 358. Pistil of Geranium or Cranesbill.

FIG. 359. The same, ripe, with the five carpels splitting away from the long beak (carpophore), and hanging from its top by their recurving styles.

323. **The Torus** or Receptacle of the flower (237, Fig. 223) is the portion which belongs to the stem or axis. In all preceding illustrations it is small and short. But it sometimes lengthens, sometimes thickens or variously enlarges, and takes on various forms. Some of these have received special names, very few of which are in common use. A lengthened portion of the receptacle is called

A STIPE. This name, which means simply a trunk or stalk, is used in botany for various stalks, even for the leaf-stalk in Ferns. It is also applied to the stalk or petiole of a carpel, in the rare cases when there is any, as in [Pg 113]Goldthread. Then it is technically distinguished as a THECAPHORE. When there is a stalk, or lengthened internode of receptacle, directly under a compound pistil, as in Stanleya and some other Cruciferæ, it is called a GYNOPHORE. When the stalk is developed below the stamens, as in most species of Silene (Fig. 356), it has been called an ANTHOPHORE or GONOPHORE. In Fig. 357 the torus is dilated above the calyx where it bears the petals, then there is a long internode (gonophore) between it and the stamens; then a shorter one (gynophore) between these and the pistil.

324. **A Carpophore** is a prolongation of receptacle or axis between the carpels and bearing them. Umbelliferous plants and Geranium (Fig. 358, 359) afford characteristic examples.

FIG. 360. Longitudinal section of a young strawberry, enlarged.

FIG. 361. Similar section of a young Rose-hip.

FIG. 362. Enlarged and top-shaped receptacle of Nelumbium, at maturity.

325. Flowers with very numerous simple pistils generally have the receptacle enlarged so as to give them room; sometimes becoming broad and flat, as in the Flowering Raspberry, sometimes elongated, as in the Blackberry, the Magnolia, etc. It is the receptacle in the Strawberry (Fig. 360), much enlarged and pulpy when ripe, which forms the eatable part of the fruit, and bears the small seed-like pistils on its surface. In the Rose (Fig. 361), instead of being convex or conical, the receptacle is deeply concave, or urn-shaped. Indeed, a Rose-hip may be likened to a strawberry turned inside out, like the finger of a glove reversed, and the whole covered by the adherent tube of the calyx. The calyx remains beneath in the strawberry.

326. In Nelumbium, of the Water-Lily family, the singular and greatly enlarged receptacle is shaped like a top, and bears the small pistils immersed in separate cavities of its flat upper surface (Fig. 362).

FIG. 363. Hypogynous disk in Orange.

327. **A Disk** is an enlarged low receptacle or an outgrowth from it, *hypogynous* when underneath the pistil, as in Rue and the Orange (Fig. 363), and *perigynous* when adnate to calyx-tube (as in Buckthorn, Fig. 364, 365), and Cherry (Fig. 271), or [Pg 114]to both calyx-tube and

ovary, as in Hawthorn (Fig. 273). A flattened hypogynous disk, underlying the ovary or ovaries, and from which they fall away at maturity, is sometimes called a GYNOBASE, as in the Rue family. In some Borragineous flowers, such as Houndstongue, the gynobase runs up in the centre between the carpels into a carpophore. The so-called *epigynous* disk (orSTYLOPODIUM) crowning the summit of the ovary in flowers of Umbelliferæ, etc., cannot be said to belong to the receptacle.

FIG. 364. Flower of a Buckthorn showing a conspicuous perigynous disk.
FIG. 365. Vertical section of same flower.

SECTION XIII. FERTILIZATION.

328. The end of the flower is attained when the ovules become seeds. A flower remains for a certain time (longer or shorter according to the species) in *anthesis*, that is, in the proper state for the fulfilment of this end. During anthesis, the ovules have to be fertilized by the pollen; or at least some pollen has to reach the stigma, or in gymnospermy the ovule itself, and to set up the peculiar growth upon its moist and permeable tissue, which has for result the production of an embryo in the ovules. By this the ovules are said to be *fertilized.* The first step is *pollination*, or, so to say, the sowing of the proper pollen upon the stigma, where it is to germinate.

§ 1. ADAPTATIONS FOR POLLINATION OF THE STIGMA.

329. These various and ever-interesting adaptations and processes are illustrated in the "Botanical Text Book, Structural Botany," chap. VI. sect. iv., also in a brief and simple way in "Botany for Young People, How Plants Behave." So mere outlines only are given here.

330. Sometimes the application of pollen to the stigma is left to chance, as in diœcious wind-fertilized flowers; sometimes it is rendered very sure, as in flowers that are fertilized in the bud; sometimes the pollen is prevented from reaching the stigma of the same flower, although placed very near to it, but then there are always arrangements for its transference to the stigma of some other blossom of the kind. It is among these last that the most exquisite adaptations are met with.

331. Accordingly, some flowers are particularly adapted to close or self-fertilization; others to cross fertilization; some for either, according to circumstances.

[Pg 115]

Close Fertilization occurs when the pollen reaches and acts upon a stigma of the very same flower (this is also called self-fertilization), or, less closely, upon other blossoms of the same cluster or the same individual plant.

Cross Fertilization occurs when ovules are fertilized by pollen of other individuals of the same species.

Hybridization occurs when ovules are fertilized by pollen of some other (necessarily some nearly related) species.

332. **Close Fertilization** would seem to be the natural result in ordinary hermaphrodite flowers; but it is by no means so in all of them. More commonly the arrangements are such that it takes place only after some opportunity for cross fertilization has been afforded. But close fertilization is inevitable in what are called

Cleistogamous Flowers, that is, in those which are fertilized in the flower-bud, while still unopened. Most flowers of this kind, indeed, never open at all; but the closed floral coverings are forced off by the growth of the precociously fertilized pistil. Common examples of this are found in the earlier blossoms of Specularia perfoliata, in the later ones of most Violets, especially the stemless species, in our wild Jewel weeds or Impatiens, in the subterranean shoots of Amphicarpæa. Every plant which produces these cleistogamous or bud-fertilized flowers bears also more conspicuous and open flowers, usually of bright colors. The latter very commonly fail to set seed, the former are prolific.

333. **Cross Fertilization** is naturally provided for in diœcious plants (249), is much favored in monœcious plants (249), and hardly less so in dichogamous and in heterogonous flowers (338). Cross fertilization depends upon the transportation of pollen; and the two principal agents of conveyance are winds and insects. Most flowers are in their whole structure adapted either to the one or to the other.

334. **Wind-fertilizable or Anemophilous** flowers are more commonly diœcious or monœcious, as in Pines and all coniferous trees, Oaks, and Birches, and Sedges; yet sometimes hermaphrodite, as in Plantains and most Grasses; they produce a superabundance of very light pollen, adapted to be wind-borne; and they offer neither nectar to feed winged insects, nor fragrance nor bright colors to attract them.

335. **Insect-fertilizable or Entomophilous** flowers are those which are sought by insects, for pollen or for nectar, or for both. Through their visits pollen is conveyed from one

flower and from one plant to another. Insects are attracted to such blossoms by their bright colors, or their fragrance, or by the nectar (the material of honey) there provided for them. While supplying their own needs, they carry pollen from anthers to stigmas and from plant to plant, thus bringing about a certain amount of cross fertilization. Willows and some other diœcious flowers are so fertilized, chiefly by bees. But most insect-visited flowers have the stamens and pistils associated either in the same or in contiguous blossoms. Even when in the same blossom, anthers and stigmas are very commonly so situated [Pg 116]that under insect-visitation, some pollen is more likely to be deposited upon other than upon own stigmas, so giving a chance for cross as well as for close fertilization. On the other hand, numerous flowers, of very various kinds, have their parts so arranged that they must almost necessarily be cross-fertilized or be barren, and are therefore dependent upon the aid of insects. This aid is secured by different exquisite adaptations and contrivances, which would need a volume for full illustration. Indeed, there is a good number of volumes devoted to this subject.[1]

336. Some of the adaptations which favor or ensure cross fertilization are peculiar to the particular kind of blossom. Orchids, Milkweeds, Kalmia, Iris, and papilionaceous flowers each have their own special contrivances, quite different for each.

337. Irregular flowers (253) and especially irregular corollas are usually adaptations to insect-visitation. So are all *Nectaries*, whether hollow spurs, sacs, or other concavities in which nectar is secreted, and all *nectariferous glands*.

338. Moreover, there are two arrangements for cross fertilization common to hermaphrodite flowers in various different families of plants, which have received special names, *Dichogamy* and *Heterogony*.

339. **Dichogamy** is the commoner case. Flowers are *dichogamous* when the anthers discharge their pollen either before or after the stigmas of that flower are in a condition to receive it. Such flowers are

Proterandrous, when the anthers are earlier than the stigmas, as in Gentians, Campanula, Epilobium, etc.

Proterogynous, when the stigmas are mature and moistened for the reception of pollen, before the anthers of that blossom are ready to supply it, and are withered before that pollen can be supplied. Plantains or Ribworts (mostly wind-fertilized) are strikingly proterogynous: so is Amorpha, our Papaws, Scrophularia, and in a less degree the blossom of Pears, Hawthorns, and Horse-chestnut.

340. In Sabbatia, the large-flowered species of Epilobium, and strikingly in Clerodendron, the dichogamy is supplemented and perfected by movements of the stamens and style, one or both, adjusted to make sure of cross fertilization.

341. **Heterogony.** This is the case in which hermaphrodite and fertile flowers of two sorts are produced on different individuals of the same species; one sort having higher anthers and lower stigmas, the other having higher stigmas and lower anthers. Thus reciprocally disposed, a visiting insect carries pollen from the high anthers of the one to the high stigma of the other, and from the low anthers of the one to the low stigma of the other. These plants are practically as if diœcious, with the advantage that [Pg 117]both kinds are fruitful. Houstonia and Mitchella, or Partridge-berry, are excellent and familiar examples. These are cases of

Heterogone Dimorphism, the relative lengths being only short and long reciprocally.

Heterogone Trimorphism, in which there is a mid-length as well as a long and a short set of stamens and style; occurs in Lythrum Salicaria and some species of Oxalis.

342. There must be some essential advantage in cross fertilization or cross breeding. Otherwise all these various, elaborate, and exquisitely adjusted adaptations would be aimless. Doubtless the advantage is the same as that which is realized in all the higher animals by the distinction of sexes.

§ 2. ACTION OF POLLEN, AND FORMATION OF THE EMBRYO.

343. **Pollen-growth.** A grain of pollen may be justly likened to one of the simple bodies (*spores*) which answer for seeds in Cryptogamous plants. Like one of these, it is capable of germination. When deposited upon the moist surface of the stigma (or in some cases even when at a certain distance) it grows from some point, its living inner coat breaking through the inert outer coat, and protruding in the form of a delicate tube. This as it lengthens penetrates the loose tissue of the stigma and of a loose conducting tissue in the style, feeds upon the nourishing liquid matter there provided, reaches the cavity of the ovary, enters the orifice of an ovule, and attaches its extremity to a sac, or the lining of a definite cavity, in the ovule, called the *Embryo-Sac*.

344. **Origination of the Embryo.** A globule of living matter in the embryo-sac is formed, and is in some way placed in close proximity to the apex of the pollen tube; it probably absorbs the contents of the latter; it then sets up a special growth, and the *Embryo* (8-10) or rudimentary plantlet in the seed is the result.

FOOTNOTES:

[1]Beginning with one by C. C. Sprengel in 1793, and again in our day with Darwin, "On the Various Contrivances by which Orchids are fertilized by Insects," and in succeeding works.

SECTION XIV. THE FRUIT.

345. **Its Nature.** The ovary matures into the Fruit. In the strictest sense the fruit is the seed-vessel, technically named the PERICARP. But practically it may include other parts organically connected with the pericarp. Especially the calyx, or a part of it, is often incorporated with the ovary, so as to be undistinguishably a portion of the pericarp, and it even forms along with the receptacle the whole bulk of such edible fruits as apples and pears. The receptacle is an obvious part in blackberries, and is the whole edible portion in the strawberry.

346. Also a cluster of distinct carpels may, in ripening, be consolidated or compacted, so as practically to be taken for one fruit. Such are raspberries, [Pg 118]blackberries, the Magnolia fruit, etc. Moreover, the ripened product of many flowers may be compacted or grown together so as to form a single compound fruit.

347. **Its kinds** have therefore to be distinguished. Also various names of common use in descriptive botany have to be mentioned and defined.

348. In respect to composition, accordingly, fruits may be classified into

Simple, those which result from the ripening of a single pistil, and consist only of the matured ovary, either by itself, as in a cherry, or with calyx-tube completely incorporated with it, as in a gooseberry or cranberry.

Aggregate, when a cluster of carpels of the same flower are crowded into a mass; as in raspberries and blackberries.

FIG. 366. Forming fruit (capsule) of Gaultheria, with calyx thickening around its base. 367. Section of same mature, the berry-like calyx nearly enclosing the capsule.

FIG. 368. Section of a part of a strawberry. Compare with Fig. 360.

FIG. 369. Similar section of part of a blackberry. 370. One of its component simple fruits (drupe) in section, showing the pulp, stone, and contained seed; more enlarged. Compare with Fig. 375.

Accessory or *Anthocarpous*, when the surroundings or supports of the pistil make up a part of the mass; as does the loose calyx changed into a fleshy and berry-like envelope of our Wintergreen (Gaultheria, Fig. 366, 367) and Buffalo-berry, which are otherwise simple fruits. In an aggregate fruit such as the strawberry the great mass is receptacle (Fig. 360, 368); and in the blackberry (Fig. 369) the juicy receptacle forms the central part of the savory mass.

Multiple or *Collective*, when formed from several flowers consolidated into one mass, of which the common receptacle or axis of inflorescence, the floral envelopes, and even the bracts, etc., make a part. A mulberry (Fig. 408, which superficially much resembles a blackberry) is of this multiple sort. A pine-apple is another example.

349. In respect to texture or consistence, fruits may be distinguished into three kinds, viz.—

Fleshy Fruits, those which are more or less soft and juicy throughout;

[Pg 119]

Stone Fruits, or *Drupaceous*, the outer part fleshy like a berry, the inner hard or stony, like a nut; and

Dry Fruits, those which have no flesh or pulp.

350. In reference to the way of disseminating the contained seed, fruits are said to be

Indehiscent when they do not open at maturity. Fleshy fruits and stone fruits are of course indehiscent. The seed becomes free only through decay or by being fed upon by animals. Those which escape digestion are thus disseminated by the latter. Of dry fruits many are indehiscent; and these are variously arranged to be transported by animals. Some burst irregularly; many are

Dehiscent, that is, they split open regularly along certain lines, and discharge the seeds. A dehiscent fruit almost always contains many or several seeds, or at least more than one seed.

FIG. 371. Leafy shoot and berry (cut across) of the larger Cranberry, Vaccinium macrocarpon.

FIG. 372, 373. Pepo of Gourd, in section. 373. One carpel of same in diagram.

FIG. 374. Longitudinal and transverse sections of a pear (pome).

351. The principal kinds of fruit which have received substantive names and are of common use in descriptive botany are the following. Of fleshy fruits the leading kind is

352. **The Berry**, such as the gooseberry and currant, the blueberry and cranberry (Fig. 371), the tomato, and the grape. Here the whole flesh is soft throughout. The orange is a berry with a leathery rind.

353. **The Pepo**, or *Gourd-fruit*, is a hard-rinded berry, belonging to the Gourd family, such as the pumpkin, squash, cucumber, and melon, Fig. 372, 373.

354. **The Pome** is a name applied to the apple, pear (Fig. 374), and quince; fleshy fruits, like a berry, but the principal thickness is calyx, only [Pg 120]the papery pods arranged like a star in the core really belonging to the carpels. The fruit of the Hawthorn is a drupaceous pome, something between pome and drupe.

355. Of fruits which are externally fleshy and internally hard the leading kind is

356. **The Drupe**, or *Stone-fruit*, of which the cherry, plum, and peach (Fig. 375) are familiar examples. In this the outer part of the thickness of the pericarp becomes fleshy, or softens like a berry, while the inner hardens, like a nut. From the way in which the pistil is constructed, it is evident that the fleshy part here answers to the lower, and the stone to the upper face of the component leaf. The layers or concentric portions of a drupe, or of any pericarp which is thus separable, are named, when thus distinguishable into three portions,—

Epicarp, the external layer, often the mere skin of the fruit,

Mesocarp, the middle layer, which is commonly the fleshy part, and

Endocarp, the innermost layer, the stone. But more commonly only two portions of a drupe are distinguished, and are named, the outer one

Sarcocarp or *Exocarp*, for the flesh, the first name referring to the fleshy character, the second to its being an external layer; and

Putamen or *Endocarp*, the *Stone*, within.

FIG. 375. Longitudinal section of a peach, showing flesh, stone, and seed.

357. The typical or true drupe is of a single carpel. But, not to multiply technical names, this name is extended to all such fruits when fleshy without and stony within, although of compound pistil,—even to those having several or separable stones, such as the fruit of Holly. These stones in such drupes, or drupaceous fruits, are called *Pyrenæ*, or *Nucules*, or simply *Nutlets* of the drupe.

358. Of Dry fruits, there is a greater diversity of kinds having distinct names. The indehiscent sorts are commonly one-seeded.

FIG. 376. Akene of a Buttercup. 377. The same, divided lengthwise, to show the contained seed.

FIG. 378. Akene of Virgin's-bower, retaining the feathered style, which aids in dissemination.

359. **The Akene or Achenium** is a small, dry and indehiscent one-seeded fruit, often so seed-like in appearance that it is popularly taken for a naked seed. The fruit of the Buttercup or Crowfoot is a good example, Fig. 376, 377. Its nature, as a ripened pistil (in this [Pg 121]case a simple carpel), is apparent by its bearing the remains of a style or stigma, or a scar from which this has fallen. It may retain the style and use it in various ways for dissemination (Fig. 378).

360. The fruit of Compositæ (though not of a single carpel) is also an akene. In this case the pericarp is invested by an adherent calyx-tube; the limb of which, when it has any, is called the PAPPUS. This name was first given to the down like that of the Thistle, but is applied to all forms under which the limb of the calyx of the "compound flower" appears. In Lettuce, Dandelion (Fig. 384), and the like, the achenium as it matures tapers upwards into a slender beak, like a stalk to the pappus.

FIG. 379. Akene of Mayweed (no pappus). 380. That of Succory (its pappus a shallow cup). 381. Of Sunflower (pappus of two deciduous scales). 382. Of Sneezeweed (Helenium), with its pappus of five scales. 383. Of Sow-Thistle, with its pappus of delicate downy hairs. 384. Of the Dandelion, its pappus raised on a long beak.

361. **A Cremocarp** (Fig. 385), a name given to the fruit of Umbelliferæ, consists as it were of a pair of akenes united completely in the blossom, but splitting apart when ripe into the two closed carpels. Each of these is a *Mericarp* or *Hemicarp*, names seldom used.

362. **A Utricle** is the same as an akene, but with a thin and bladdery loose pericarp; like that of the Goosefoot or Pigweed (Fig. 386). When ripe it may burst open irregularly to discharge the seed; or it may open by a circular line all round, the upper part falling off like a lid; as in the Amaranth (Fig. 387).

FIG. 385. Fruit (cremocarp) of Osmorrhiza; the two akene-like ripe carpels separating at maturity from a slender axis or carpophore.

FIG. 386. Utricle of the common Pigweed (Chenopodium album).

FIG. 387. Utricle (pyxis) of Amaranth, opening all round (circumscissile).

363. **A Caryopsis, or Grain,** is like an akene with the seed adhering to the thin pericarp throughout, so that fruit and seed are incorporated into one body; as in wheat, Indian corn, and other kinds of grain.

364. **A Nut** is a dry and indehiscent fruit, commonly one-celled and one-seeded, [Pg 122]with a hard, crustaceous, or bony wall, such as the cocoa-nut, hazelnut, chestnut, and the acorn (Fig. 37, 388.) Here the involucre, in the form of a cup at the base, is called the CUPULE. In the Chestnut the cupule forms the bur; in the Hazel, a leafy husk.

FIG. 388. Nut (acorn) of the Oak, with its cup or cupule.

365. **A Samara, or Key-fruit,** is either a nut or an akene, or any other indehiscent fruit, furnished with a wing, like that of Ash (Fig. 389), and Elm (Fig. 390). The Maple-fruit is a pair of keys (Fig. 391).

366. Dehiscent Fruits, or Pods, are of two classes, viz., those of a simple pistil or carpel, and those of a compound pistil. Two common sorts of the first are named as follows:—

367. **The Follicle** is a fruit of a simple carpel, which dehisces down one side only, i. e. by the inner or ventral suture. The fruits of Marsh Marigold (Fig. 392), Pæony, Larkspur, and Milkweed are of this kind.

FIG. 389. Samara or key of the White Ash, winged at end. 390. Samara of the American Elm, winged all round.

FIG. 391. Pair of samaras of Sugar Maple.

FIG. 392. Follicle of Marsh Marigold (Caltha palustris).

FIG. 393. Legume of a Sweet Pea, opened.

FIG. 394. Loment or jointed legume of a Tick-Trefoil (Desmodium).

368. **The Legume** or true Pod, such as the peapod (Fig. 393), and the fruit of the Leguminous or Pulse family generally, is one which opens along the dorsal as well as the ventral suture. The two pieces into which it splits are called VALVES. A LOMENT is a legume which is constricted between the seeds, and at length breaks up crosswise into distinct joints, as in Fig. 394.

369. The pods or dehiscent fruits belonging to a compound ovary have several technical names: but they all may be regarded as kinds of

370. **The Capsule,** the dry and dehiscent fruit of any compound pistil. The capsule may discharge its seeds through chinks or pores, as in the [Pg 123]Poppy, or burst irregularly in some part, as in Lobelia and the Snapdragon; but commonly it splits open (or is *dehiscent*) lengthwise into regular pieces, called VALVES.

FIG. 395. Capsule of Iris, with loculicidal dehiscence; below, cut across.

FIG. 396. Pod of a Marsh St. John's-wort, with septicidal dehiscence.

371. Regular *Dehiscence* in a capsule takes place in two ways, which are best illustrated in pods of two or three cells. It is either

Loculicidal, or, splitting directly into the *loculi* or cells, that is, down the back (or the dorsal suture) of each cell or carpel, as in Iris (Fig. 395); or

Septicidal, that is, splitting through the partitions or *septa*, as in St. John's-wort (Fig. 396), Rhododendron, etc. This divides the capsule into its component carpels, which then open by their ventral suture.

FIG. 397, 398. Diagrams of the two modes.

FIG. 399. Diagram of septifragal dehiscence of the loculicidal type. 400. Same of the septicidal or *marginicidal* type.

372. In loculicidal dehiscence the valves naturally bear the partitions on their middle; in the septicidal, half the thickness of a partition is borne on the margin of each valve. See the annexed diagrams. A variation of either mode occurs when the valves break away from the partitions, these remaining attached in the axis of the fruit. This is called *Septifragal* dehiscence. One form is seen in the Morning-Glory (Fig. 400).

373. The capsules of Rue, Spurge, and some others, are both loculicidal and septicidal, and so split into half-carpellary valves or pieces.

52

374. **The Silique** (Fig. 401) is the technical name of the peculiar pod of the Mustard family; which is two-celled by a false partition stretched across between two parietal placentæ. It generally opens by two valves from below upward, and the placentæ with the partition are left behind when the valves fall off.

375. **A Silicle or Pouch** is only a short and broad silique, like that of the Shepherd's Purse, Fig. 402, 403.

[Pg 124]

FIG. 401. Silique of a Cadamine or Spring Cress.
FIG. 402. Silicle of Shepherd's Purse.
FIG. 403. Same, with one valve removed.
FIG. 404. Pyxis of Purslane, the lid detaching.

376. **The Pyxis** is a pod which opens by a circular horizontal line, the upper part forming a lid, as in Purslane (Fig. 404), the Plantain, Henbane, etc. In these the dehiscence extends all round, or is *circumscissile*. So it does in Amaranth (Fig. 387), forming a one-seeded utricular pyxis. In Jeffersonia, the line does not separate quite round, but leaves a portion for a hinge to the lid.

377. Of Multiple or Collective Fruits, which are properly masses of fruits aggregated into one body (as is seen in the Mulberry (Fig. 408), Pine-apple, etc.), there are two kinds with special names and of peculiar structure.

FIG. 405. A fig-fruit when young. 406. Same in section. 407. Magnified portion, a slice, showing some of the flowers.
FIG. 408. A mulberry. 409. One of the grains younger, enlarged; seen to be a pistillate flower with calyx becoming fleshy. 410. Same, with fleshy calyx cut across.

378. **The Syconium or Fig-fruit** (Fig. 405, 406) is a fleshy axis or summit of stem, hollowed out, and lined within by a multitude of minute flowers, the whole becoming pulpy, and in the common fig, luscious.

379. **The Strobile or Cone** (Fig. 411), is the peculiar multiple fruit of Pines, Cypresses, and the like; hence named *Coniferæ*, viz. cone-bearing [Pg 125]plants. As already shown (313), these cones are *open pistils*, mostly in the form of flat scales, regularly overlying each other, and pressed together in a spike or head. Each scale bears one or two naked seeds on its inner face. When ripe and dry, the scales turn back or diverge, and in the Pine the seed peels off and falls, generally carrying with it a wing, a part of the lining of the scale, which facilitates the dispersion of the seeds by the wind (Fig. 412, 413). In Arbor-Vitæ, the scales of the small cone are few, and not very unlike the leaves. In Cypress they are very thick at the top and narrow at the base, so as to make a peculiar sort of closed cone. In Juniper and Red Cedar, the few scales of the very small cone become fleshy, and ripen into a fruit which closely resembles a berry.

FIG. 411. Cone of a common Pitch Pine. 412. Inside view of a separated scale or open carpel; one seed in place: 413, the other seed.

SECTION XV. THE SEED.

380. Seeds are the final product of the flower, to which all its parts and offices are subservient. Like the ovule from which it originates, a seed consists of coats and kernel.

FIG. 414. Seed of a Linden or Basswood cut through lengthwise, and magnified, the parts lettered: *a*, the hilum or scar; *b*, the outer coat; *c*, the inner; *d*, the albumen; *e*, the embryo.

381. **The Seed-coats** are commonly two (320), the outer and the inner. Fig. 414 shows the two, in a seed cut through lengthwise. The outer coat is often hard or crustaceous, whence it is called the *Testa*, or shell of the seed; the inner is almost always thin and delicate.

FIG. 415. A winged seed of the Trumpet-Creeper.
FIG. 416. One of Catalpa, the kernel cut to show the embryo.

FIG. 417. Seed of Milkweed, with a *Coma* or tuft of long silky hairs at one end.

382. The shape and the markings, so various in different seeds, depend mostly on the outer coat. Sometimes this fits the kernel closely; sometimes it is expanded into a *wing*, as in the Trumpet-Creeper (Fig. 415), and occasionally this wing is cut up into shreds or tufts, as in the Catalpa (Fig. 416); or instead of a wing it may bear a *Coma*, or tuft of long and soft hairs, as in the Milkweed or Silkweed (Fig. 417). The use of wings, or downy tufts is to render the seeds buoyant [Pg 126]for dispersion by the winds. This is clear, not only from their evident adaptation to this purpose, but also from the fact that winged and tufted seeds are found only in fruits that

53

split open at maturity, never in those that remain closed. The coat of some seeds is beset with long hairs or wool. *Cotton*, one of the most important vegetable products, since it forms the principal clothing of the larger part of the human race, consists of the long and woolly hairs which thickly cover the whole surface of the seed. There are also crests or other appendages of various sorts on certain seeds. A few seeds have an additional, but more or less incomplete covering, outside of the real seed-coats called an

383. Aril, or Arillus. The loose and transparent bag which encloses the seed of the White Water-Lily (Fig. 418) is of this kind. So is the *mace* of the nutmeg; and also the scarlet pulp around the seeds of the Waxwork (Celastrus) and Strawberry-bush (Euonymus). The aril is a growth from the extremity of the seed-stalk, or from the placenta when there is no seed-stalk.

FIG. 418. Seed of White Water Lily, enclosed in its aril.

384. A short and thickish appendage at or close to the hilum in certain seeds is called a CARUNCLE or STROPHIOLE (Fig. 419).

FIG. 419. Seed of Ricinus or Castor oil plant, with caruncle.

385. The various terms which define the position or direction of the ovule (erect, ascending, etc.) apply equally to the seed: so also the terms anatropous, orthotropous, campylotropous, etc., as already defined (320, 321), and such terms as

HILUM, or *Scar* left where the seed-stalk or funiculus falls away, or where the seed was attached directly to the placenta when there is no seed-stalk.

RHAPHE, the line or ridge which runs from the hilum to the chalaza in anatropous and amphitropous seeds.

CHALAZA, the place where the seed-coats and the kernel or nucleus are organically connected,—at the hilum in orthotropous and campylotropous seeds, at the extremity of the rhaphe or tip of the seed in other kinds.

MICROPYLE, answering to the *Foramen* or orifice of the ovule. Compare the accompanying figures and those of the ovules, Fig. 341-355.

[Pg 127]

FIG. 420. Seed of a Violet (anatropous): *a*, hilum; *b*, rhaphe; *c*, chalaza.

FIG. 421. Seed of a Larkspur (also anatropous); the parts lettered as in the last.

FIG. 422. The same, cut through lengthwise: *a*, the hilum; *c*, chalaza; *d*, outer seed coat; *e*, inner seed-coat; *f*, the albumen; *g*, the minute embryo.

FIG. 423. Seed of a St. John's-wort, divided lengthwise; here the whole kernel is embryo.

386. **The Kernel, or Nucleus,** is the whole body of the seed within the coats. In many seeds the kernel is all *Embryo*; in others a large part of it is the *Albumen*. For example, in Fig. 423, it is wholly embryo; in Fig. 422, all but the small speck (*g*) is albumen.

387. **The Albumen or Endosperm** of the seed is sufficiently characterized and its office explained in Sect. III., 31-35.

388. **The Embryo** or *Germ*, which is the rudimentary plantlet and the final result of blossoming, and its development in germination have been extensively illustrated in Sections II. and III. Its essential parts are the *Radicle* and the *Cotyledons*.

389. **Its Radicle or Caulicle** (the former is the term long and generally used in botanical descriptions, but the latter is the more correct one, for it is the initial stem, which merely gives origin to the root), as to its position in the seed, always points to and lies near the micropyle. In relation to the pericarp it is

Superior, when it points to the apex of the fruit or cell, and

Inferior, when it points to its base, or downward.

FIG. 424. Embryo of Calycanthus; upper part cut away, to show the convolute cotyledons.

390. **The Cotyledons** have already been illustrated as respects their number,—giving the important distinction of *Dicotyledonous, Polycotyledonous* and*Monocotyledonous* embryos (36-43),—also as regards their thickness, whether *foliaceous* or *fleshy*; and some of the very various shapes and adaptations to the seed have been figured. They may be straight, or folded, or rolled up. In the latter case the cotyledons may be rolled up as it were from one margin, as in Calycanthus (Fig. 424), or from apex to base in a flat spiral, or they may be both folded (*plicate*) and rolled up (*convolute*), as in Sugar Maple (Fig. 11.) In one very natural family, the Cruciferæ, two different modes prevail in the way the two cotyledons are brought round against the radicle. In one series they are

[Pg 128]

54

Accumbent, that is, the edges of the flat cotyledons lie against the radicle, as in Fig. 425, 426. In another they are

FIG. 425. Seed of Bitter Cress, Barbarea, cut across to show the accumbent cotyledons. 426. Embryo of same, whole.

Incumbent, or with the plane of the cotyledons brought up in the opposite direction, so that the back of one of them lies against the radicle, as shown in Fig. 427, 428.

FIG. 427. Seed of a Sisymbrium, cut across to show the incumbent cotyledons. 428. Embryo of the same, detached whole.

391. As to the situation of the embryo with respect to the albumen of the seed, when this is present in any quantity, the embryo may be *Axile*, that is occupying the axis or centre, either for most of its length, as in Violet (Fig. 429), Barberry (Fig. 48), and Pine (Fig. 56); and in these it is straight. But it may be variously curved or coiled in the albumen, as in Helianthemum (Fig. 430), in a Potato-seed (Fig. 50), or Onion-seed (Fig. 60), and Linden (Fig. 414); or it may be coiled around the outside of the albumen, partly or into a circle, as in Chickweed (Fig. 431, 432) and in Mirabilis (Fig. 52). The latter mode prevails in Campylotropous seeds. In the cereal grains, such as Indian Corn (Fig. 67) and Rice (Fig. 430²), and in all other Grasses, the embryo is straight and applied to the outside of the abundant albumen.

FIG. 429. Section of seed of Violet; anatropous with straight axile embryo in the albumen. 430. Section of seed of Rock Rose, Helianthemum Canadense; orthotropous, with curved embryo in the albumen. 430². Section of a grain of Rice, lengthwise, showing the embryo outside the albumen, which forms the principal bulk.

FIG. 431. Seed of a Chickweed, campylotropous. 432. Section of same, showing slender embryo coiled around the outside of the albumen of the kernel.

392. The matured seed, with embryo ready to germinate and reproduce the kind, completes the cycle of the vegetable life in a phanerogamous plant, the account of which began with the seed and seedling.

SECTION XVI. VEGETABLE LIFE AND WORK.

393. The following simple outlines of the anatomy and physiology of plants (3) are added to the preceding structural part for the better preparation of students in descriptive and systematic botany; also to give to all learners some general idea of the life, growth, intimate structure, and action of the beings which compose so large a part of organic nature. Those who would extend and verify the facts and principles here outlined will use the Physiological Botany of the "Botanical Text Book," by Professor Goodale, or some similar book.

[Pg 129]

§ 1. ANATOMICAL STRUCTURE AND GROWTH.

394. **Growth** *is the increase of a living thing in size and substance*. It appears so natural that plants and animals should grow, that one rarely thinks of it as requiring explanation. It seems enough to say that a thing is so because it grew so. Growth from the seed, the germination and development of an embryo into a plantlet, and at length into a mature plant (as illustrated in Sections II. and III.), can be followed by ordinary observation. But the embryo is already a miniature plantlet, sometimes with hardly any visible distinction of parts, but often one which has already made very considerable growth in the seed. To investigate the formation and growth of the embryo itself requires well-trained eyes and hands, and the expert use of a good compound microscope. So this is beyond the reach of a beginner.

395. Moreover, although observation may show that a seedling, weighing only two or three grains, may double its bulk and weight every week of its early growth, and may in time produce a huge amount of vegetable matter, it is still to be asked what this vegetable matter is, where it came from, and by what means plants are able to increase and accumulate it, and build it up into the fabric of herbs and shrubs and lofty trees.

396. **Protoplasm.** All this fabric was built up under life, but only a small portion of it is at any one time alive. As growth proceeds, life is passed on from the old to the new parts, much as it has passed on from parent to offspring, from generation to generation in unbroken continuity. *Protoplasm* is the common name of that plant-stuff in which life essentially resides. All growth depends upon it; for it has the peculiar power of growing and multiplying and building up a living structure,—the animal no less than the vegetable structure, for it is essentially the same in both. Indeed, all the animal protoplasm comes primarily from the vegetable, which has the

55

prerogative of producing it; and the protoplasm of plants furnishes all that portion of the food of animals which forms their flesh and living fabric.

397. The very simplest plants (if such may specifically be called plants rather than animals, or one may say, the simplest living things) are mere particles, or pellets, or threads, or even indefinite masses of protoplasm of vague form, which possess powers of motion or of changing their shape, of imbibing water, air, and even other matters, and of assimilating these into plant-stuff for their own growth and multiplication. Their growth is increase in substance by incorporation of that which they take in and assimilate. Their multiplication is by spontaneous division of their substance or body into two or more, each capable of continuing the process.

398. The embryo of a phanerogamous plant at its beginning (344) is essentially such a globule of protoplasm, which soon constricts itself into two and more such globules, which hold together inseparably in a row; then the last of the row divides without separation in the two other planes, to [Pg 130]form a compound mass, each grain or globule of which goes on to double itself as it grows; and the definite shaping of this still increasing mass builds up the embryo into its form.

FIG. 433-436. Figures to illustrate the earlier stages in the formation of an embryo; a single mass of protoplasm (Fig. 433) dividing into two, three, and then into more incipient cells, which by continued multiplication build up an embryo.

399. **Cell-walls.** While this growth was going on, each grain of the forming structure formed and clothed itself with a coat, thin and transparent, of something different from protoplasm,—something which hardly and only transiently, if at all, partakes of the life and action. The protoplasm forms the living organism; the coat is a kind of protective covering or shell. The protoplasm, like the flesh of animals which it gives rise to, is composed of four chemical elements: Carbon, Hydrogen, Oxygen, and Nitrogen. The coating is of the nature of wood (is, indeed, that which makes wood), and has only the three elements, Carbon, Hydrogen, and Oxygen, in its composition.

FIG. 437. Magnified view of some of a simple fresh water Alga, the Tetraspora lubrica, each sphere of which may answer to an individual plant.

400. Although the forming structure of an embryo in the fertilized ovule is very minute and difficult to see, there are many simple plants of lowest grade, abounding in pools of water, which more readily show the earlier stages or simplest states of plant-growth. One of these, which is common in early spring, requires only moderate magnifying power to bring to view what is shown in Fig. 437. In a slimy mass which holds all loosely together, little spheres of green vegetable matter are seen, assembled in fours, and these fours themselves in clusters of fours. A transient inspection shows, what prolonged watching would confirm, that each sphere divides first in one plane, then in the other, to make four, soon acquiring the size of the original, and so on, producing successive groups of fours. These pellets each form on their surface a transparent wall, like that just described. The delicate wall is for some time capable of expansive growth, but is from the first much firmer than the protoplasm within; through it the latter imbibes surrounding moisture, which becomes a watery sap, occupying vacuities in the protoplasmic mass which enlarge or run together as the periphery increases and distends. When full grown the protoplasm may become a mere lining to the wall, or some of it central, as a nucleus, this usually connected with the wall-lining by delicate threads of the same substance. So, when full grown, the wall with its lining—a vesicle, containing liquid or some [Pg 131]solid matters and in age mostly air—naturally came to be named a Cell. But the name was suggested by, and first used only for, cells in combination or built up into a fabric, much as a wall is built of bricks, that is, into a

401. **Cellular Structure or Tissue.** Suppose numerous cells like those of Fig. 437 to be heaped up like a pile of cannon-balls, and as they grew, to be compacted together while soft and yielding; they would flatten where they touched, and each sphere, being touched by twelve surrounding ones would become twelve-sided. Fig. 438 would represent one of them. Suppose the contiguous faces to be united into one wall or partition between adjacent cavities, and a *cellular structure*would be formed, like that shown in Fig. 439. Roots, stems, leaves, and the whole of phanerogamous plants are a fabric of countless numbers of such cells. No such exact regularity in size and shape is ever actually found; but a nearly truthful magnified view of a small portion of a slice of the flower-stalk of a Calla Lily (Fig. 440) shows a fairly corresponding structure; except that, owing to the great air-spaces of the interior, the fabric may be likened rather to a stack of chimneys than to a solid fabric. In young and partly transparent parts one may discern the cellular structure by looking down directly on the surface, as of a forming root. (Fig. 82, 441, 442).

FIG. 438. Diagram of a vegetable cell, such as it would be if when spherical it were equally pressed by similar surrounding cells in a heap.

FIG. 439. Ideal construction of cellular tissue so formed, in section.

FIG. 440. Magnified view of a portion of a transverse slice of stem of Calla Lily. The great spaces are tubular air-channels built up by the cells.

402. The substance of which cell-walls are mainly composed is called CELLULOSE. It is essentially the same in the stem of a delicate leaf or petal and in the wood of an Oak, except that in the latter the walls are [Pg 132]much thickened and the calibre small. The protoplasm of each living cell appears to be completely shut up and isolated in its shell of cellulose; but microscopic investigation has brought to view, in many cases, minute threads of protoplasm which here and there traverse the cell-wall through minute pores, thus connecting the living portion of one cell with that of adjacent cells. (See Fig. 447, &c.)

FIG. 441. Much magnified small portion of young root of a seedling Maple (such as of Fig. 82); and 442, a few cells of same more magnified. The prolongations from the back of some of the cells are root hairs.

403. The hairs of plants are cells formed on the surface; either elongated single cells (like the root-hairs of Fig. 441, 442), or a row of shorter cells. Cotton fibres are long and simple cells growing from the surface of the seed.

404. The size of the cells of which common plants are made up varies from about the thirtieth to the thousandth of an inch in diameter. An ordinary size of short or roundish cells is from 1/300 to 1/500 of an inch; so that there may generally be from 27 to 125 millions of cells in the compass of a cubic inch!

405. Some parts are built up as a compact structure; in others cells are arranged so as to build up regular air-channels, as in the stems of aquatic and other water-loving plants (Fig. 440), or to leave irregular spaces, as in the lower part of most leaves, where the cells only here and there come into close contact (Fig. 443).

FIG. 443. Magnified section through the thickness of a leaf of Florida Star-Anise.

406. All such soft cellular tissue, like this of leaves, that of pith, and of the green bark, is called PARENCHYMA, while fibrous and woody parts are composed ofPROSENCHYMA, that is, of peculiarly transformed

407. **Strengthening Cells.** Common cellular tissue, which makes up the whole structure of all very young plants, and the whole of Mosses and other vegetables of the lowest grade, even when full grown, is too tender or too brittle to give needful strength and toughness for plants which are to rise to any considerable height and support themselves. In these needful strength is imparted, and the conveyance of sap through the plant is facilitated, by the change, as they are formed, of some cells into thicker-walled and tougher tubes, and by the running together of some of [Pg 133]these, or the prolongation of others, into hollow fibres or tubes of various size. Two sorts of such transformed cells go together, and essentially form the

408. **Wood.** This is found in all common herbs, as well as in shrubs and trees, but the former have much less of it in proportion to the softer cellular tissue. It is formed very early in the growth of the root, stem, and leaves,—traces of it appearing in large embryos even while yet in the seed. Those cells that lengthen, and at the same time thicken their walls form the proper WOODY FIBRE or WOOD-CELLS; those of larger size and thinner walls, which are thickened only in certain parts so as to have peculiar markings, and which often are seen to be made up of a row of cylindrical cells, with the partitions between absorbed or broken away, are calledDUCTS, or sometimes VESSELS. There are all gradations between wood-cells and ducts, and between both these and common cells. But in most plants the three kinds are fairly distinct.

FIG. 444. Magnified wood-cells of the bark (bast-cells) of Basswood, one and part of another. 445. Some wood cells from the wood (and below part of a duct); and 446, a detached wood-cell of the same; equally magnified.

FIG. 447. Some wood cells from Buttonwood, Platanus, highly magnified, a whole cell and lower end of another on the left; a cell cut half away lengthwise, and half of another on the right; some pores or pits (a) seen on the left; while b b mark sections through these on the cut surface. When living and young the protoplasm extends into these and by minuter perforations connects across them. In age the pits become open passages, facilitating the passage of sap and air.

409. The proper cellular tissue, or *parenchyma*, is the ground-work of root, stem, and leaves; this is traversed, chiefly lengthwise, by the strengthening and conducting tissue, wood-cells and duct-cells, in the form of bundles or threads, which, in the stems and stalks of herbs are fewer

57

and comparatively scattered, but in shrubs and trees so numerous and crowded that in the stems and all permanent parts they make a solid mass of wood. They extend into and ramify in the leaves, spreading out in a horizontal plane, as the framework of ribs and veins, which supports the softer cellular portion or parenchyma.

410. **Wood-Cells, or Woody Fibres**, consist of tubes, commonly between one and two thousandths, but in Pine-wood sometimes two or three hundredths, of an inch in diameter. Those from the tough bark of the Basswood, [Pg 134]shown in Fig. 444, are only the fifteen-hundredth of an inch wide. Those of Buttonwood (Fig. 447) are larger, and are here highly magnified besides. The figures show the way wood-cells are commonly put together, namely, with their tapering ends overlapping each other,—spliced together, as it were,—thus giving more strength and toughness. In hard woods, such as Hickory and Oak, the walls of these tubes are very thick, as well as dense; while in soft woods, such as White Pine and Basswood, they are thinner.

411. Wood-cells in the bark are generally longer, finer, and tougher than those of the proper wood, and appear more like fibres. For example, Fig. 446 represents a cell of the wood of Basswood of average length, and Fig. 444 one (and part of another) of the fibrous bark, both drawn to the same scale. As these long cells form the principal part of fibrous bark, or *bast*, they are named *Bast-cells* or *Bast-fibres*. These give the great toughness and flexibility to the inner bark of Basswood (i. e. Bast-wood) and of Leatherwood; and they furnish the invaluable fibres of flax and hemp; the proper wood of their stems being tender, brittle, and destroyed by the processes which separate for use the tough and slender bast-cells. In Leatherwood (Dirca) the bast-cells are remarkably slender. A view of one, if magnified on the scale of Fig. 444, would be a foot and a half long.

FIG. 448. Magnified bit of a pine shaving, taken parallel with the silver grain. 449. Separate whole wood-cell, more magnified. 450. Same, still more magnified; both sections represented: *a*, disks in section, *b*, in face.

412. The wood-cells of Pines, and more or less of all other Coniferous trees, have on two of their sides very peculiar disk-shaped markings (Fig. 448-450) by which that kind of wood is recognizable.

FIG. 451, 452. A large and a smaller dotted duct from Grape-Vine.

413. **Ducts**, also called VESSELS, are mostly larger than wood-cells: indeed, some of them, as in Red Oak, have calibre large enough to be discerned on a cross section by the naked eye. They make the visible porosity of such kinds of wood. This is particularly the case with

Dotted ducts (Fig. 451, 452), the surface of which appears as if riddled with round or oval pores. Such ducts are commonly made up of a row of large cells more or less confluent into a tube.

Scalariform ducts (Fig. 458, 459), common in Ferns, and generally angled by mutual pressure in the bundles, [Pg 135]have transversely elongated thin places, parallel with each other, giving a ladder-like appearance, whence the name.

Annular ducts (Fig. 457) are marked with cross lines or rings, which are thickened portions of the cell-wall.

FIG. 453, 454. Spiral ducts which uncoil into a single thread. 455. Spiral duct which tears up as a band. 456. An annular duct, with variations above. 457. Loose spiral duct passing into annular. 458. Scalariform ducts of a Fern; part of a bundle, prismatic by pressure. 459. One torn into a band.

Spiral ducts or vessels (Fig. 453-455) have thin walls, strengthened by a spiral fibre adherent within. This is as delicate and as strong as spider-web: when uncoiled by pulling apart, it tears up and annihilates the cell-wall. The uncoiled threads are seen by gently pulling apart many leaves, such as those of Amaryllis, or the stalk of a Strawberry leaflet.

FIG. 460. Milk Vessels of Dandelion, with cells of the common cellular tissue. 461. Others from the same older and gorged with milky juice. All highly magnified.

Laticiferous ducts, *Vessels of the Latex*, or *Milk-vessels* are peculiar branching tubes which hold *latex* or milky juice in certain plants. It is very difficult to see them, and more so to make out their nature. They are peculiar in branching and inosculating, so as to make a net-work of tubes, running in among the cellular tissue; and they are very small, except when gorged and old (Fig. 460, 461).

[Pg 136]

§ 2. CELL-CONTENTS.

414. The living contents of young and active cells are mainly protoplasm with water or watery sap which this has imbibed. Old and effete cells are often empty of solid matter, containing only water with whatever may be dissolved in it, or air, according to the time and circumstances. All the various products which plants in general elaborate, or which particular plants specially elaborate, out of the common food which they derive from the soil and the air, are contained in the cells, and in the cells they are produced.

415. **Sap** is a general name for the principal liquid contents,—*Crude sap*, for that which the plant takes in, *Elaborated sap* for what it has digested or assimilated. They must be undistinguishably mixed in the cells.

416. Among the solid matters into which cells convert some of their elaborated sap two are general and most important. These are *Chlorophyll* and *Starch*.

417. **Chlorophyll** (meaning *leaf-green*) is what gives the green color to herbage. It consists of soft grains of rather complex nature, partly wax-like, partly protoplasmic. These abound in the cells of all common leaves and the green rind of plants, wherever exposed to the light. The green color is seen through the transparent skin of the leaf and the walls of the containing cells. Chlorophyll is essential to ordinary assimilation in plants: by its means, under the influence of sunlight, the plant converts crude sap into vegetable matter.

418. Far the largest part of all vegetable matter produced is that which goes to build up the plant's fabric or cellular structure, either directly or indirectly. There is no one good name for this most important product of vegetation. In its final state of cell-walls, the permanent fabric of herb and shrub and tree, it is called *Cellulose*(408): in its most soluble form it is *Sugar* of one or another kind; in a less soluble form it is *Dextrine*, a kind of liquefied starch: in the form of solid grains stored up in the cells it is *Starch*. By a series of slight chemical changes (mainly a variation in the water entering into the composition), one of these forms is converted into another.

419. **Starch** (*Farina* or *Fecula*) is the form in which this common plant material is, as it were, laid by for future use. It consists of solid grains, somewhat different in form in different plants, in size varying from 1/300 to 1/4000 of an inch, partly translucent when wet, and of a pearly lustre. From the concentric lines, which commonly appear under the microscope, the grains seem to be made up of layer over layer. When loose they are commonly oval, as in potato-starch (Fig. 462): when much compacted the grains may become angular (Fig. 463).

FIG. 462. Some magnified starch-grains, in two cells of a potato. 463. Some cells of the albumen or floury part of Indian Corn, filled with starch-grains.

420. The starch in a potato was produced in the foliage. In the soluble form of dextrine, or that of sugar, it was conveyed through the cells of the herbage and stalks to a subterranean shoot, and there stored up in the [Pg 137]tuber. When the potato sprouts, the starch in the vicinity of developing buds or eyes is changed back again, first into mucilaginous dextrine, then into sugar, dissolved in the sap, and in this form it is made to flow to the growing parts, where it is laid down into cellulose or cell-wall.

FIG. 464. Four cells from dried Onion-peel, each holding a crystal of different shape, one of them twinned. 465. Some cells from stalk of Rhubarb-plant, three containing chlorophyll; two (one across) with rhaphides. 466. Rhaphides in a cell, from Arisæma, with small cells surrounding. 467. Prismatic crystals from the bark of Hickory. 468. Glomerate crystal in a cell, from Beet-root. 469. A few cells of Locust-bark, a crystal in each. 470. A detached cell, with rhaphides being forced out, as happens when put in water.

421. Besides these cell-contents which are in obvious and essential relation to nutrition, there are others the use of which is problematical. Of such the commonest are

422. **Crystals.** These when slender or needle-shaped are called RHAPHIDES. They are of inorganic matter, usually of oxalate or phosphate or sulphate of lime. Some, at least of the latter, may be direct crystallizations of what is taken in dissolved in the water absorbed, but others must be the result of some elaboration in the plant. Some plants have hardly any; others abound in them, especially in the foliage and bark. In Locust-bark almost every cell holds a crystal; so that in a square inch not thicker than writing-paper there may be over a million and a half of them. When [Pg 138]needle-shaped (rhaphides), as in stalks of Calla-Lily, Rhubarb, or Four-o'clock, they are usually packed in sheaf-like bundles. (Fig. 465, 466.)

§ 3. ANATOMY OF ROOTS AND STEMS.

423. This is so nearly the same that an account of the internal structure of stems may serve for the root also.

424. At the beginning, either in the embryo or in an incipient shoot from a bud, the whole stem is of tender cellular tissue or parenchyma. But wood (consisting of wood-cells and ducts or vessels) begins to be formed in the earliest growth; and is from the first arranged in two ways,

making two general kinds of wood. The difference is obvious even in herbs, but is more conspicuous in the enduring stems of shrubs and trees.

425. On one or the other of these two types the stems of all phanerogamous plants are constructed. In one, the wood is made up of separate threads, scattered here and there throughout the whole diameter of the stem. In the other, the wood is all collected to form a layer (in a slice across the stem appearing as a ring) between a central cellular part which has none in it, the *Pith*, and an outer cellular part, the *Bark*.

FIG. 471. Diagram of structure of Palm or Yucca. 472. Structure of a Corn stalk, in transverse and longitudinal section. 473. Same of a small Palm stem. The dots on the cross sections represent cut ends of the woody bundles or threads.

426. An Asparagus-shoot and a Corn-stalk for herbs, and a rattan for a woody kind, represent the first kind. To it belong all plants with monocotyledonous embryo (40). A Bean-stalk and the stem of any common shrub or tree represent the second; and to it belong all plants with dicotyledonous or polycotyledonous embryo. The first has been called, not very properly, *Endogenous*, which means inside-growing; the second, properly enough, *Exogenous*, or outside-growing.

427. **Endogenous Stems**, those of Monocotyls (40), attain their greatest size and most characteristic development in Palms and Dragon-trees, therefore chiefly in warm climates, although the Palmetto and some [Pg 139]Yuccas become trees along the southern borders of the United States. In such stems the woody bundles are more numerous and crowded toward the circumference, and so the harder wood is outside; while in an exogenous stem the oldest and hardest wood is toward the centre. An endogenous stem has no clear distinction of pith, bark, and wood, concentrically arranged, no silver grain, no annual layers, no bark that peels off clean from the wood. Yet old stems of Yuccas and the like, that continue to increase in diameter, do form a sort of layers and a kind of scaly bark when old. Yuccas show well the curving of the woody bundles (Fig. 471) which below taper out and are lost at the rind.

FIG. 474. Short piece of stem of Flax, magnified, showing the bark, wood, and pith in a cross section.

428. **Exogenous Stems**, those of Dicotyls (37), or of plants coming from dicotyledonous and also polycotyledonous embryos, have a structure which is familiar in the wood of our ordinary trees and shrubs. It is the same in an herbaceous shoot (such as a Flax-stem, Fig. 474) as in a Maple-stem of the first year's growth, except that the woody layer is commonly thinner or perhaps reduced to a circle of bundles. It was so in the tree-stem at the beginning. The wood all forms in a cylinder,—in cross section a ring—around a central cellular part, dividing the cellular core within, the pith, from a cellular bark without. As the wood-bundles increase in number and in size, they press upon each other and become wedge-shaped in the cross section; and they continue to grow from the outside, next the bark, so that they become very thin wedges or plates. Between the plates or wedges are very thin plates (in cross section lines) of much compressed cellular tissue, which connect the pith with the bark. The plan of a one-year-old woody stem of this kind is exhibited in the figures, which are essentially diagrams.

FIG. 475. Diagram of a cross section of a very young exogenous stem, showing six woody bundles or wedges. 476. Same later, with wedges increased to twelve. 477. Still later, the wedges filling the space, separated only by the thin lines, or medullary rays, running from pith to bark.

429. When such a stem grows on from year to year, it adds annually a [Pg 140]layer of wood outside the preceding one, between that and the bark. This is exogenous growth, or outside-growing, as the name denotes.

FIG. 478. Piece of a stem of Soft Maple, of a year old, cut crosswise and lengthwise.
FIG. 479. A portion of the same, magnified.
FIG. 480. A small piece of the same, taken from one side, reaching from the bark to the pith, and highly magnified: *a*, a small bit of the pith; *b*, spiral ducts of what is called the *medullary sheath*; *c*, the wood; *d, d*, dotted ducts in the wood; *e, e*, annular ducts; *f*, the liber or inner bark; *g*, the green bark; *h*, the corky layer; *i*, the skin, or epidermis; *j*, one of the medullary rays, or plates of silver grain, seen on the cross-section.

430. Some new bark is formed every year, as well as new wood, the former inside, as the latter is outside of that of the year preceding. The ring or zone of tender forming tissue between the bark and the wood has been called the *Cambium Layer*. *Cambium* is an old name of the physiologists for nutritive juice. And this thin layer is so gorged with rich nutritive sap when spring growth is renewed, that the bark then seems to be loose from the wood and a layer of

viscid sap (or *cambium*) to be poured out between the two. But there is all the while a connection of the bark and the wood by delicate cells, rapidly multiplying and growing.

431. **The Bark** of a year-old stem consists of three parts, more or less distinct, namely,—beginning next the wood,—

1. The LIBER or FIBROUS BARK, the *Inner Bark*. This contains some wood-cells, or their equivalent, commonly in the form of bast or bast-cells (411, Fig. 444), such as those of Basswood or Linden, and among herbs those of flax and hemp, which are spun and woven or made into cordage. It also contains cells which are named *sieve*-cells, on account of numerous slits and pores in their walls, by which the protoplasm of contiguous cells communicates. In woody stems, whenever a new layer of wood is formed, some new liber or inner bark is also formed outside of it.

[Pg 141]

2. The GREEN BARK or *Middle Bark*. This consists of cellular tissue only, and contains the same green matter (*chlorophyll*, 417) as the leaves. In woody stems, before the season's growth is completed, it becomes covered by

3. The CORKY LAYER or *Outer Bark*, the cells of which contain no chlorophyll, and are of the nature of *cork*. Common cork is the thick corky layer of the bark of the Cork-Oak of Spain. It is this which gives to the stems or twigs of shrubs and trees the aspect and the color peculiar to each,—light gray in the Ash, purple in the Red Maple, red in several Dogwoods, etc.

4. The EPIDERMIS, or skin of the plant, consisting of a layer of thick-sided empty cells, which may be considered to be the outermost layer, or in most herbaceous stems the only layer, of cork-cells.

FIG. 481. Magnified view of surface of a bit of young Maple wood from which the bark has been torn away, showing the wood-cells and the bark-ends of medullary rays.

FIG. 482. Section in the opposite direction, from bark (on the left) to beginning of pith (on the right), and a medullary ray extending from one to the other.

432. The green layer of bark seldom grows much after the first season. Sometimes the corky layer grows and forms new layers, inside of the old, for years, as in the Cork-Oak, the Sweet Gum-tree, and the White and the Paper Birch. But it all dies after a while; and the continual enlargement of the wood within finally stretches it more than it can bear, and sooner or later cracks and rends it, while the weather acts powerfully upon its surface; so the older bark perishes and falls away piecemeal year by year.

433. So on old trunks only the inner bark remains. This is renewed every year from within and so kept alive, while the older and outer layers die, are fissured and rent by the distending trunk, weathered and worn, and thrown off in fragments,—in some trees slowly, so that the bark of old trunks may acquire great thickness; in others, more rapidly. In Honeysuckles and Grape-Vines, the layers of liber loosen and die when only a year or two old. The annual layers of liber are sometimes as distinct as those of the wood, but often not so.

[Pg 142]

434. **The Wood** of an exogenous trunk, having the old growths covered by the new, remains nearly unchanged in age, except from decay. Wherever there is an annual suspension and renewal of growth, as in temperate climates, the annual growths are more or less distinctly marked, in the form of concentric rings on the cross section, so that the age of the tree may be known by counting them. Over twelve hundred layers have been counted on the stumps of Sequoias in California, and it is probable that some trees now living antedate the Christian era.

435. The reason why the annual growths are distinguishable is, that the wood formed at the beginning of the season is more or less different in the size or character of the cells from that of the close. In Oak, Chestnut, etc., the first wood of the season abounds in dotted ducts, the calibre of which is many times greater than that of the proper wood-cells.

436. **Sap-wood, or Alburnum.** This is the newer wood, living or recently alive, and taking part in the conveyance of sap. Sooner or later, each layer, as it becomes more and more deeply covered by the newer ones and farther from the region of growth, is converted into

437. **Heart-wood, or Duramen.** This is drier, harder, more solid, and much more durable as timber, than sap-wood. It is generally of a different color, and it exhibits in different species the hue peculiar to each, such as reddish in Red-Cedar, brown in Black-Walnut, black in Ebony, etc. The change of sap-wood into heart-wood results from the thickening of the walls of the wood-cells by the deposition of hard matter, lining the tubes and diminishing their calibre; and by the deposition of a vegetable coloring-matter peculiar to each species. The heart-wood, being no longer a living part, may decay, and often does so, without the least injury to the tree, except by diminishing the strength of the trunk, and so rendering it more liable to be overthrown.

61

438. The Living Parts of a Tree, of the exogenous kind, are only these: first, the rootlets at one extremity; second, the buds and leaves of the season at the other; and third, a zone consisting of the newest wood and the newest bark, connecting the rootlets with the buds or leaves, however widely separated these may be,—in the tallest trees from two to four hundred feet apart. And these parts of the tree are all renewed every year. No wonder, therefore, that trees may live so long, since they annually reproduce everything that is essential to their life and growth, and since only a very small part of their bulk is alive at once. The tree survives, but nothing now living has been so long. In it, as elsewhere, life is a transitory thing, ever abandoning the *old*, and renewed in the *young*.

§ 4. ANATOMY OF LEAVES.

439. The wood in leaves is the framework of ribs, veins, and veinlets (125), serving not only to strengthen them, but also to bring in the sap, and to distribute it throughout every part. The cellular portion is the [Pg 143]green pulp, and is nearly the same as the green layer of the bark. So that the leaf may properly enough be regarded as a sort of expansion of the fibrous and green layers of the bark. It has no proper corky layer; but the whole is covered by a transparent skin or *epidermis*, resembling that of the stem.

440. The cells of the leaf are of various forms, rarely so compact as to form a close cellular tissue, usually loosely arranged, at least in the lower part, so as to give copious intervening spaces or air passages, communicating throughout the whole interior (Fig. 443, 483). The green color is given by the chlorophyll (417), seen through the very transparent walls of the cells and through the translucent epidermis of the leaf.

FIG. 483. Magnified section of a leaf of White Lily, to exhibit the cellular structure, both of upper and lower stratum, the air-passages of the lower, and the epidermis or skin, in section, also a little of that of the lower face, with some of its stomates.

441. In ordinary leaves, having an upper and under surface, the green cells form two distinct strata, of different arrangement. Those of the upper stratum are oblong or cylindrical, and stand endwise to the surface of the leaf, usually close together, leaving hardly any vacant spaces; those of the lower are commonly irregular in shape, most of them with their longer diameter parallel to the face of the leaf, and are very loosely arranged, leaving many and wide air-chambers. The green color of the lower is therefore diluted, and paler than that of the upper face of the leaf. The upper part of the leaf is so constructed as to bear the direct action of the sunshine; the lower so as to afford freer circulation of air, and to facilitate transpiration. It communicates more directly than the upper with the external air by means of *Stomates*.

442. **The Epidermis** or skin of leaves and all young shoots is best seen in the foliage. It may readily be stripped off from the surface of a Lily-leaf, and still more so from more fleshy and soft leaves, such as those [Pg 144]of Houseleek. The epidermis is usually composed of a single layer, occasionally of two or three layers, of empty cells, mostly of irregular outline. The sinuous lines which traverse it, and may be discerned under low powers of the microscope (Fig. 487), are the boundaries of the epidermal cells.

FIG. 484. Small portion of epidermis of the lower face of a White-Lily leaf, with stomata.
FIG. 485. One of these, more magnified, in the closed state. 486. Another stoma, open.
FIG. 487. Small portion of epidermis of the Garden Balsam, highly magnified, showing very sinuous-walled cells, and three stomata.

443. **Breathing-pores, or Stomates, Stomata** (singular, a *Stoma*,—literally, a mouth) are openings through the epidermis into the air-chambers or intercellular passages, always between and guarded by a pair of thin-walled guardian cells. Although most abundant in leaves, especially on their lower face (that which is screened from direct sunlight), they are found on most other green parts. They establish a direct communication between the external air and that in the loose interior of the leaf. Their guardian cells or lips, which are soft and delicate, like those of the green pulp within, by their greater or less turgidity open or close the orifice as the moisture or dryness varies.

444. In the White Lily the stomata are so remarkably large that they may be seen by a simple microscope of moderate power, and may be discerned even by a good hand lens. There are about 60,000 of them to the square inch of the epidermis of the lower face of this Lily-leaf, and only about 3000 to the same space on the upper face. It is computed that an average leaf of an Apple-tree has on its lower face about 100,000 of these mouths.

§ 5. PLANT FOOD AND ASSIMILATION.

445. Only plants are capable of originating organizable matter, or the materials which compose the structure of vegetables and animals. The essential and peculiar work of plants is to take up portions of earth and air (water belonging to both) upon which animals cannot live at all,

and to convert them into something organizable; that is, into something that, under life, may be built up into vegetable and animal structures. All the food of animals is produced by plants. Animals live upon vegetables, [Pg 145]directly or at second hand, the carnivorous upon the herbivorous; and vegetables live upon earth and air, immediately or at second hand.

446. **The Food of plants**, then, primarily, is earth and air. This is evident enough from the way in which they live. Many plants will flourish in pure sand or powdered chalk, or on the bare face of a rock or wall, watered merely with rain. And almost any plant may be made to grow from the seed in moist sand, and increase its weight many times, even if it will not come to perfection. Many naturally live suspended from the branches of trees high in the air, and nourished by it alone, never having any connection with the soil; and some which naturally grow on the ground, like the Live-forever of the gardens, when pulled up by the roots and hung in the air will often flourish the whole summer long.

447. It is true that fast-growing plants, or those which produce much vegetable matter in one season (especially in such concentrated form as to be useful as food for man or the higher animals) will come to maturity only in an enriched soil. But what is a rich soil? One which contains decomposing vegetable matter, or some decomposing animal matter; that is, in either case, some decomposing organic matter formerly produced by plants. Aided by this, grain-bearing and other important vegetables will grow more rapidly and vigorously, and make a greater amount of nourishing matter, than they could if left to do the whole work at once from the beginning. So that in these cases also all the organic or organizable matter was made by plants, and made out of earth and air. Far the larger and most essential part was air and water.

448. Two kinds of material are taken in and used by plants; of which the first, although more or less essential to perfect plant-growth, are in a certain sense subsidiary, if not accidental, viz.:—

Earthy constituents, those which are left in the form of ashes when a leaf or a stick of wood is burned in the open air. These consist of some *potash* (or *soda* in a marine plant), some *silex* (the same as flint), and a little *lime, alumine,* or *magnesia, iron* or *manganese, sulphur, phosphorus*, etc.,—some or all of these in variable and usually minute proportions. They are such materials as happen to be dissolved, in small quantity, in the water taken up by the roots; and when that is consumed by the plant, or flies off pure (as it largely does) by exhalation, the earthy matter is left behind in the cells,—just as it is left incrusting the sides of a teakettle in which much hard water has been boiled. Naturally, therefore, there is more earthy matter (i. e. more ashes) in the leaves than in any other part (sometimes as much as seven per cent, when the wood contains only two per cent); because it is through the leaves that most of the water escapes from the plant. Some of this earthy matter incrusts the cell-walls, some goes to form crystals or rhaphides, which abound in many plants (422), some enters into certain special vegetable products, and some appears to be necessary to the well-being of the higher orders of plants, although forming no necessary part of the proper vegetable structure.

[Pg 146]

The essential constituents of the organic fabric are those which are dissipated into air and vapor in complete burning. They make up from 88 to 99 per cent of the leaf or stem, and essentially the whole both of the cellulose of the walls and the protoplasm of the contents. Burning gives these materials of the plant's structure back to the air, mainly in the same condition in which the plant took them, the same condition which is reached more slowly in natural decay. The chemical elements of the cell-walls (or cellulose, 402), as also of starch, sugar, and all that class of organizable cell-material, are carbon, hydrogen, and oxygen (399). The same, with nitrogen, are the constituents of protoplasm, or the truly vital part of vegetation.

449. These chemical elements out of which organic matters are composed are supplied to the plant by water, carbonic acid, and some combinations of nitrogen.

Water, far more largely than anything else, is imbibed by the roots; also more or less by the foliage in the form of vapor. Water consists of oxygen and hydrogen; and cellulose or plant-wall, starch, sugar, etc., however different in their qualities, agree in containing these two elements in the same relative proportions as in water.

Carbonic acid gas (Carbon dioxide) is one of the components of the atmosphere,—a small one, ordinarily only about 1/2500 of its bulk,—sufficient for the supply of vegetation, but not enough to be injurious to animals, as it would be if accumulated. Every current or breeze of air brings to the leaves expanded in it a succession of fresh atoms of carbonic acid, which it absorbs through its multitudinous breathing-pores. This gas is also taken up by water. So it is brought to the ground by rain, and is absorbed by the roots of plants, either as dissolved in the water they imbibe, or in the form of gas in the interstices of the soil. Manured ground, that is, soil containing decomposing vegetable or animal matters, is constantly giving out this gas into the interstices of the soil, whence the roots of the growing crop absorb it. Carbonic acid thus supplied, primarily from the air, is the source of the carbon which forms much the largest part of the substance of every plant. The proportion of carbon may be roughly estimated by charring some wood or foliage; that is, by heating it out of contact with the air, so as to decompose and drive off all the other constituents of the fabric, leaving the large bulk of charcoal or carbon behind.

Nitrogen, the remaining plant-element, is a gas which makes up more than two thirds of the atmosphere, is brought into the foliage and also to the roots (being moderately soluble in water) in the same ways as is carbonic acid. The nitrogen which, mixed with oxygen, a little carbonic acid, and vapor of water, constitutes the air we breathe, is the source of this fourth plant-element. But it is very doubtful if ordinary plants can use any nitrogen gas directly as food; that is, if they can directly cause it to combine with the other elements so as to form protoplasm. But when combined with hydrogen (forming ammonia), or when combined with oxygen [Pg 147](nitric acid and nitrates) plants appropriate it with avidity. And several natural processes are going on in which nitrogen of the air is so combined and supplied to the soil in forms directly available to the plant. The most efficient is *nitrification*, the formation of nitre (nitrate of potash) in the soil, especially in all fertile soils, through the action of a bacterial ferment.

450. **Assimilation** in plants is the conversion of these inorganic substances—essentially, water, carbonic acid, and some form of combined or combinable nitrogen—into vegetable matter. This most dilute food the living plant concentrates and assimilates to itself. Only plants are capable of converting these mineral into organizable matters; and this all-important work is done by them (so far as all ordinary vegetation is concerned) only

451. *Under the light of the sun, acting upon green parts or foliage*, that is, upon the chlorophyll, or upon what answers to chlorophyll, which these parts contain. The sun in some way supplies a power which enables the living plant to originate these peculiar chemical combinations,—to organize matter into forms which are alone capable of being endowed with life. The proof of this proposition is simple; and it shows at the same time, in the simplest way, what a plant does with the water and carbonic acid it consumes. Namely, 1st, it is only in sunshine or bright daylight that the green parts of plants give out oxygen gas,—then they regularly do so; and 2d, the giving out of this oxygen gas is required to render the chemical composition of water and carbonic acid the same as that of *cellulose*, that is, of the plant's permanent fabric. This shows why plants spread out so large a surface of foliage. Leaves are so many workshops, full of machinery worked by sun-power. The emission of oxygen gas from any sun-lit foliage is seen by placing some of this under water, or by using an aquatic plant, by collecting the air bubbles which rise, and by noting that a taper burns brighter in this air. Or a leafy plant in a glass globe may be supplied with a certain small percentage of carbonic acid gas, and after proper exposure to sunshine, the air on being tested will be found to contain less carbonic acid and just so much the more oxygen gas.

452. Now if the plant is making cellulose or any equivalent substance,—that is, is making the very materials of its fabric and growth, as must generally be the case,—all this oxygen gas given off by the leaves comes from the decomposition of carbonic acid taken in by the plant. For cellulose, and also starch, dextrine, sugar, and the like are composed of carbon along with oxygen and hydrogen in just the proportions to form water. And the carbonic acid and water taken in, less the oxygen which the carbon brought with it as carbonic acid, and which is given off from the foliage in sunshine, just represents the manufactured article, cellulose.

453. It comes to the same if the first product of assimilation is sugar, or dextrine which is a sort of soluble starch, or starch itself. And in the plant all these forms are readily changed into one another. In the tiny seedling, as fast as this assimilated matter is formed it is used in growth, that is, in the formation of cell-walls. After a time some or much of [Pg 148]the product may be accumulated in store for future growth, as in the root of the turnip, or the tuber of the potato, or the seed of corn or pulse. This store is mainly in the form of starch. When growth begins anew, this starch is turned into dextrine or into sugar, in liquid form, and used to nourish and build up the germinating embryo or the new shoot, where it is at length converted into cellulose and used to build up plant-structure.

454. But that which builds plant-fabric is not the cellular structure itself; the work is done by the living protoplasm which dwells within the walls. This also has to take and to assimilate its proper food, for its own maintenance and growth. Protoplasm assimilates, along with the other three elements, the nitrogen of the plant's food. This comes primarily from the vast stock in the atmosphere, but mainly through the earth, where it is accumulated through various processes in a fertile soil,—mainly, so far as concerns crops, from the decomposition of former vegetables and animals. This protoplasm, which is formed at the same time as the simpler cellulose, is essentially the same as the flesh of animals, and the source of it. It is the common basis of vegetable and of animal life.

455. *So plant-assimilation produces all the food and fabric of animals.* Starch, sugar, the oils (which are, as it were, these farinaceous matters more deoxidated), chlorophyll, and the like, and even cellulose itself, form the food of herbivorous animals and much of the food of man. When digested they enter into the blood, undergo various transformations, and are at length decomposed into carbonic acid and water, and exhaled from the lungs in respiration,—in other words, are given back to the air by the animal as the very same materials which the plant took from the air as its food,—are given back to the air in the same form that they would have taken if the vegetable matter had been left to decay where it grew, or if it had been set on fire and burned; and with the same result, too, as to the heat,—the heat in this case producing and maintaining the proper temperature of the animal.

456. The protoplasm and other products containing nitrogen (gluten, legumine, etc.), and which are most accumulated in grains and seeds (for the nourishment of their embryos when they germinate), compose the most nutritious vegetable food consumed by animals; they form their proper flesh and sinews, while the earthy constituents of the plant form the earthy matter of the bones, etc. At length decomposed, in the secretions and excretions, these nitrogenous constituents are through successive changes finally resolved into mineral matter, into carbonic acid, water, and ammonia or some nitrates,—into exactly or essentially the same materials which the plants took up and assimilated. Animals depend upon vegetables absolutely and directly for their subsistence; also indirectly, because

457. *Plants purify the air for animals.* In the very process by which they create food they take from the air carbonic acid gas, injurious to animal respiration, which is continually poured into it by the breathing of all animals, by all decay, by the burning of fuel and all other ordinary combustion; and [Pg 149]they restore an equal bulk of life-sustaining oxygen needful for the respiration of animals,—needful, also, in a certain measure, for plants in any work they do. For in plants, as well as in animals, work is done at a certain cost.

§ 6. PLANT WORK AND MOVEMENT.

458. As the organic basis and truly living material of plants is identical with that of animals, so is the life at bottom essentially the same; but in animals something is added at every rise from the lowest to highest organisms. Action and work in living beings require movement.

459. Living things move; those not living are only moved. Plants move as truly as do animals. The latter, nourished as they are upon organized food, which has been prepared for them by plants, and is found only here and there, must needs have the power of going after it, of collecting it, or at least of taking it in; which requires them to make spontaneous movements. But ordinary plants, with their wide-spread surface, always in contact with the earth and air on which they feed,—the latter everywhere the same, and the former very much so,—might be thought to have no need of movement. Ordinary plants, indeed, have no locomotion; some float, but most are rooted to the spot where they grew. Yet probably all of them execute various movements which must be as truly self-caused as are those of the lower grades of animals,—movements which are overlooked only because too slow to be directly observed. Nevertheless, the motion of the hour-hand and of the minute-hand of a watch is not less real than that of the second-hand.

FIG. 488. Two individuals of an Oscillaria, magnified.

460. **Locomotion.** Moreover, many microscopic plants living in water are seen to move freely, if not briskly, under the microscope; and so likewise do more conspicuous aquatic plants in their embryo-like or seedling state. Even at maturity, species of Oscillaria (such as in Fig. 488, minute worm-shaped plants of fresh waters, taking this name from their oscillating motions) freely execute three different kinds of movement, the very delicate investing coat of cellulose not impeding the action of the living protoplasm within. Even when this coat is firmer and hardened with a siliceous deposit, such crescent-shaped or boat-shaped one-celled plants as *Closterium* or *Naricula* are able in some way to move along from place to place in the water.

FIG. 489. A few cells of a leaf of Naias flexilis, highly magnified: the arrows indicate the courses of the circulating currents.

461. **Movements in Cells, or Cell-circulation**, sometimes called *Cyclosis*, has been detected in so many plants, especially in comparatively [Pg 150]transparent aquatic plants and in hairs on the surface of land plants (where it is easiest to observe), that it may be inferred to take place in all cells during the most active part of their life. This motion is commonly a streaming movement of threads of protoplasm, carrying along solid granules by which the action may be observed and the rate measured, or in some cases it is a rotation of the whole protoplasmic contents of the cell. A comparatively low magnifying power will show it in the cells of Nitella and Chara (which are cryptogamous plants); and under a moderate power it is well seen in the Tape Grass of fresh water, Vallisneria, and in Naias flexilis (Fig.489). Minute particles and larger

greenish globules are seen to be carried along, as if in a current, around the cell, passing up one side, across the end, down the other and across the bottom, completing the circuit sometimes within a minute or less when well warmed. To see it well in the cell, which like a string of beads form the hairs on the stamens of Spiderwort, a high magnifying power is needed.

462. **Transference of Liquid from Cell to Cell**, and so from place to place in the plant, the absorption of water by the rootlets, and the exhalation of the greater part of it from the foliage,—these and similar operations are governed by the physical laws which regulate the diffusion of fluids, but are controlled by the action of living protoplasm. Equally under vital control are the various chemical transformations which attend assimilation and growth, and which involve not only molecular movements but conveyance. Growth itself, which is the formation and shaping of new parts, implies the direction of internal activities to definite ends.

463. **Movements of Organs.** The living protoplasm, in all but the lowest grade of plants, is enclosed and to common appearance isolated in separate cells, the walls of which can only in their earliest state be said to be alive. Still plants are able to cause the protoplasm of adjacent cells to act in concert, and by their combined action to effect movements in roots, stems, or leaves, some of them very slow and gradual, some manifest and striking. Such movements are brought about through individually minute changes in the form or tension in the protoplasm of the innumerable cells which make up the structure of the organ. Some of the slower movements are effected during growth, and may be explained by inequality of growth on the two sides of the bending organ. But the more rapid changes of position, and some of the slow ones, cannot be so explained.

[Pg 151]

464. **Root-movements.** In its growth a root turns or bends away from the light and toward the centre of the earth, so that in lengthening it buries itself in the soil where it is to live and act. Every one must have observed this in the germination of seeds. Careful observations have shown that the tip of a growing root also makes little sweeps or short movements from side to side. By this means it more readily insinuates itself into yielding portions of the soil. The root-tips will also turn toward moisture, and so secure the most favorable positions in the soil.

465. **Stem-movements.** The root end of the caulicle or first joint of stem (that below the cotyledons) acts like the root, in turning downward in germination (making a complete bend to do so if it happens to point upward as the seed lies in the ground), while the other end turns or points skyward. These opposite positions are taken in complete darkness as readily as in the light, in dryness as much as in moisture: therefore, so far as these movements are physical, the two portions of the same internode appear to be oppositely affected by gravitation or other influences.

466. Rising into the air, the stem and green shoots generally, while young and pliable, bend or direct themselves toward the light, or toward the stronger light when unequally illuminated; while roots turn toward the darkness.

467. Many growing stems have also a movement of *Nutation*, that is, of nodding successively in different directions. This is brought about by a temporary increase of turgidity of the cells along one side, thus bowing the stem over to the opposite side; and this line of turgescence travels round the shoot continually, from right to left or from left to right according to the species: thus the shoot bends to all points of the compass in succession. Commonly this nutation is slight or hardly observable. It is most marked in

468. **Twining Stems** (Fig. 90). The growing upper end of such stems, as is familiar in the Hop, Pole Beans, and Morning-Glory, turns over in an inclined or horizontal direction, thus stretching out to reach a neighboring support, and by the continual change in the direction of the nodding, sweeps the whole circle, the sweeps being the longer as the stem lengthens. When it strikes against a support, such as a stem or branch of a neighboring plant, the motion is arrested at the contact, but continues at the growing apex beyond, and this apex is thus made to wind spirally around the supporting body.

469. **Leaf-movements** are all but universal. The presentation by most leaves of their upper surface to the light, from whatever direction that may come, is an instance; for when turned upside down they twist or bend round on the stalk to recover this normal position. Leaves, and the leaflets of compound leaves, change this position at nightfall, or when the light is withdrawn; they then take what is called their sleeping posture, resuming the diurnal position when daylight returns. This is very striking [Pg 152]in Locust-trees, in the Sensitive Plant (Fig. 490), and in Woodsorrel. Young seedlings droop or close their leaves at night in plants which are not thus affected in the adult foliage. All this is thought to be a protection against the cold by nocturnal radiation.

470. Various plants climb by a coiling movement of their leaves or their leaf-stalks. Familiar examples are seen in Clematis, Maurandia, Tropæolum, and in a Solanum which is much

cultivated in greenhouses (Fig. 172). In the latter, and in other woody plants which climb in this way, the petioles thicken and harden after they have grasped their support, thus securing a very firm hold.

471. **Tendril movements.** Tendrils are either leaves or stems (98, 168), specially developed for climbing purposes. Cobæa is a good example of partial transformation; some of the leaflets are normal, some of the same leaf are little tendrils, and some intermediate in character. The Passion-flowers give good examples of simple stem-tendrils (Fig. 92); Grape-Vines, of branched ones. Most tendrils make revolving sweeps, like those of twining stems. Those of some Passion-flowers, in sultry weather, are apt to move fast enough for the movement actually to be seen for a part of the circuit, as plainly as that of the second-hand of a watch. Two herbaceous species, Passiflora gracilis and P. sicyoides (the first an annual, the second a strong-rooted perennial of the easiest cultivation), are admirable for illustration both of revolving movements and of sensitive coiling.

FIG. 490. Piece of stem of Sensitive Plant (Mimosa pudica), with two leaves, the lower open, the upper in the closed state.

472. **Movements under Irritation.** The most familiar case is that of the Sensitive Plant (Fig. 490). The leaves suddenly take their nocturnal position when roughly touched or when shocked by a jar. The leaflets close in pairs, the four outspread partial petioles come closer together, and the common petiole is depressed. The seat of the movements is at the base of the leaf-stalk and stalklets. Schrankia, a near relative of the Sensitive Plant, acts in the same way, but is slower. These are not anomalous actions, but only extreme manifestations of a faculty more or less common in foliage. In Locust and Honey-Locusts for example, repeated jars will slowly produce similar effects.

[Pg 153]

473. Leaf-stalks and tendrils are adapted to their uses in climbing by a similar sensitiveness. The coiling of the leaf-stalk is in response to a kind of irritation produced by contact with the supporting body. This may be shown by gentle rubbing or prolonged pressure upon the upper face of the leaf-stalk, which is soon followed by a curvature. Tendrils are still more sensitive to contact or light friction. This causes the free end of the tendril to coil round the support, and the sensitiveness, propagated downward along the tendril, causes that side of it to become less turgescent or the opposite side more so, thus throwing the tendril into coils. This shortening draws the plant up to the support. Tendrils which have not laid hold will at length commonly coil spontaneously, in a simple coil, from the free apex downward. In Sicyos, Echinocystis, and the above mentioned Passion-flowers (471), the tendril is so sensitive, under a high summer temperature, that it will curve and coil promptly after one or two light strokes by the hand.

FIG. 491. Portion of stem and leaves of Telegraph-plant (Desmodium gyrans), almost of natural size.

474. Among spontaneous movements the most singular are those of Desmodium gyrans of India, sometimes called Telegraph-plant, which is cultivated on account of this action. Of its three leaflets, the larger (terminal) one moves only by drooping at nightfall and rising with the dawn. But its two small lateral leaflets, when in a congenial high temperature, by day and by night move upward and downward in a succession of jerks, stopping occasionally, as if to recover from exhaustion. In most plant-movements some obviously useful purpose is subserved: this of Desmodium gyrans is a riddle.

475. **Movements in Flowers** are very various. The most remarkable are in some way connected with fertilization (Sect. XIII.). Some occur under irritation: the stamens of Barberry start forward when touched at the base inside: those of many polyandrous flowers (of Sparmannia very strikingly) spread outwardly when lightly brushed: the two lips or lobes [Pg 154]of the stigma in Mimulus close after a touch. Some are automatic and are connected with dichogamy (339): the style of Sabbatia and of large-flowered species of Epilobium bends over strongly to one side or turns downward when the blossom opens, but slowly erects itself a day or two later.

476. **Extraordinary Movements connected with Capture of Insects.** The most striking cases are those of Drosera and Dionæa; for an account of which see "How Plants Behave," and Goodale's "Physiological Botany."

477. The upper face of the leaves of the common species of Drosera, or Sundew, is beset with stout bristles, having a glandular tip. This tip secretes a drop of a clear but very viscid liquid, which glistens like a dew-drop in the sun; whence the popular name. When a fly or other small insect, attracted by the liquid, alights upon the leaf, the viscid drops are so tenacious that they

hold it fast. In struggling it only becomes more completely entangled. Now the neighboring bristles, which have not been touched, slowly bend inward from all sides toward the captured insect, and bring their sticky apex against its body, thus increasing the number of bonds. Moreover, the blade of the leaf commonly aids in the capture by becoming concave, its sides or edges turning inward, which brings still more of the gland-tipped bristles into contact with the captive's body. The insect perishes; the clear liquid disappears, apparently by absorption into the tissue of the leaf. It is thought that the absorbed secretion takes with it some of the juices of the insect or the products of its decomposition.

FIG. 492. Plant of Dionæa muscipula, or Venus's Fly-trap, reduced in size.

478. Dionæa muscipula, the most special vegetable fly-trap (Fig. 176, 492), is related to the Sundews, and has a more special and active apparatus for fly-catching, formed of the summit of the leaf. The two halves of this rounded body move as if they were hinged upon the midrib; their edges are fringed with spiny but not glandular bristles, which interlock when the organ closes. Upon the face are two or three short and delicate bristles, which are sensitive. They do not themselves move when touched, but they propagate the sensitiveness to the organ itself, causing it to close with a quick movement. In a fresh [Pg 155]and vigorous leaf, under a high summer temperature, and when the trap lies widely open, a touch of any one of the minute bristles on the face, by the finger or any extraneous body, springs the trap (so to say), and it closes suddenly; but after an hour or so it opens again. When a fly or other small insect alights on the trap, it closes in the same manner, and so quickly that the intercrossing marginal bristles obstruct the egress of the insect, unless it be a small one and not worth taking. Afterwards and more slowly it completely closes, and presses down upon the prey; then some hidden glands pour out a glairy liquid, which dissolves out the juices of the insect's body; next all is re-absorbed into the plant, and the trap opens to repeat the operation. But the same leaf perhaps never captures more than two or three insects. It ages instead, becomes more rigid and motionless, or decays away.

479. That some few plants should thus take animal food will appear less surprising when it is considered that hosts of plants of the lower grade, known as Fungi, moulds, rusts, ferments, Bacteria, etc., live upon animal or other organized matter, either decaying or living. That plants should execute movements in order to accomplish the ends of their existence is less surprising now when it is known that the living substance of plants and animals is essentially the same; that the beings of both kingdoms partake of a common life, to which, as they rise in the scale, other and higher endowments are successively superadded.

480. **Work uses up material and energy** in plants as well as in animals. The latter live and work by the consumption and decomposition of that which plants have assimilated into organizable matter through an energy derived from the sun, and which is, so to say, stored up in the assimilated products. In every internal action, as well as in every movement and exertion, some portion of this assimilated matter is transformed and of its stored energy expended. The steam-engine is an organism for converting the sun's radiant energy, stored up by plants in the fuel, into mechanical work. An animal is an engine fed by vegetable fuel in the same or other forms, from the same source, by the decomposition of which it also does mechanical work. The plant is the producer of food and accumulator of solar energy or force. But the plant, like the animal, is a consumer whenever and by so much as it does any work except its great work of assimilation. Every internal change and movement, every transformation, such as that of starch into sugar and of sugar into cell-walls, as well as every movement of parts which becomes externally visible, is done at the expense of a certain amount of its assimilated matter and of its stored energy; that is, by the decomposition or combustion of sugar or some such product into carbonic acid and water, which is given back to the air, just as in the animal it is given back to the air in respiration. So the respiration of plants is as real and as essential as that of animals. But what plants consume or decompose in their life and action is of insignificant amount in comparison with what they compose.

[Pg 156]
SECTION XVII. CRYPTOGAMOUS OR FLOWERLESS PLANTS.

481. Even the beginner in botany should have some general idea of what cryptogamous plants are, and what are the obvious distinctions of the principal families. Although the lower grades are difficult, and need special books and good microscopes for their study, the higher orders, such as Ferns, may be determined almost as readily as phanerogamous plants.

482. Linnæus gave to this lower grade of plants the name of *Cryptogamia*, thereby indicating that their organs answering to stamens and pistils, if they had any, were recondite and unknown. There is no valid reason why this long-familiar name should not be kept up, along with the

counterpart one of *Phanerogamia* (6), although organs analogous to stamens and pistil, or rather to pollen and ovule, have been discovered in all the higher and most of the lower grades of this series of plants. So also the English synonymous name of *Flowerless Plants* is both good and convenient: for they have not flowers in the proper sense. The essentials of flowers are stamens and pistils, giving rise to seeds, and the essential of a seed is an embryo (8). Cryptogamous or Flowerless plants are propagated by SPORES; and a spore is not an embryo-plantlet, but mostly a single plant-cell (399).

483. **Vascular Cryptogams**, which compose the higher orders of this series of plants, have stems and (usually) leaves, constructed upon the general plan of ordinary plants; that is, they have wood (wood-cells and vessels, 408) in the stem and leaves, in the latter as a frame work of veins. But the lower grades, having only the more elementary cellular structure, are called *Cellular Cryptogams*. Far the larger number of the former are Ferns: wherefore that class has been called

484. **Pteridophyta, Pteridophytes** in English form, meaning *Fern-plants,*—that is, Ferns and their relatives. They are mainly Horsetails, Ferns, Club-Mosses, and various aquatics which have been called *Hydropterides*, i. e. Water-Ferns.

485. **Horsetails**, *Equisetaceæ,* is the name of a family which consists only (among now-living plants) of *Equisetum,* the botanical name of Horsetail and Scouring Rush. They have hollow stems, with partitions at the nodes; the leaves consist only of a whorl of scales at each node, these coalescent into a sheath: from the axils of these leaf-scales, in many species, branches grow out, which are similar to the stem but on a much smaller scale, close-jointed, and with the tips of the leaves more apparent. At the apex of the stem appears the *fructification*, as it is called for lack of a better term, in the form of a short spike or head. This consists of a good number of stalked shields, bearing on their inner or under face several wedge-shaped spore-cases. The spore-cases when they ripen open down the inner [Pg 157]side and discharge a great number of green spores of a size large enough to be well seen by a hand-glass. The spores are aided in their discharge and dissemination by four club-shaped threads attached to one part of them. These are hygrometric: when moist they are rolled up over the spore; when dry they straighten, and exhibit lively movements, closing over the spore when breathed upon, and unrolling promptly a moment after as they dry. (See Fig. 493-498.)

FIG. 493. Upper part of a stem of a Horsetail, Equisetum sylvaticum. 494. Part of the head or spike of spore-cases, with some of the latter taken off. 495. View (more enlarged) of under side of the shield-shaped body, bearing a circle of spore-cases. 496. One of the latter detached and more magnified. 497. A spore with the attached arms moistened. 498. Same when dry, the arms extended.

FIG. 499. A Tree-Fern, Dicksonia arborescens, with a young one near its base. In front a common herbaceous Fern (Polypodium vulgare) with its creeping stem or rootstock.

FIG. 500. A section of the trunk of a Tree-Fern.

486. **Ferns, or Filices**, a most attractive family of plants, are very numerous and varied. In warm and equable climates some rise into forest-trees, with habit of Palms; but most of them are perennial herbs. The wood of a Fern-trunk is very different, however, from that of a palm, or of any exogenous stem either. A section is represented in Fig. 500. The curved plates of wood each terminate [Pg 158]upward in a leaf-stalk. The subterranean trunk or stem of any strong-growing herbaceous Fern shows a similar structure. Most Ferns are circinate in the bud; that is, are rolled up in the manner shown in Fig. 197. Uncoiling as they grow, they have some likeness to a crosier.

FIG. 501. The Walking-Fern, Camptosorus, reduced in size, showing its fruit-dots on the veins approximated in pairs. 502. A small piece (pinnule) of a Shield-Fern: a row of fruit-dots on each side of the midrib, each covered by its kidney-shaped indusium. 503. A spore-case bursting the latter, just bursting by the partial straightening of the incomplete ring; well magnified. 504. Three of the spores of 509, more magnified. 505. Schizæa pusilla, a very small and simple-leaved Fern, drawn nearly of natural size. 506. One of the lobes of its fruit-bearing portion, magnified, bearing two rows of spore-cases. 507. Spore-case of the latter, detached, opening lengthwise. 508. Adder-tongue, Ophioglossum; spore-cases in a kind of spike: *a*, a portion of the fruiting part, about natural size; showing two rows of the firm spore-cases, which open transversely into two valves.

487. The fructification of Ferns is borne on the back or under side of the leaves. The early botanists thought this such a peculiarity that they always called a Fern-leaf a FROND, and its petiole a STIPE. Usage continues these terms, although they are superfluous. The fruit of Ferns consists of SPORE-CASES, technically SPORANGIA, which grow out of the veins of the leaf. Sometimes these are distributed over the whole lower [Pg 159]surface of the leaf or frond, or

over the whole surface when there are no proper leaf-blades to the frond, but all is reduced to stalks. Commonly the spore-cases occupy only detached spots or lines, each of which is called a SORUS, or in English merely a Fruit-dot. In many Ferns these fruit-dots are naked; in others they are produced under a scale-like bit of membrane, called an INDUSIUM. In Maidenhair-Ferns a little lobe of the leaf is folded back over each fruit-dot, to serve as its shield or indusium. In the true Brake or Bracken (Pteris) the whole edge of the fruit-bearing part of the leaf is folded back over it like a hem.

488. The form and structure of the spore-cases can be made out with a common hand magnifying glass. The commonest kind (shown in Fig. 503) has a stalk formed of a row of jointed cells, and is itself composed of a layer of thin-walled cells, but is incompletely surrounded by a border of thicker-walled cells, forming the RING. This extends from the stalk up one side of the spore-case, round its summit, descends on the other side, but there gradually vanishes. In ripening and drying the shrinking of the cells of the ring on the outer side causes it to straighten; in doing so it tears the spore-case open on the weaker side and discharges the minute spores that fill it, commonly with a jerk which scatters them to the wind. Another kind of spore-case (Fig. 507) is stalkless, and has its ring-cells forming a kind of cap at the top: at maturity it splits from top to bottom by a regular dehiscence. A third kind is of firm texture and opens across into two valves, like a clam-shell (Fig. 508⁴): this kind makes an approach to the next family.

FIG. 509. A young prothallus of a Maiden-hair, moderately enlarged, and an older one with the first fern-leaf developed from near the notch. 510. Middle portion of the young one, much magnified, showing below, partly among the rootlets, the *antheridia* or fertilizing organs, and above, near the notch, three *pistillidia* to be fertilized.

489. The spores germinate on moistened ground. In a conservatory they may be found germinating on a damp wall or on the edges of a well-watered flower-pot. Instead of directly forming a fern-plantlet, the spore grows first into a body which [Pg 160]closely resembles a small Liverwort. This is named a PROTHALLUS (Fig. 509): from some point of this a bud appears to originate, which produces the first fern-leaf, soon followed by a second and third, and so the stem and leaves of the plant are set up.

FIG. 511. Lycopodium Carolinianum, of nearly natural size. 512. Inside view of one of the bracts and spore-case, magnified.

FIG. 513. Open 4-valved spore-case of a Selaginella, and its four large spores (macrospores), magnified. 514. Macrospores of another Selaginella. 515. Same separated.

FIG. 516. Plant of Isoetes. 517. Base of a leaf and contained sporocarp filled with microspores cut across, magnified. 518. Same divided lengthwise, equally magnified; some microspores seen at the left. 519. Section of a spore-case containing macrospores, equally magnified; at the right three macrospores more magnified.

490. Investigation of this prothallus under the microscope resulted in the discovery of a wholly unsuspected kind of fertilization, taking place at this germinating stage of the plant. On the under side of the prothallus two kinds of organs appear (Fig. 510). One may be likened to an open and depressed ovule, with a single cell at bottom answering to nucleus; the other, to an anther; but instead of pollen, it discharges corkscrew-shaped microscopic filaments, which bear some cilia of extreme tenuity, by the rapid vibration of which the filaments move freely over a wet surface. These filaments travel over the surface of the prothallus, and even to other prothalli (for there are natural hybrid Ferns), reach and enter the ovule-like [Pg 161]cavities, and fertilize the cell. This thereupon sets up a growth, forms a vegetable bud, and so develops the new plant.

491. An essentially similar process of fertilization has been discovered in the preceding and the following families of Pteridophytes; but it is mostly subterranean and very difficult to observe.

492. **Club-Mosses or Lycopodiums.** Some of the common kinds, called Ground Pine, are familiar, being largely used for Christmas wreaths and other decoration. They are low evergreens, some creeping, all with considerable wood in their stems: this thickly beset with small leaves. In the axils of some of these leaves, or more commonly, in the axils of peculiar leaves changed into bracts (as in Fig. 511, 512) spore-cases appear, as roundish or kidney-shaped bodies, of firm texture, opening round the top into two valves, and discharging a great quantity of a very fine yellow powder, the spores.

493. The Selaginellas have been separated from Lycopodium, which they much resemble, because they produce two kinds of spores, in separate spore-cases. One kind (MICROSPORES) is just that of Lycopodium; the other consists of only four large spores (MACROSPORES), in a spore-case which usually breaks in pieces at maturity (Fig. 513-515).

494. **The Quillworts, Isoetes** (Fig. 516-519), are very unlike Club Mosses in aspect, but have been associated with them. They look more like Rushes, and live in water, or partly out of it. A very short stem, like a corm, bears a cluster of roots underneath; above it is covered by the broad bases of a cluster of awl-shaped or thread-shaped leaves. The spore-cases are immersed in the bases of the leaves. The outer leaf-bases contain numerous macrospores; the inner are filled with innumerable microspores.

FIG. 520. Plant of Marsilia quadrifoliata, reduced in size; at the right a pair of sporocarps of about natural size.

495. **The Pillworts** (*Marsilia* and *Pilularia*) are low aquatics, which [Pg 162]bear globular or pill-shaped fruit (SPOROCARPS) on the lower part of their leaf-stalks or on their slender creeping stems. The leaves of the commoner species of Marsilia might be taken for four-leaved Clover. (See Fig. 520.) The sporocarps are usually raised on a short stalk. Within they are divided lengthwise by a partition, and then crosswise by several partitions. These partitions bear numerous delicate sacs or spore-cases of two kinds, intermixed. The larger ones contain each a large spore, or macrospore; the smaller contain numerous microspores, immersed in mucilage. At maturity the fruit bursts or splits open at top, and the two kinds of spores are discharged. The large ones in germination produce a small prothallus; upon which the contents of the microspores act in the same way as in Ferns, and with a similar result.

496. **Azolla** is a little floating plant, looking like a small Liverwort or Moss. Its branches are covered with minute and scale-shaped leaves. On the under side of the branches are found egg-shaped thin-walled sporocarps of two kinds. The small ones open across and discharge microspores; the larger burst irregularly, and bring to view globose spore-cases, attached to the bottom of the sporocarp by a slender stalk. These delicate spore-cases burst and set free about four macrospores, which are fertilized at germination, in the manner of the Pillworts and Quillworts. (See Fig. 521-526.)

FIG. 521. Small plant of Azolla Caroliniana. 522. Portion magnified, showing the two kinds of sporocarp; the small ones contain microspores. 523 represents one more magnified. 524. The larger sporocarp more magnified. 525. Same more magnified and burst open, showing stalked spore-cases. 526. Two of the latter highly magnified; one of them bursting shows four contained macrospores; between the two, three of these spores highly magnified.

497. **Cellular Cryptogams** (483) are so called because composed, even in their higher forms, of cellular tissue only, without proper wood-cells or vessels. Many of the lower kinds are mere plates, or ribbons, or simple rows of cells, or even single cells. But their highest orders follow the plan of Ferns and phanerogamous plants in having stem and leaves for their upward growth, and commonly roots, or at least rootlets, [Pg 163]to attach them to the soil, or to trunks, or to other bodies on which they grow. Plants of this grade are chiefly Mosses. So as a whole they take the name of

498. **Bryophyta, Bryophytes** in English form, Bryum being the Greek name of a Moss. These plants are of two principal kinds: true Mosses (*Musci*, which is their Latin name in the plural); and Hepatic Mosses, or Liverworts (*Hepaticæ*).

FIG. 527. Single plant of Physcomitrium pyriforme, magnified. 528. Top of a leaf, cut across; it consists of a single layer of cells.

499. **Mosses or Musci.** The pale Peat-mosses (species of Sphagnum, the principal component of sphagnous bogs) and the strong-growing Hair-cap Moss (Polytrichum) are among the larger and commoner representatives of this numerous family; while Fountain Moss (Fontinalis) in running water sometimes attains the length of a yard or more. On the other hand, some are barely individually distinguishable to the naked eye. Fig. 527 represents a common little Moss, enlarged to about twelve times its natural size; and by its side is part of a leaf, much magnified, showing that it is composed of cellular tissue (parenchyma-cells) only. The leaves of Mosses are always simple, distinct, and sessile on the stem. The fructification is an urn-shaped spore-case, in this as in most cases raised on a slender stalk. The spore-case loosely bears on its summit a thin and pointed cap, like a candle-extinguisher, called a *Calyptra*. Detaching this, it is found that the spore-case is like a pyxis (376), that is, the top at maturity comes off as a lid (*Operculum*); and that the interior is filled with a green powder, the spores, which are discharged through the open mouth. In most Mosses there is a fringe of one or two rows of teeth or membrane around this mouth or orifice, the *Peristome*. When moist the peristome closes hygrometrically over the orifice more or less; when drier the teeth or processes commonly bend outward or recurve; and then the spores more readily escape. In Hair-cap Moss a membrane is

71

stretched quite across the mouth, like a drum-head, retaining the spores until this wears away. See Figures 527-541 for details.

500. Fertilization in Mosses is by the analogues of stamens and pistils, which are hidden in the axils of leaves, or in the cluster of leaves at the [Pg 164]end of the stem. The analogue of the anther (*Antheridium*) is a cellular sac, which in bursting discharges innumerable delicate cells floating in a mucilaginous liquid; each of these bursts and sets free a vibratile self-moving thread. These threads, one or more, reach the orifice of the pistil-shaped body, the *Pistillidium*, and act upon a particular cell at its base within. This cell in its growth develops into the spore-case and its stalk (when there is any), carrying on its summit the wall of the pistillidium, which becomes the calyptra.

FIG. 529. Mnium cuspidatum, smaller than nature. 530. Its calyptra, detached, enlarged. 531. Its spore-case, with top of stalk, magnified, the lid (532) being detached, the outer peristome appears. 533. Part of a cellular ring (*annulus*) which was under the lid, outside of the peristome, more magnified. 534. Some of the outer and of the inner peristome (consisting of jointed teeth) much magnified. 535. Antheridia and a pistillidium (the so-called flower) at end of a stem of same plant, the leaves torn away (♂, antheridia, ♀, pistillidium), magnified. 536. A bursting antheridium, and some of the accompanying jointed threads, highly magnified. 537. Summit of an open spore-case of a Moss, which has a peristome of 16 pairs of teeth. 538. The double peristome of a Hypnum. 539-541. Spore-case, detached calyptra, and top of more enlarged spore-case and detached lid, of Physcomitrium pyriforme (Fig. 527): orifice shows that there is no peristome.

501. **Liverworts or Hepatic Mosses** (*Hepaticæ*) in some kinds resemble true Mosses, having distinct stem and leaves, although their leaves occasionally run together; while in others there is no distinction of stem and leaf, but the whole plant is a leaf-like body, which produces rootlets on the lower face and its fructification on the upper. Those of the moss-like kind (sometimes called Scale-Mosses) have their tender spore-cases splitting into four valves; and with their spores are intermixed some slender spiral [Pg 165]and very hygrometric threads (called *Elaters*) which are thought to aid in the dispersion of the spores. (Fig. 542-544.)

FIG. 542. Fructification of a Jungermannia, magnified; its cellular spore-stalk, surrounded at base by some of the leaves, at summit the 4-valved spore-case opening, discharging spores and elaters. 543. Two elaters and some spores from the same, highly magnified.

FIG. 544. One of the frondose Liverworts, Steetzia, otherwise like a Jungermannia; the spore-case not yet protruded from its sheath.

502. Marchantia, the commonest and largest of the true Liverworts, forms large green plates or fronds on damp and shady ground, and sends up from some part of the upper face a stout stalk, ending in a several-lobed umbrella-shaped body, under the lobes of which hang several thin-walled spore-cases, which burst open and discharge spores and elaters. Riccia natans (Fig. 545) consists of wedge-shaped or heart-shaped fronds, which float free in pools of still water. The under face bears copious rootlets; in the substance of the upper face are the spore-cases, their pointed tips merely projecting: there they burst open, and discharge their spores. These are comparatively few and large, and are in fours; so they are very like the macrospores of Pillworts or Quillworts.

503. **Thallophyta, or Thallophytes** in English form. This is the name for the lower class of Cellular Cryptogams,—plants in which there is no marked distinction into root, stem, and leaves. Roots in any proper sense they never have, as organs for absorbing, although some of the larger Seaweeds (such as the Sea Colander, Fig. 553) have them as holdfasts. Instead of axis and foliage, there is a stratum of frond, in such plants commonly called a THALLUS (by a strained use of a Greek and Latin word which means a green shoot or bough), which may have any kind of form, leaf-like, stem-like, branchy, extended to a flat plate, or gathered into a sphere, or drawn out into threads, or reduced to a single row of cells, or even reduced to single cells. Indeed, Thallophytes are so multifarious, so numerous in kinds, so protean in their stages and transformations, so recondite in their fructification, and many so microscopic in size, either of [Pg 166]the plant itself or its essential organs, that they have to be elaborately described in separate books and made subjects of special study.

FIG. 545, 546. Two plants of Riccia natans, about natural size. 547. Magnified section of a part of the frond, showing two immersed spore-cases, and one emptied space. 548. Magnified section of a spore-case with some spores. 549. Magnified spore-case torn out, and spores; one figure of the spores united; the other of the four separated.

504. Nevertheless, it may be well to try to give some general idea of what Algæ and Lichens and Fungi are. Linnæus had them all under the orders of Algæ and Fungi. Afterwards the Lichens were separated; but of late it has been made most probable that a Lichen consists of an Alga and a Fungus conjoined. At least it must be so in some of the ambiguous forms. Botanists are in the way of bringing out new classifications of the Thallophytes, as they come to understand their structure and relations better. Here, it need only be said that

505. Lichens live in the air, that is, on the ground, or on rocks, trunks, walls, and the like, and grow when moistened by rains. They assimilate air, water, and some earthy matter, just as do ordinary plants. Algæ, or Seaweeds, live in water, and live the same kind of life as do ordinary plants. Fungi, whatever medium they inhabit, live as animals do, upon organic matter,—upon what other plants have assimilated, or upon the products of [Pg 167]their decay. True as these general distinctions are, it is no less true that these orders run together in their lowest forms; and that Algæ and Fungi may be traced down into forms so low and simple that no clear line can be drawn between them; and even into forms of which it is uncertain whether they should be called plants or animals. It is as well to say that they are not high enough in rank to be distinctively either the one or the other. On the other hand there is a peculiar group of plants, which in simplicity of composition resemble the simpler Algæ, while in fructification and in the arrangements of their simple cells into stem and branches they seem to be of a higher order, viz.:—

FIG. 550. Branch of a Chara, about natural size. 551. A fruiting portion, magnified, showing the structure; a sporocarp, and an antheridium. 552. Outlines of a portion of the stem in section, showing the central cell and the outer or cortical cells.

506. **Characeæ.** These are aquatic herbs, of considerable size, abounding in ponds. The simpler kinds (Nitella) have the stem formed of a single row of tubular cells, and at the nodes, or junction of the cells, a whorl of similar branches. Chara (Fig. 550-552) is the same, except that the cells which make up the stem and the principal branches are strengthened by a coating of many smaller tubular cells, applied to the surface of the main or central cell. The fructification consists of a globular sporocarp of considerable size, which is spirally enwrapped by tubular cells twisted around it: by the side of this is a smaller and globular antheridium. The latter breaks up into eight shield-shaped [Pg 168]pieces, with an internal stalk, and bearing long and ribbon shaped filaments, which consist of a row of delicate cells, each of which discharges a free-moving microscopic thread (the analogue of the pollen or pollen-tube), nearly in the manner of Ferns and Mosses. One of these threads reaches and fertilizes a cell at the apex of the nucleus or solid body of the sporocarp. This subsequently germinates and forms a new individual.

507. **Algæ or Seaweeds.** The proper Seaweeds may be studied by the aid of Professor Farlow's "Marine Algæ of New England;" the fresh-water species, by Prof. H. C. Woods's "Fresh-water Algæ of North America," a larger and less accessible volume. A few common forms are here very briefly mentioned and illustrated, to give an idea of the family. But they are of almost endless diversity.

FIG. 553. Agarum Turneri, Sea Colander (so called from the perforations with which the frond, as it grows, becomes riddled); very much reduced in size.

FIG. 554. Upper end of a Rockweed, Fucus vesiculosus, reduced half or more, *b*, the fructification.

508. The common Rockweed (Fucus vesiculosus, Fig. 554, abounding between high and low water mark on the coast), the rarer Sea Colander (Agarum Turneri, Fig. 553), and Laminaria, of which the larger forms are called Devil's Aprons, are good representatives of the olive green or brownish Seaweeds. They are attached either by a disk-like base or by root-like holdfasts to the rocks or stones on which they grow.

FIG. 555. Magnified section through a fertile conceptacle of Rockweed, showing the large spores in the midst of threads of cells. 556. Similar section of a sterile conceptacle, containing slender antheridia. From Farlow's "Marine Algæ of New England."

509. The hollow and inflated places in the Fucus vesiculosus or Rockweed (Fig. 554) are air-bladders for buoyancy. The fructification forms in the substance of the tips of the frond: the rough dots mark the places where the conceptacles open. The spores and the fertilizing cells are in different plants. Sections of the two kinds of conceptacles are given in Fig. 555 and 556. The contents of the conceptacles are discharged through [Pg 169]a small orifice which in each figure is at the margin of the page. The large spores are formed eight together in a mother-cell. The minute motile filaments of the antheridia fertilize the large spores after injection into the water: and then the latter promptly acquire a cell-wall and germinate.

73

510. The Florideæ or Rose-red series of marine Algæ (which, however, are sometimes green or brownish) are the most attractive to amateurs. The delicate Porphyra or Laver is in some countries eaten as a delicacy, and the cartilaginous Chondrus crispus has been largely used for jelly. Besides their conceptacles, which contain true spores (Fig. 560), they mostly have a fructification in *Tetraspores*, that is, of spores originating in fours (Fig. 559).

FIG. 557. Small plant of Chondrus crispus, or Carrageen Moss, reduced in size, in fruit; the spots represent the fructification, consisting of numerous tetraspores in bunches in the substance of the plant. 558. Section through the thickness of one of the lobes, magnified, passing through two of the imbedded fruit-clusters. 559. Two of its tetraspores (spores in fours), highly magnified.

FIG. 560. Section through a conceptacle of Delesseria Leprieurei, much magnified, showing the spores, which are single specialized cells, two or three in a row.

FIG. 561. A piece of the rose-red Delesseria Leprieurei, double natural size. 562. A piece cut out and much magnified, showing that it is composed of a layer of cells. 563. A few of the cells more highly magnified: the cells are gelatinous and thick-walled.

511. The Grass-green Algæ sometimes form broad membranous fronds, such as those of the common Ulva of the sea-shore, but most of them form mere threads, either simple or branched. To this division belong almost [Pg 170]all the Fresh-water Algæ, such as those which constitute the silky threads or green slime of running streams or standing pools, and which were all called Confervas before their immense diversity was known. Some are formed of a single row of cells, developed each from the end of another. Others branch, the top of one cell producing more than one new one (Fig. 564). Others, of a kind which is very common in fresh water, simple threads made of a line of cells, have the chlorophyll and protoplasm of each cell arranged in spiral lines or bands. They form spores in a peculiar way, which gives to this family the designation of conjugating Algæ.

FIG. 564. The growing end of a branching Conferva (Cladophora glomerata), much magnified; showing how, by a kind of budding growth, a new cell is formed by a cross partition separating the newer tip from the older part below; also, how the branches arise.

FIG. 565. Two magnified individuals of a Spirogyra, forming spores by conjugation; a completed spore at base: above, successive stages of the conjugation are represented.

512. At a certain time two parallel threads approach each other more closely; contiguous parts of a cell of each thread bulge or grow out, and unite when they meet; the cell-wall partitions between them are absorbed so as to open a free communication; the spiral band of green matter in both cells breaks up; the whole of that of one cell passes over into the other; and of the united contents a large green spore is formed. Soon the old cells decay, and the spore [Pg 171]set free is ready to germinate. Fig. 565 represents several stages of the conjugating process, which, however, would never be found all together like this in one pair of threads.

FIG. 566. Closterium acutum, a common Desmid, moderately magnified. It is a single firm-walled cell, filled with green protoplasmic matter.

FIG. 567. More magnified view of three stages of the conjugation of a pair of the same.

513. Desmids and Diatomes, which are microscopic one-celled plants of the same class, conjugate in the same way, as is shown in a Closterium by Fig. 566, 567. Here the whole living contents of two individuals are incorporated into one spore, for a fresh start. A reproduction which costs the life of two individuals to make a single new one would be fatal to the species if there were not a provision for multiplication by the prompt division of the new-formed individual into two, and these again into two, and so on in geometrical ratio. And the costly process would be meaningless if there were not some real advantage in such a fresh start, that is, in sexes.

FIG. 568. Early stage of a species of Botrydium, a globose cell. 569, 570. Stages of growth. 571. Full-grown plant, extended and ramified below in a root-like way. 572. A Vaucheria; single cell grown on into a much-branched thread; the end of some branches enlarging, and the green contents in one (*a*) there condensed into a spore. 573. More magnified view of *a*, and the mature spore escaping. 574. Bryopsis plumosa; apex of a stem with its branchlets; all the extension of one cell. Variously magnified.

514. There are other Algæ of the grass-green series which consist of single cells, but which by continued growth form plants of considerable size. Three kinds of these are represented in Fig. 568-574.

74

515. **Lichens**, Latin *Lichenes*, are to be studied in the works of the late Professor Tuckerman, but a popular exposition is greatly needed. The subjoined illustrations (Fig. 575-580) may simply indicate what some of the commoner forms are like. The cup, or shield-shaped spot, or knob, which bears the fructification is named the *Apothecium*. This is mainly [Pg 172]composed of slender sacs (*Asci*), having thread-shaped cells intermixed; and each ascus contains few or several spores, which are commonly double or treble. Most Lichens are flat expansions of grayish hue; some of them foliaceous in texture, but never of bright green color; more are crustaceous; some are wholly pulverulent and nearly formless. But in several the vegetation lengthens into an axis (as in Fig. 580), or imitates stem and branches or threads, as in the Reindeer-Moss on the ground in our northern woods, and the Usnea hanging from the boughs of old trees overhead.

FIG. 575. A stone on which various Lichens are growing, such as (passing from left to right) a Parmelia, a Sticta, and on the right, Lecidia geographica, so called from its patches resembling the outline of islands or continents as depicted upon maps. 576. Piece of thallus of Parmelia conspersa, with section through an apothecium. 577. Section of a smaller apothecium, enlarged. 578. Two asci of same, and contained spores, and accompanying filaments; more magnified. 579. Piece of thallus of a Sticta, with section, showing the immersed apothecia; the small openings of these dot the surface. 580. Cladonia coccinea; the fructification is in the scarlet knobs, which surround the cups.

516. **Fungi.** For this immense and greatly diversified class, it must here suffice to indicate the parts of a Mushroom, a Sphæria, and of one or two common Moulds. The true vegetation of common Fungi consists of slender cells which form what is called a *Mycelium*. These filamentous [Pg 173]cells lengthen and branch, growing by the absorption through their whole surface of the decaying, or organizable, or living matter which they feed upon. In a Mushroom (Agaricus), a knobby mass is at length formed, which develops into a stout stalk (*Stipe*), bearing the cap (*Pileus*): the under side of the cap is covered by the *Hymenium*, in this genus consisting of radiating plates, the gills or *Lamellæ*; and these bear the powdery spores in immense numbers. Under the microscope, the gills are found to be studded with projecting cells, each of which, at the top, produces four stalked spores. These form the powder which collects on a sheet of paper upon which a mature Mushroom is allowed to rest for a day or two. (Fig. 581-586.)

517. The esculent Morel, also Sphæria (Fig. 585, 586), and many other Fungi bear their spores in sacs (asci) exactly in the manner of Lichens (515).

FIG. 581. Agaricus campestris, the common edible Mushroom. 582. Section of cap and stalk. 583. Minute portion of a section of a gill, showing some spore-bearing cells, much magnified. 584. One of these, with its four spores, more magnified.

FIG. 585. Sphæria rosella. 586. Two of the asci and contained double spores, quite like those of a Lichen; much magnified.

518. Of the Moulds, one of the commoner is the Bread-Mould (Fig. 587). In fruiting it sends up a slender stalk, which bears a globular sac; [Pg 174]this bursts at maturity and discharges innumerable spores. The blue Cheese-Mould (Fig. 588) bears a cluster of branches at top, each of which is a row of naked spores, like a string of beads, all breaking apart at maturity. Botrytis (Fig. 589), the fruiting stalk of which branches, and each branch is tipped with a spore, is one of the many moulds which live and feed upon the juices of other plants or of animals, and are often very destructive. The extremely numerous kinds of smut, rust, mildew, the ferments, bacteria, and the like, many of them very destructive to other vegetable and to animal life, are also low forms of the class of Fungi.[1]

FIG. 587. Ascophora, the Bread-Mould. 588. Aspergillus glaucus, the mould of cheese, but common on mouldy vegetables. 589. A species of Botrytis. All magnified.

FOOTNOTES:

[1]The "Introduction to Cryptogamous Botany," or third volume of "The Botanical Text Book," now in preparation by the author's colleague, Professor Farlow, will be the proper guide in the study of the Flowerless Plants, especially of the Algæ and Fungi.

[Pg 175]
SECTION XVIII. CLASSIFICATION AND NOMENCLATURE.

519. Classification, in botany, is the consideration of plants in respect to their kinds and relationships. Some system of Nomenclature, or naming, is necessary for fixing and expressing botanical knowledge so as to make it available. The vast multiplicity of plants and the various degrees of their relationship imperatively require order and system, not only as to *names* for designating the kinds of plants, but also as to *terms* for defining their differences. Nomenclature is

concerned with the names of plants. Terminology supplies names of organs or parts, and terms to designate their differences.

§ 1. KINDS AND RELATIONSHIP.

520. Plants and animals have two great peculiarities: 1st, they form themselves; and 2d, they multiply themselves. They reproduce their kind in a continued succession of

521. **Individuals.** Mineral things occur as *masses*, which are divisible into smaller and still smaller ones without alteration of properties. But organic things (vegetables and animals) exist as *individual beings*. Each owes its existence to a parent, and produces similar individuals in its turn. So each individual is a link of a chain; and to this chain the natural-historian applies the name of

522. **Species.** All the descendants from the same stock therefore compose one species. And it was from our observing that the several sorts of plants or animals steadily reproduce themselves, or, in other words, keep up a succession of similar individuals, that the idea of species originated. There are few species, however, in which man has actually observed the succession for many generations. It could seldom be proved that all the White Pine trees or White Oaks of any forest came from the same stock. But observation having familiarized us with the general fact that individuals proceeding from the same stock are essentially alike, we infer from their close resemblance that these similar individuals belong to the same species. That is, we infer it when the individuals are as much like each other as those are which we know, or confidently suppose, to have sprung from the same stock.

523. Identity in species is inferred from close similarity in all essential respects, or whenever the differences, however considerable, are not known or reasonably supposed to have been originated in the course of time under changed conditions. No two individuals are exactly alike; a tendency to variation pervades all living things. In cultivation, where variations are looked after and cared for, very striking differences come to light; and if in wild nature they are less common or less conspicuous, it is partly because they are uncared for. When such variant forms are pretty well marked they are called

[Pg 176]

524. **Varieties.** The White Oak, for example, presents two or three varieties in the shape of the leaves, although they may be all alike upon each particular tree. The question often arises, and it is often hard to answer, whether the difference in a particular case is that of a variety, or is specific. If the former, it may commonly be proved by finding such intermediate degrees of difference in various individuals as to show that no clear distinction can be drawn between them; or else by observing the variety to vary back again in some of its offspring. The sorts of Apples, Pears, Potatoes, and the like, show that differences which are permanent in the individual, and continue unchanged through a long series of generations when propagated by division (as by offsets, cuttings, grafts, bulbs, tubers, etc.), are not likely to be reproduced by seed. Still they sometimes are so, and perhaps always tend in that direction. For the fundamental law in organic nature is that offspring shall be like parent.

RACES are such strongly marked varieties, capable of coming true to seed. The different sorts of Wheat, Maize, Peas, Radishes, etc., are familiar examples. By selecting those individuals of a species which have developed or inherited any desirable peculiarity, keeping them from mingling with their less promising brethren, and selecting again the most promising plants raised from their seeds, the cultivator may in a few generations render almost any variety transmissible by seed, so long as it is cared for and kept apart. In fact, this is the way the cultivated domesticated races, so useful to man, have been fixed and preserved. Races, in fact, can hardly, if at all, be said to exist independently of man. But man does not really produce them. Such peculiarities—often surprising enough—now and then originate, we know not how (the plant *sports*, as the gardeners say); they are only preserved, propagated, and generally further developed, by the cultivator's skilful care. If left alone, they are likely to dwindle and perish, or else revert to the original form of the species. Vegetable races are commonly annuals, which can be kept up only by seed, or herbs of which a succession of generations can be had every year or two, and so the education by selection be completed without great lapse of time. But all fruit-trees could probably be fixed into races in an equal number of generations.

BUD-VARIETIES are those which spring from buds instead of seed. They are uncommon to any marked extent. They are sometimes called *Sports*, but this name is equally applied to variations among seedlings.

CROSS-BREEDS, strictly so-called, are the variations which come from cross-fertilizing one variety of a species with another.

HYBRIDS are the varieties, if they may be so called,—which come from the crossing of species (331). Only nearly related species can be hybridized; and the resulting progeny is usually self-sterile, but not always. Hybrid plants, however, may often be fertilized and made prolific by the pollen of one or the other parent. This produces another kind of cross-breeds.

525. Species are the units in classification. Varieties, although of [Pg 177]utmost importance in cultivation and of considerable consequence in the flora of any country, are of less botanical significance. For they are apt to be indefinite and to shade off one form into another. But species, the botanist *expects* to be distinct. Indeed, the practical difference to the botanist between species and varieties is the definite limitation of the one and the indefiniteness of the other. The botanist's determination is partly a matter of observation, partly of judgment.

526. In an enlarged view, varieties may be incipient species; and nearly related species probably came from a common stock in earlier times. For there is every reason to believe that existing vegetation came from the more or less changed vegetation of a preceding geological era. However that may be, species are regarded as permanent and essentially unchanged in their succession of individuals through the actual ages.

527. There are, at nearly the lowest computation, as many as one hundred thousand species of phanerogamous plants, and the cryptogamous species are thought to be still more numerous. They are all connected by resemblances or relationships, near and remote, which show that they are all parts of one system, realizations in nature, as we may affirm, of the conception of One Mind. As we survey them, they do not form a single and connected chain, stretching from the lowest to the highest organized species, although there obviously are lower and higher grades. But the species throughout group themselves, as it were, into clusters or constellations, and these into still more comprehensive clusters, and so on, with gaps between. It is this clustering which is the ground of the recognition of *kinds* of species, that is, of groups of species of successive grades or degree of generality; such as that of similar species into *Genera*, of genera into *Families* or *Orders*, of orders into *Classes*. In classification the sequence, proceeding from higher   or   more   general   to   lower   or   special,   is always CLASS, ORDER, GENUS, SPECIES, VARIETY(if need be).

528. **Genera** (in the singular, *Genus*) are assemblages of closely related species, in which the essential parts are all constructed on the same particular type or plan. White Oak, Red Oak, Scarlet Oak, Live Oak, etc., are so many species of the Oak genus (Latin, *Quercus*). The Chestnuts compose another genus; the Beeches another. The Apple, Pear, and Crab are species of one genus, the Quince represents another, the various species of Hawthorn a third. In the animal kingdom the common cat, the wild-cat, the panther, the tiger, the leopard, and the lion are species of the cat kind or genus; while the dog, the jackal, the different species of wolf, and the foxes, compose another genus. Some genera are represented by a vast number of species, others by few, very many by only one known species. For the genus may be as perfectly represented in one species as in several, although, if this were the case throughout, genera and species would of course be identical. The Beech genus and the Chestnut genus would be just as distinct from the Oak genus even if but one Beech and Chestnut were known; as indeed was once the case.

[Pg 178]

529. **Orders** are groups of genera that resemble each other; that is, they are to genera what genera are to species. As familiar illustrations, the Oak, Chestnut, and Beech genera, along with the Hazel genus and the Hornbeams, all belong to one order. The Birches and the Alders make another; the Poplars and Willows, another; the Walnuts (with the Butternut) and the Hickories, still another. The Apple genus, the Quince and the Hawthorns, along with the Plums and Cherries and the Peach, the Raspberry with the Blackberry, the Strawberry, the Rose, belong to a large order, which takes its name from the Rose. Most botanists use the names "Order" and "Family" synonymously; the latter more popularly, as "the Rose Family," the former more technically, as "Order *Rosaceæ*."

530. But when the two are distinguished, as is common in zoölogy, Family is of lower grade than Order.

531. **Classes** are still more comprehensive assemblages, or great groups. Thus, in modern botany, the Dicotyledonous plants compose one class, the Monocotyledonous plants another (36-40).

532. These four grades, Class, Order, Genus, Species, are of universal use. Variety comes in upon occasion. For, although a species may have no recognized varieties, a genus implies at least one species belonging to it; every genus is of some order, and every order of some class.

533. But these grades by no means exhaust the resources of classification, nor suffice for the elucidation of all the distinctions which botanists recognize. In the first place, a higher grade than that of class is needful for the most comprehensive of divisions, that of all plants into the two *Series* of Phanerogamous and Cryptogamous (6); and in natural history there are the two *Kingdoms* or *Realms*, the Vegetable and the Animal.

534. Moreover, the stages of the scaffolding have been variously extended, as required, by the recognition of assemblages lower than class but higher than order, viz. *Subclass* and *Cohort*; or lower than order, a *Suborder*; or between this and genus, a *Tribe*; or between this and tribe,

a *Subtribe*; or between genus and species, a *Subgenus*; and by some a species has been divided into *Subspecies*, and a variety into *Subvarieties*. Last of all are *Individuals*. Suffice it to remember that the following are the principal grades in classification, with the proper sequence; also that only those here printed in small capitals are fundamental and universal in botany:—

- SERIES,
- CLASS, Subclass, Cohort,
- ORDER, or FAMILY, Suborder, Tribe, Subtribe,
- GENUS, Subgenus or Section,
- SPECIES, Variety.

[Pg 179]

§ 2. NAMES, TERMS, AND CHARACTERS.

535. The name of a plant is the name of its genus followed by that of the species. The name of the genus answers to the surname (or family name); that of the species to the baptismal name of a person. Thus *Quercus* is the name of the Oak genus; *Quercus alba*, that of the White Oak, *Q. rubra*, that of Red Oak, *Q. nigra*, that of the Black-Jack, etc. Botanical names being Latin or Latinized, the adjective name of the species comes after that of the genus.

536. **Names of Genera** are of one word, a substantive. The older ones are mostly classical Latin, or Greek adopted into Latin; such as *Quercus* for the Oak genus, *Fagus* for the Beech, *Corylus*, the Hazel, and the like. But as more genera became known, botanists had new names to make or borrow. Many are named from some appearance or property of the flowers, leaves, or other parts of the plant. To take a few examples from the early pages of the "Manual of the Botany of the Northern United States,"—the genus *Hepatica* comes from the shape of the leaf, resembling that of the liver. *Myosurus* means mouse-tail. *Delphinium* is from delphin, a dolphin, and alludes to the shape of the flower, which was thought to resemble the classical figures of the dolphin. *Xanthorrhiza* is from two Greek words meaning yellow-root, the common name of the plant. *Cimicifuga* is formed of two Latin words meaning to drive away bugs, i. e. Bugbane, the Siberian species being used to keep away such vermin. *Sanguinaria*, the Bloodroot, is named from the blood-like color of its juice. Other genera are dedicated to distinguished botanists or promoters of science, and bear their names: such are *Magnolia*, which commemorates the early French botanist, Magnol; and *Jeffersonia*, named after President Jefferson, who sent the first exploring expedition over the Rocky Mountains. Others bear the name of the discoverer of the plant; as, *Sarracenia*, dedicated to Dr. Sarrazin, of Quebec, who was one of the first to send the common Pitcher-plant to the botanists of Europe; and *Claytonia*, first made known by the early Virginian botanist Clayton.

537. **Names of Species.** The name of a species is also a single word, appended to that of the genus. It is commonly an adjective, and therefore agrees with the generic name in case, gender, etc. Sometimes it relates to the country the species inhabits; as, Claytonia *Virginica*, first made known from Virginia; Sanguinaria *Canadensis*, from Canada, etc. More commonly it denotes some obvious or characteristic trait of the species; as, for example, in Sarracenia, our northern species is named *purpurea*, from the purple blossoms, while a more southern one is named *flava*, because its petals are yellow; the species of Jeffersonia is called *diphylla*, meaning two-leaved, because its leaf is divided into two leaflets. Some species are named after the discoverer, or in compliment to a botanist who has made them known; as, Magnolia *Fraseri*, named after the botanist Fraser, one [Pg 180]of the first to find this species; and Sarracenia *Drummondii*, for a Pitcher-plant found by Mr. Drummond in Florida. Such personal specific names are of course written with a capital initial letter. Occasionally some old substantive name is used for the species; as Magnolia *Umbrella*, the Umbrella tree, and Ranunculus *Flammula*. These are also written with a capital initial, and need not accord with the generic name in gender. Geographical specific names, such as *Canadensis, Caroliniana, Americana*, in the later usage are by some written without a capital initial, but the older usage is better, or at least more accordant with English orthography.

538. **Varietal Names**, when any are required, are made on the plan of specific names, and follow these, with the prefix *var.* Ranunculus Flammula, var. *reptans*, the creeping variety: R. abortivus, var. *micranthus*, the small-flowered variety of the species.

539. In recording the name of a plant it is usual to append the name, or an abbreviation of the name, of the botanist who first published it; and in a flora or other systematic work, this reference to the source of the name is completed by a further citation of the name of the book, the volume and page where it was first published. So "*Ranunculus acris*, L.," means that this Buttercup was first so named and described by Linnæus; "R. *multifidus*, Pursh," that this species was so named and published by Pursh. The suffix is no part of the name, but is an abbreviated reference, to be added or omitted as convenience or definiteness may require. The authority for a generic name is similarly recorded. Thus, "*Ranunculus*, L.," means that the genus was so named by

78

Linnæus; "*Myosurus*, Dill.," that the Mouse-tail was established as a genus under this name by Dillenius; *Caulophyllum*, Michx., that the Blue Cohosh was published under this name by Michaux. The full reference in the last-named instance would be, "in Flora Boreali-Americana, first volume, 205th page,"—in the customary abbreviation, "Michx. Fl. i. 205."

540. **Names of Orders** are given in the plural number, and are commonly formed by prolonging the name of a genus of the group taken as a representative of it. For example, the order of which the Buttercup or Crowfoot genus, *Ranunculus*, is the representative, takes from it the name of *Ranunculaceæ*; meaning *Plantæ Ranunculaceæ* when written out in full, that is, Ranunculaceous Plants. Some old descriptive names of orders are kept up, such as *Cruciferæ* for the order to which Cress and Mustard belong, from the cruciform appearance of their expanded corolla, and *Umbelliferæ*, from the flowers being in umbels.

541. **Names of Tribes**, also of suborders, subtribes, and the like, are plurals of the name of the typical genus, less prolonged, usually in *eæ*, *ineæ*, *ideæ*, etc. Thus the proper Buttercup tribe is *Ranunculeæ*, of the Clematis tribe, *Clematideæ*. While the Rose family is *Rosaceæ*, the special Rose tribe is *Roseæ*.

542. **Names of Classes, etc.** For these see the following synopsis of the actual classification adopted, p. 183.

[Pg 181]

543. So a plant is named in two words, the generic and the specific names, to which may be added a third, that of the variety, upon occasion. The generic name is peculiar: obviously it must not be used twice over in botany. The specific name must not be used twice over in the same genus, but is free for any other genus. A *Quercus alba*, or White Oak, is no hindrance to *Betula alba*, or White Birch; and so of other names.

544. **Characters and Descriptions.** Plants are *characterized* by a terse statement, in botanical terms, of their peculiarities or distinguishing marks. The character of the order should include nothing which is common to the whole class it belongs to; that of the genus, nothing which is common to the order; that of the species nothing which is shared with all other species of the genus; and so of other divisions. *Descriptions* may enter into complete details of the whole structure.

545. **Terminology**, also called *Glossology*, is nomenclature applied to organs or parts, and their forms or modifications. Each organ or special part has a substantive name of its own: shapes and other modifications of an organ or part are designated by adjective terms, or, when the forms are peculiar, substantive names are given to them. By the correct use of such botanical terms, and by proper subordination of the characters under the order, genus, species, etc., plants may be described and determined with much precision. The classical language of botany is Latin. While modern languages have their own names and terms, these usually lack the precision of the Latin or Latinized botanical terminology. Fortunately, this Latinized terminology has been largely adopted and incorporated into the English technical language of botany, thus securing precision. And these terms are largely the basis of specific names of plants.

546. A glossary or vocabulary of the principal botanical terms used in phanerogamous and vascular cryptogamous botany is appended to this volume, to which the student may refer, as occasion arises.

§ 3. SYSTEM.

547. Two systems of classification used to be recognized in botany,—the artificial and the natural; but only the latter is now thought to deserve the name of a system.

548. Artificial classifications have for object merely the ascertaining of the name and place of a plant. They do not attempt to express relationships, but serve as a kind of dictionary. They distribute the genera and species according to some one peculiarity or set of peculiarities (just as a dictionary distributes words according to their first letters), disregarding all other considerations. At present an artificial classification in botany is needed only as a key to the natural orders,—as an aid in referring an unknown plant to its proper family; and such keys are still very needful, at least for the beginner. Formerly, when the orders themselves were not clearly made out, an artificial classification was required to lead the [Pg 182]student down to the genus. Two such classifications were long in vogue: First, that of Tournefort, founded mainly on the leaves of the flower, the calyx and corolla: this was the prevalent system throughout the first half of the eighteenth century; but it has long since gone by. It was succeeded by the well-known

549. **Artificial System of Linnæus**, which was founded on the stamens and pistils. It consists of twenty-four classes, and of a variable number of orders; the classes founded mainly on the number and disposition of the stamens; the orders partly upon the number of styles or stigmas, partly upon other considerations. Useful and popular as this system was down to a time within the memory of still surviving botanists, it is now completely obsolete. But the tradition of it survives in the names of its classes, Monandria, Diandria, Triandria, etc., which are familiar in

79

terminology in the adjective terms monandrous, diandrous, triandrous, etc. (284); also of the orders, Monogynia, Digynia, Trigynia, etc., preserved in the form of monogynous, digynous, trigynous, etc. (301); and in the name Cryptogamia, that of the 24th class, which is continued for the lower series in the natural classification.

550. **Natural System.** A genuine system of botany consists of the orders or families, duly arranged under their classes, and having the tribes, the genera, and the species arranged in them according to their relationships. This, when properly carried out, is the *Natural System;* because it is intended to express, as well as possible, the various degrees of relationship among plants, as presented in nature; that is, to rank those species and those genera, etc., next to each other in the classification which are really most alike in all respects, or, in other words, which are constructed most nearly on the same particular plan.

551. There can be only *one* natural system of botany, if by this term is meant the plan according to which the vegetable creation was called into being, with all its grades and diversities among the species, as well of past as of the present time. But there may be many natural systems, if we mean the attempts of men to interpret and express that plan,—systems which will vary with advancing knowledge, and with the judgment and skill of different botanists. These must all be very imperfect, bear the impress of individual minds, and be shaped by the current philosophy of the age. But the endeavor always is to make the classification answer to Nature, as far as any system can which has to be expressed in a definite and serial arrangement.

552. So, although the classes, orders, genera, etc., are natural, or as natural as the systematist can make them, their grouping or order of arrangement in a book, must necessarily be in great measure artificial. Indeed, it is quite impossible to arrange the orders, or even the few classes, in a single series, and yet have each group stand next to its nearest relatives on both sides.

553. Especially it should be understood that, although phanerogamous [Pg 183]plants are of higher grade than cryptogamous, and angiospermous or ordinary phanerogamous higher than the gymnospermous, yet there is no culmination in the vegetable kingdom, nor any highest or lowest order of phanerogamous plants.

554. The particular system most largely used at present in the classification of the orders is essentially the following:—

- SERIES I. PHANEROGAMIA: PHANEROGAMOUS OR FLOWERING PLANTS.
  - CLASS I. DICOTYLEDONES ANGIOSPERMEÆ, called for shortness in English, DICOTYLEDONS or DICOTYLS. Ovules in a closed ovary. Embryo dicotyledonous. Stem with exogenous plan of growth. Leaves reticulate-veined,
    - *Artificial Division I.* POLYPETALÆ, with petals mostly present and distinct. Orders about 80 in number, *Ranunculaceæ* to *Cornaceæ.*
    - *Artificial Division II.* GAMOPETALÆ, with gamopetalous corolla. Orders about 45, *Caprifoliaceæ* to *Plantaginaceæ.*
    - *Artificial Division III.* APETALÆ or INCOMPLETÆ, with perianth, when present, of calyx only. Orders about 35 in number, from *Nyctaginaceæ* to*Salicaceæ.*
  - CLASS II. DICOTYLEDONES GYMNOSPERMEÆ, in English GYMNOSPERMS. No ovary or pericarp, but ovules and seeds naked, and no proper calyx nor corolla. Embryo dicotyledonous or polycotyledonous. Stem with exogenous plan of growth. Leaves mostly parallel-veined. Consists of order *Gnetaceæ,* which strictly connects with Angiospermous Dicotyls, of *Coniferæ,* and of *Cycadaceæ.*
  - CLASS III. MONOCOTYLEDONES, in English MONOCOTYLEDONS or MONOCOTYLS. Angiospermous. Embryo monocotyledonous. Stem with endogenous plan of growth. Leaves mostly parallel-veined.
    - *Division I.* PETALOIDEÆ. Perianth complete, having the equivalent of both calyx and corolla, and all the inner series corolline. About 18 orders.
    - *Division II.* CALYCINÆ. Perianth complete (in two series) but not corolline, mostly thickish or glumaceous. Chiefly two orders, *Juncaceæ,* the true Rushes, and *Palmæ,* Palms.
    - *Division III.* SPADICIFLORÆ or NUDIFLORÆ. Perianth none, or rudimentary and incomplete: inflorescence spadiceous. Of five orders, *Typhaceæ*and *Aroideæ* the principal.
    - *Division IV.* GLUMACEÆ. Perianth none, or very rudimentary: glumaceous bracts to the flowers. Orders mainly *Cyperaceæ* and *Gramineæ.*
- SERIES II. CRYPTOGAMIA: CRYPTOGAMOUS OR FLOWERLESS PLANTS.
  - CLASS I. PTERIDOPHYTA, PTERIDOPHYTES (484).

80

[Pg 184]

SECTION XIX. BOTANICAL WORK.

555. Some hints and brief instructions for the collection, examination, and preservation of specimens are added. They are especially intended for the assistance of those who have not the advantage of a teacher. They apply to phanerogamous plants and Ferns only, and to systematic botany.[1]

§ 1. COLLECTION, OR HERBORIZATION.

556. As much as possible, plants should be examined in the living state, or when freshly gathered. But dried specimens should be prepared for more leisurely examination and for comparison. To the working botanist good dried specimens are indispensable.

557. **Botanical Specimens**, to be complete, should have root or rootstock, stem, leaves, flowers, both open and in bud, and fruit. Sometimes these may all be obtained at one gathering; more commonly two or three gatherings at different times are requisite, especially for trees and shrubs.

558. **In Herborizing**, a good knife and a narrow and strong trowel are needed; but a very strong knife will serve instead of a trowel or small pick for digging out bulbs, tubers, and the like. To carry the specimens, either the tin box (*vasculum*) or a portfolio, or both are required. The tin box is best for the collection of specimens to be used fresh, as in the class-room; also for very thick or fleshy plants. The portfolio is indispensable for long expeditions, and is best for specimens which are to be preserved in the herbarium.

559. The *Vasculum*, or *Botanical Collecting-box*, is made of tin, in shape like a candle-box, only flatter, or the smaller sizes like an English sandwich-case; the lid opening for nearly the whole length of one side of the box. Any portable tin box of convenient size, and capable of holding specimens a foot or fifteen inches long, will answer the purpose. The box should shut close, so that the specimens may not wilt: then it will keep leafy branches and most flowers perfectly fresh for a day or two, especially if slightly moistened. They should not be wet.

560. *The Portfolio* is best made of two pieces of solid binder's-board, covered with enamel cloth, which also forms the back, and fastened by straps and buckles. It may be from a foot to twenty inches long, from nine to eleven or twelve inches wide. It should contain a needful quantity of smooth but strong and pliable paper (thin so-called Manilla paper is best), either fastened at the back as in a book, or loose in folded sheets when not very many specimens are required. As soon as gathered, the specimens should be separately laid between the leaves or in the folded sheets, and kept under moderate pressure in the closed portfolio.

[Pg 185]

561. Of small herbs, especially annuals, the whole plant, root and all, should be taken for a specimen. Of larger ones branches will suffice, with some leaves from near the root. Enough of the root or subterranean part of the plant should be collected to show whether it is an annual, a biennial, or a perennial. Thick roots, bulbs, tubers, or branches of specimens intended to be pressed should be thinned with a knife, or cut into slices. Keep the specimens within the length of fifteen or sixteen inches, by folding, or when that cannot be done, by cutting into lengths.

562. **For Drying Specimens** a good supply of soft and unsized paper is wanted; and some convenient means of applying considerable pressure. To make good dried botanical specimens, dry them as rapidly as possible between many thicknesses of sun-dried paper to absorb their moisture, under as much pressure as can be given without crushing the more delicate parts. This pressure may be had by a botanical press, of which various forms have been contrived; or by weights placed upon a board,—from forty to eighty or a hundred pounds, according to the quantity of specimens drying at the time. For use while travelling, a good portable press may be made of thick binders' boards for the sides, and the pressure may be applied by strong straps with buckles. Still better, on some accounts, are portable presses made of wire network, which allow the dampness to escape by evaporation between the meshes. For herborization in a small way, a light wire-press may be taken into the field and made to serve also as a portfolio.

563. It is well to have two kinds of paper, namely, *driers* of bibulous paper, stitched into pads (or the pads may be of thick carpet-paper, cut to size) and thin smooth paper, folded once; the specimens to be laid into the fold, either when gathered or on returning from the excursion. These sheets are to hold the specimens until they are quite dry. Every day, or at first even twice a day, the specimens, left undisturbed in their sheets, are to be shifted into fire-dried or sun-dried fresh driers, and the pressure renewed, while the moist sheets are spread out to dry, so as to take their turn again at the next shifting. This course must be continued until the specimens are no

longer moist to the touch. Good and comely specimens are either made or spoiled within the first twenty-four or thirty-six hours. After that, when plenty of driers are used, it may not be necessary to change them so frequently.

564. Succulent plants, which long refuse to part with life and moisture, and Spruces and some other evergreens which are apt to cast off their leaves, may be plunged for a moment into boiling water, all but the flowers. Delicate flowers may be encased in thin tissue paper when put into the press. Thick parts, like the heads of Sunflowers and Thistles, may be cut in two or into slices.

565. Dried specimens may be packed in bundles, either in folded paper or upon single half-sheets. It is better that such paper should not be bibulous. The packages should be well wrapped or kept in close cases.

[Pg 186]

566. **Poisoning** is necessary if specimens are to be permanently preserved from the depredation of insects. The usual application is an almost saturated solution of corrosive sublimate in 95 per cent alcohol, freely applied with a large and soft brush, or the specimens dipped into some of the solution poured into a large and flat dish; the wetted specimens to be transferred for a short time to driers.

§ 2. HERBARIUM.

567. The botanist's collection of dried specimens, ticketed with their names, place, and time of collection, and systematically arranged under their genera, orders, etc., forms a *Hortus Siccus* or *Herbarium*. It comprises not only the specimens which the proprietor has himself collected, but those which he acquires through friendly exchanges, or in other ways. The specimens of an herbarium may be kept in folded sheets of paper; or they may be fastened on half-sheets of thick and white paper, either by gummed slips, or by glue applied to the specimens themselves. The former is best for private and small herbaria; the latter for large ones which are much turned over. Each sheet should be appropriated to one species; two or more different plants should never be attached to the same sheet. The generic and specific name of the plant should be added to the lower right-hand corner, either written on the sheet, or on a ticket pasted down; and the time of collection, the locality, the color of the flowers, and any other information which the specimens themselves do not afford, should be duly recorded upon the sheet or the ticket. The sheets of the herbarium should all be of exactly the same dimensions. The herbarium of Linnæus is on paper of the common foolscap size, about eleven inches long and seven wide. This is too small. Sixteen and three eighths inches by eleven and a half inches is an approved size.

568. The sheets containing the species of each genus are to be placed in *genus-covers*, made of a full sheet of thick paper (such as the strongest Manilla-hemp paper), to be when folded of the same dimensions as the species-sheet but slightly wider: the name of the genus is to be written on one of the lower corners. These are to be arranged under the orders to which they belong, and the whole kept in closed cases or cabinets, either laid flat in compartments, like "pigeon-holes," or else placed in thick portfolios, arranged like folio volumes. All should be kept, as much as practicable, in dust-proof and insect-proof cases or boxes.

569. Fruits, tubers, and other hard parts, too thick for the herbarium, may be kept in pasteboard or light wooden boxes, in a collection apart. Small loose fruits, seeds, detached flowers, and the like may be conveniently preserved in paper capsules or envelopes, attached to the herbarium-sheets.

[Pg 187]

§ 3. INVESTIGATION AND DETERMINATION OF PLANTS.

570. **The Implements** required are a hand magnifying glass, a pocket lens of an inch or two focus, or a glass of two lenses, one of the lower and the other of the higher power; and a sharp penknife for dissection. With these and reasonable perseverance the structure of the flowers and fructification of most phanerogamous plants and Ferns can be made out. But for ease and comfort, as well as for certainty and right training, the student should have some kind of simple stage microscope, and under this make all dissections of small parts. Without it the student will be apt to fall into the bad habit of guessing where he ought to ascertain.

571. The simple microscope may be reduced to a good lens or doublet, of an inch focus, mounted over a glass stage, so that it can be moved up and down and also sidewise, and with (or without) a little mirror underneath. A better one would have one or two additional lenses (say of half and of a quarter inch focus), a pretty large stage, on the glass of which several small objects can be placed and conveniently brought under the lens; and its height or that of the lens should be adjustable by a rack-work; also a swivel-mounted little mirror beneath, which is needed for minute objects to be viewed by transmitted light.

572. For dissecting and displaying small parts on the stage of the microscope, besides a thin-bladed knife, the only tools needed are a good stock of common needles of various sizes,

mounted in handles, and one or more saddler's-needles, which, being triangular, may be ground to sharp edges convenient for dissection. Also a pair of delicate-pointed forceps; those with curved points used by the dentist are most convenient. A cup of clean water is indispensable, with which to moisten or wet, or in which occasionally to float delicate parts. Small flowers, buds, fruits, and seeds of dried specimens can be dissected quite as well as fresh ones. They have only to be soaked in warm or boiling water.

573. The compound microscope is rarely necessary except in cryptogamic botany and vegetable anatomy; but it is very useful and convenient, especially for the examination of pollen. To the advanced botanist it is a necessity, to all students of botany an aid and delight.

574. **Analysis.** A few directions and hints may be given. The most important is this: In studying an unknown plant, make a complete examination of all its parts, and form a clear idea of its floral structure and that of its fruit, from pericarp down to the embryo, or as far as the materials in hand allow, before taking a step toward finding out its name and relationship by means of the keys or other helps which the Manuals and Floras provide. If it is the name merely that is wanted, the shorter way is to ask some one who already knows it. To verify the points of structure one by one as they happen to occur in an artificial key, without any preparatory investigation, is a usual but is not the best nor the surest [Pg 188]way. It is well to make drawings or outline sketches of the smaller parts, and especially diagrams of the plan of the flower, such as those of Fig. 225, 227, 241, 244, 275-277. For these, cross sections of the flower-bud or flower are to be made: and longitudinal sections, such as Fig. 270-274, are equally important. The dissection even of small seeds is not difficult after some practice. Commonly they need to be soaked or boiled.

575. The right appreciation of characters and terms used in description needs practice and calls for judgment. Plants do not grow exactly by rule and plummet, and measurements must be taken loosely. Difference of soil and situation are responded to by considerable variations, and other divergences occur which cannot be accounted for by the surroundings, nor be anticipated in general descriptions. Annuals may be very depauperate in dry soils or seasons, or very large when particularly well nourished. Warm and arid situations promote, and wet ones are apt to diminish pubescence. Salt water causes increased succulence. The color of flowers is apt to be lighter in shade, and brighter in open and elevated situations. A color or hue not normal to the species now and then occurs, which nothing in the conditions will account for. *A white-flowered variation of any other colored blossom may always be expected*; this, though it may be notable, no more indicates a distinct variety of the species than an albino would a variety of the human species. The numerical plan is subject to variation in some flowers; those on the plan of five may now and then vary to four or to six. Variations of the outline or lobing of leaves are so familiar that they do not much mislead. Only wider and longer observation suffices to prevent or correct mistakes in botanical study. But the weighing of evidence and the balancing of probabilities, no less than the use of the well-ordered and logical system of classification, give as excellent training to the judgment as the search for the facts themselves does to the observing powers.

§ 4. SIGNS AND ABBREVIATIONS.

576. For a full account of these, whether of former or actual use, see "Structural Botany" of the "Botanical Text Book," pp. 367, 392, as also for the principles which govern the accentuation of names. It is needful here to explain only those used in the Manuals and Floras of this country, for which the present volume is an introduction and companion. They are not numerous.

577. In arranging the species, at least those of a large genus, the divisions are denoted and graduated as follows: The sign § is prefixed to sections of the highest rank: these sections when they have names affixed to them (as PRUNUS § CERASUS) may be called subgenera. When the divisions of a genus are not of such importance, or when divisions are made under the subgenus itself, the most comprehensive ones are marked by asterisks, * for the first, * * for the second, and so on. Subdivisions are [Pg 189]marked with a prefixed +; those under this head with ++; and those under this with =, if there be so many grades. A similar notation is followed in the synopsis of the genera of an order.

578. The interrogation point is used in botany to indicate doubt. Thus *Clematis crispa*, L.? expresses a doubt whether the plant in question is really the *Clematis crispa* of Linnæus. *Clematis? polypetala* expresses a doubt whether the plant so named is really a Clematis. On the other hand the exclamation point (!) is used to denote certainty whenever there is special need to affirm this.

579. For size or height, the common signs of degrees, minutes, and seconds, have been used, thus, 1°, 2′, 3″, stand respectively for a foot, two inches, and three lines or twelfths of an inch. A better way, when such brevity is needed, is to write 1^{ft}. 2^{in}. 3^{l}.

580. Signs for duration used by Linnæus were ⊙ for an annual, ♂ for a biennial, ♃ for a perennial herb, [Symbol like numeral 5 without top bar] for a shrub or tree. DeCandolle brought in ⊙ for a plant that died after once flowering, ① if annual, ② if biennial.[1]

581. To indicate sexes, ♂ means staminate or male plant or blossom; ♀, pistillate or female; [Symbol like ☿ with two inverted breves], perfect or hermaphrodite.

582. To save room it is not uncommon to use ∞ in place of "many;" thus, "Stamens ∞," for stamens indefinitely numerous: "∞ flora" for pluriflora or many-flowered. Still more common is the form "Stamens 5-20," or "Calyx 4-5-parted," for stamens from five to twenty, calyx four-parted or five-parted, and the like. Such abbreviations hardly need explanation.

583. The same may be said of such abbreviations as *Cal.* for calyx, *Cor.* for corolla, *Pet.* for petals, *St.* for stamens, *Pist.* for pistil, *Hab.* for habitat, meaning place of growth, *Herb.* for herbarium, *Hort.* for garden. Also *l. c.*, loco citato, which avoids repetition of volume and page.

584. "Structural Botany" has six pages of abbreviations of the names of botanists, mostly of botanical authors. As they are not of much consequence to the beginner, while the more advanced botanist will know the names in full, or know where to find them, only a selection is here appended.

FOOTNOTES:

[1]For fuller directions in many particulars, see "Structural Botany," pp. 370-374.

ABBREVIATIONS OF THE NAMES OF BOTANISTS.

Adans.	Adanson.
Ait.	Aiton.
All.	Allioni.
Andr.	Andrews.
Arn.	Arnott.
Aub.	Aublet.
Bartr.	Bartram.
Beauv.	Palisot de Beauvois.
Benth.	Bentham.
Bernh.	Bernhardi.
Bigel.	Jacob Bigelow.
Bong.	Bongard.
Bonpl.	Bonpland.
Br. or *R. Br.*	Robert Brown.
Cass.	Cassini.
Cav.	Cavanilles.
Cham.	Chamisso.
Chapm.	Chapman.
Chois.	Choisy.
Clayt.	Clayton.
Curt.	Curtis.
Curt. (M. A.)	M. A. Curtis.
Darl.	Darlington.
DC. *DeCand*	DeCandolle.
A. DC.	Alphonse DeCandolle.
Desc.	Descourtilz.
Desf.	Desfontaines.
Desv.	Desvaux.
Dill.	Dillenius.
Dougl.	Douglas.

84

Duham.	Duhamel.
Dun.	Dunal.
Eat.	Eaton (Amos) or D. C.
Ehrh.	Ehrhart.
Ell.	Elliott.
Endl.	Endlicher.
Engelm.	Engelmann.
Engl.	Engler.
Fisch.	Fischer.
Frœl.	Frœlich.
Gærtn.	Gærtner.
Gaud.	Gaudin.
Gaudich.	Gaudichaud.
Ging.	Gingins.
Gmel.	Gmelin.
Good.	Goodenough.
Grev.	Greville.
Griseb.	Grisebach.
Gron. *Gronov.*	Gronovius.
Hall.	Haller.
Hartm.	Hartmann.
Hartw.	Hartweg.
Harv.	Harvey.
Haw.	Haworth.
Hegelm.	Hegelmaier.
Hemsl.	Hemsley.
Herb.	Herbert.
Hoffm.	Hoffmann.
Hoffmans.	Hoffmansegg.
Hook.	Hooker.
Hook. f.	J. D. Hooker.
Hornem.	Hornemann.
Huds.	Hudson.
Humb.	Humboldt.
HBK.	Humboldt, Bonpland, and Kunth.
Jacq.	Jacquin.
Jacq. f.	J. F. Jacquin.
Juss.	Jussieu.
A. Juss.	Adrien de Jussieu.
Kit.	Kitaibel.
L. or Linn.	Linnæus.
Labill.	Labillardiere.
Lag.	Lagasca.
Lam.	Lamarck.
Ledeb.	Ledebour.
Lehm.	Lehmann.

Lesq.	Lesquereux.
Less.	Lessing.
Lestib.	Lestibudois.
L'Her.	L'Heritier.
Lindb.	Lindberg.
Lindh.	Lindheimer.
Lindl.	Lindley.
Lodd.	Loddiges.
Loud.	Loudon.
M. Bieb.	Marschall von Bieberstein.
Marsh.	Marshall (Humphrey).
Mart.	Martius.
[Pg 191]*Mast.* :	Masters.
Maxim.	Maximowicz.
Meisn.	Meisner or
Meissn.	Meissner.
Michx. or *Mx.*	Michaux.
Michx. f.	F. A. Michaux.
Mill.	Miller.
Miq.	Miquel.
Mitch.	Mitchell.
Moç.	Moçino.
Moq.	Moquin-Tandon.
Moric.	Moricand.
Moris.	Morison.
Muell. Arg.	J. Mueller.
Muell. (F.)	Ferdinand Mueller.
Muhl.	Muhlenberg.
Murr.	Murray.
Naud.	Naudin.
Neck.	Necker.
Nees N. ab E.	Nees von Esenbeck.
Nutt.	Nuttall.
Œd.	Œder.
Ort.	Ortega.
P. de Beauv.	Palisot de Beauvois.
Pall.	Pallas.
Parl.	Parlatore.
Pav.	Pavon.
Pers.	Persoon.
Planch.	Planchon.
Pluk.	Plukenet.
Plum.	Plumier.

Poir.	Poiret.
Radlk.	Radlkofer.
Raf.	Rafinesque.
Red.	Redouté.
Reichen b.	Reichenbach.
Rich.	L. C. Richard.
Rich. f. or *A.*	Achille Richard.
Richard s.	Richardson.
Ridd.	Riddell.
Ræm. & Schult.	Ræmer & Schultes.
Rottb.	Rottbœll.
Rupr.	Ruprecht.
St. Hil.	Saint-Hilaire.
Salisb.	Salisbury.
Schk.	Schkuhr.
Schlecht.	Schlechtendal.
Schrad.	Schrader.
Schreb.	Schreber.
Schwein.	Schweinitz.
Scop.	Scopoli.
Spreng.	Sprengel.
Sternb.	Sternberg.
Steud.	Steudel.
Sull.	Sullivant.
Thunb.	Thunberg.
Torr.	Torrey.
Tourn.	Tournefort.
Trautv.	Trautvetter.
Trin.	Trinius.
Tuck.	Tuckerman.
Vaill.	Vaillant.
Vent.	Ventenat.
Vill.	Villars.
Wahl.	Wahlenberg.
Walds.	Waldstein.
Wall.	Wallich.
Wallr.	Wallroth.
Walp.	Walpers.
Walt.	Walter.
Wang.	Wangenheim.
Wats.	Sereno Watson, unless other initials are given.
Wedd.	Weddell.
Wendl.	Wendland.
Wiks.	Wikstrom.
Willd.	Willdenow.
Wulf.	Wulfen.

[Pg 193]

GLOSSARY AND INDEX,
OR
DICTIONARY OF THE PRINCIPAL TERMS IN DESCRIPTIVE BOTANY,
COMBINED WITH AN INDEX.

For the convenience of unclassical students, the commoner Latin and Greek words (or their equivalents in English form) which enter into the composition of botanical names, as well as of technical terms, are added to this Glossary. The numbers refer to pages.

A, at the beginning of words of Greek derivation, commonly signifies a negative, or the absence of something; as *a*petalous, without petals; *a*phyllous, leafless, &c. In words beginning with a vowel, the prefix is *an*; as *an*antherous, destitute of anther.

Abnormal, contrary to the usual or the natural structure.

Aboriginal, original in the strictest sense; same as indigenous.

Abortive, imperfectly formed, or rudimentary.

Abortion, the imperfect formation or the non-formation of some part.

Abrupt, suddenly terminating; as, for instance,

Abruptly pinnate, pinnate without an odd leaflet at the end, 58.

Acantho-, spiny.

Acaulescent (*acaulis*), apparently stemless; the proper stem, bearing the leaves and flowers, being very short or subterranean.

Accessory, something additional; as *Accessory buds*, 30, 31; *Accessory fruits*, 118.

Accrescent, growing larger after flowering.

Accrete, grown to.

Accumbent, lying against a thing. The cotyledons are accumbent when they lie with their edges against the radicle, 128.

Acephalous, headless.

Acerose, needle-shaped, as the leaves of Pines.

Acetabuliform, saucer-shaped.

Achænium, or *Achenium* (plural *achenia*), a one-seeded, seed-like fruit, 120.

Achlamydeous (flower), without floral envelopes, 86.

Acicular, needle-shaped; more slender than acerose.

Acinaciform, scimitar-shaped, like some bean-pods.

Acines, the separate grains of a fruit, such as the raspberry.

Acorn, the nut of the Oak, 122.

Acotyledonous, destitute of cotyledons or seed-leaves.

Acrogenous, growing from the apex, as the stems of Ferns and Mosses. *Acrogens*, or *Acrogenous Plants*, a name for the vascular cryptogamous plants, 156.

Aculeate, armed with prickles, i. e. *aculei*; as the Rose and Brier.

Aculeolate, armed with small prickles, or slightly prickly.

Acuminate, taper-pointed, 54.

Acute, merely sharp-pointed, or ending in a point less than a right angle, 54.

[Pg 194]

Adelphous (stamens), joined in a fraternity (*adelphia*); see *monadelphous*, &c.

Aden, Greek for gland. So *Adenophorous*, gland-bearing.

Adherent, sticking to, or more commonly, growing fast to another body.

Adnate, literally, growing fast to, born adherent, 95. The anther is adnate when fixed by its whole length to the filament or its prolongation, 101.

Adnation, the state of being adnate, 94.

Adpressed or *appressed*, brought into contact with, but not united.

Adscendent, ascendent, or *ascending*, rising gradually upwards, 39.

Adsurgent, or *assurgent*, same as ascending, 39.

Adventitious, out of the proper or usual place; e. g. *Adventitious buds*, 30.

Adventive, applied to foreign plants accidentally or sparingly introduced into a country, but hardly to be called naturalized.

Æquilateral, equal-sided; opposed to oblique.

Aerial roots, &c., 36.

Æruginous, verdigris-colored.

Æstival, produced in summer.

88

Æstivation, the arrangement of parts in a flower-bud, 97.

Agamous, sexless.

Aggregate fruits, 118.

Agrestis, growing in fields.

Air-cells or *Air-passages*, spaces in the tissue of leaves and some stems, 131.

Air-Plants, 36.

Akene or *Akenium*, 120.

Ala (plural, *alæ*), a wing; the side-petals of a papilionaceous corolla, 92.

Alabastrum, a flower-bud.

Alar, situated in the forks of a stem.

Alate, winged.

Albescent, whitish, or turning white.

Albus, Latin for white.

Albumen of the seed, nourishing matter stored up with the embryo, 21, 127.

Albumen, a vegetable product, of four elements.

Albuminous (seeds), furnished with albumen, 21.

Alburnum, young wood, sap-wood, 142.

Alliaceous, with odor of garlic.

Allogamous, close fertilization.

Alpestrine, subalpine.

Alpine, belonging to high mountains above the limit of forests.

Alternate (leaves), one after another, 29, 67. Petals are *alternate* with the sepals, or stamens with the petals, when they stand over the intervals between them, 82.

Alveolate, honeycomb-like.

Ament, the scaly spike of trees like the Birch and Willow, 75.

Amentaceous, catkin-like, or catkin-bearing.

Amorphous, shapeless, without any definite form.

Amphicarpous, producing two kinds of fruit.

Amphigastrium (plural, *amphigastria*), a peculiar stipule-like leaf of Liverworts.

Amphitropous ovules or seeds, 111.

Amphora, a pitcher-shaped organ.

Amplectant, embracing. *Amplexicaul* (leaves), clasping the stem by the base.

Ampullaceous, swelling out like a bottle or bladder (*ampulla*).

Amylaceous, *Amyloid*, composed of starch (*amylum*), or starch-like.

Anandrous, without stamens.

Anantherous, without anthers.

Ananthous, destitute of flowers; flowerless.

Anastomosing, forming a net-work (*anastomosis*), as the veins of leaves, 50.

Anatropous ovules or seeds, 111.

Ancipital (*anceps*), two-edged.

Andrœcium, a name for the stamens taken together, 98.

[Pg 195]

Andro-diœcious, flowers staminate on one plant, perfect on another.

Androgynous, having both staminate and pistillate flowers in the same cluster.

Androphore, a column of united stamens, as in a Mallow.

Androus, or *Ander, andra, andrum*, Greek in compounds for male, or stamens.

Anemophilous, wind-loving, said of wind-fertilizable flowers, 113.

Anfractuose, bent hither and thither as the anthers of the Squash, &c.

Angiospermæ, *Angiospermous*, with seeds formed in an ovary or pericarp, 109.

Angular divergence of leaves, 69.

Anisos, unequal. *Anisomerous*, parts unequal in number. *Anisopetalous*, with unequal petals. *Anisophyllous*, the leaves unequal in the pairs.

Annual (plant), flowering and fruiting the year it is raised from the seed, and then dying, 37.

Annular, in the form of a ring, or forming a circle.

Annulate, marked by rings; or furnished with an

Annulus, or ring, like that of the spore-case of most Ferns. In Mosses it is a ring of cells placed between the mouth of the spore-case and the lid in many species.

Annotinous, yearly, or in yearly growths.

Anterior, in the blossom, is the part next the bract, i. e. external; while the posterior side is that next the axis of inflorescence. Thus, in the Pea, &c., the keel is *anterior*, and the standard *posterior*, 96.

89

Anthela, an open paniculate cyme.

Anther, the essential part of the stamen, which contains the pollen, 14, 80, 101.

Antheridium (plural *antheridia*), the organ in Cryptogams which answers to the anther of Flowering Plants, 150.

Antheriferous, anther-bearing.

Anthesis, the period or the act of the expansion of a flower.

Anthocarpus (fruits), 118.

Anthophore, a stipe between calyx and corolla, 113.

Anthos, Greek for flower; in composition, *Monanthous*, one-flowered, &c.

Anticous, same as anterior.

Antrorse, directed upwards or forwards.

Apetalous, destitute of petals, 86.

Aphyllous, leafless.

Apical, belonging to the apex or point.

Apiculate, pointleted; tipped with a small point.

Apocarpous (pistils), when the several pistils of the same flower are separate.

Apophysis, any irregular swelling; the enlargement at the base of the spore-case of the Umbrella-Moss.

Apothecium, the fructification of Lichens, 171.

Appendage, any superadded part. *Appendiculate*, provided with appendages.

Appressed, close pressed to the stem, &c.

Apricus, growing in dry and sunny places.

Apterous, wingless.

Aquatic (*Aquatilis*), living or growing in water; applied to plants whether growing under water, or with all but the base raised out of it.

Arachnoid, *Araneose*, cobwebby; clothed with, or consisting of, soft downy fibres.

Arboreous, *Arborescent*, tree-like, in size or form, 39.

Arboretum, a collection of trees.

Archegonium (plural *archegonia*), the organ in Mosses, &c., which is analogous to the pistil of Flowering Plants.

Arcuate, bent or curved like a bow.

Arenose (*Arenarius*), growing in sand.

Areolate, marked out into little spaces or *areolæ*.

Argenteous, or *Argentate*, silvery-like.

Argillose, growing in clay.

Argos, Greek for pure white; *Argophyllous* or *Argyrophyllous*, white-leaved, &c.

Argutus, acutely dentate.

[Pg 196]

Arillate (seeds) furnished with an aril.

Arilliform, aril-like.

Arillus, or *Aril*, a fleshy growth from base of a seed, 126.

Aristate, awned, i. e. furnished with an *arista*, like the beard of Barley, &c., 54.

Aristulate, diminutive of the last; short-awned.

Arrect, brought into upright position.

Arrow-shaped or *Arrow-headed*, same as *sagittate*, 53.

Articulated, jointed; furnished with joints or *articulations*, where it separates or inclines to do so. *Articulated leaves*, 57.

Artificial Classification, 181.

Ascending (stems, &c.), 39; (seeds or ovules), 110.

Ascidium, a pitcher-shaped body, like leaves of Sarracenia.

Ascus (*asci*), a sac, the spore-case of Lichens and some Fungi.

Aspergilliform, shaped like the brush used to sprinkle holy water; as the stigmas of many Grasses.

Asperous, rough to touch.

Assimilation, 144, 147.

Assurgent, same as ascending, 39.

Atropous or *Atropal* (ovules), same as orthotropous.

Aurantiacous, orange-colored.

Aureous, golden.

Auriculate, furnished with *auricles* or ear-like appendages, 53.

Autogamy, self-fertilization, 115.

Awl-shaped, sharp-pointed from a broader base, 61.

Awn, the bristle or beard of Barley, Oats, &c.; or any similar appendage.

Awned or *Awn-pointed*, furnished with an awn or long bristle-shaped tip, 54.

Axil, the angle on the upper side between a leaf and the stem, 13.

Axile, belonging to the axis, or occupying the axis.

Axillary (buds, &c.), occurring in an axil, 27.

Axis, the central line of any body; the organ round which others are attached; the root and stem. *Ascending* and *Descending Axis*, 38.

Baccate, berried, berry-like, of a pulpy nature like a berry (*bacca*).

Badius, chestnut-colored.

Banner, see Standard, 92.

Barbate, bearded; bearing tufts, spots, or lines of hairs.

Barbed, furnished with a *barb* or double hook; as the apex of the bristle on the fruit of Echinospermum (Stickseed), &c.

Barbellate, said of the bristles of the pappus of some Compositæ when beset with short, stiff hairs, longer than when denticulate, but shorter than when plumose.

Barbellulate, diminutive of barbellate.

Bark, the covering of a stem outside of the wood, 138, 140.

Basal, belonging or attached to the

Base, that extremity of any organ by which it is attached to its support.

Basifixed, attached by its base.

Bast, Bast-fibres, 134.

Beaked, ending in a prolonged narrow tip.

Bearded, see *barbate*. *Beard* is sometimes used for awn, more commonly for long or stiff hairs of any sort.

Bell-shaped, of the shape of a bell, as the corolla of Harebell, 90.

Berry, a fruit pulpy or juicy throughout, as a grape, 119.

Bi- (or *Bis*), in compound words, twice; as

Biarticulate, twice-jointed, or two-jointed; separating into two pieces.

Biauriculate, having two ears, as the leaf in fig. 126.

Bicallose, having two callosities or harder spots.

Bicarinate, two-keeled.

Bicipital (*Biceps*), two-headed; dividing into two parts.

[Pg 197]

Biconjugate, twice paired, as when a petiole forks twice.

Bidentate, having two teeth (not twice or doubly dentate).

Biennial, of two years' continuance; springing from the seed one season, flowering and dying the next, 38.

Bifarious, two-ranked; arranged in two rows.

Bifid, two-cleft to about the middle.

Bifoliolate, a compound leaf of two leaflets, 59.

Bifurcate, twice forked; or more commonly, forked into two branches.

Bijugate, bearing two pairs (of leaflets, &c.).

Bilabiate, two-lipped, as the corolla of Labiatæ.

Bilamellate, of two plates (*lamellæ*), as the stigma of Mimulus.

Bilobed, the same as two-lobed.

Bilocellate, when a cell is divided into two *locelli*.

Bilocular, two-celled; as most anthers, the pod of Foxglove, &c.

Binary, in twos.

Binate, in couples, two together. *Bipartite*, the Latin form of two-parted.

Binodal, of two nodes.

Binomial, of two words, as the name of genus and species taken together, 180.

Bipalmate, twice palmately divided.

Biparous, bearing two.

Bipinnate (leaf), twice pinnate, 58. *Bipinnatifid*, twice pinnatifid, 57.

Bipinnatisect, twice pinnately divided.

Biplicate, twice folded together.

Biserial, or *Biseriate*, occupying two rows, one within the other.

Biserrate, doubly serrate, as when the teeth of a leaf are themselves serrate.

Bisexual, having both stamens and pistil.

Biternate, twice ternate; i. e. principal divisions three, each bearing three leaflets, 59.

Bladdery, thin and inflated.

Blade of a leaf, its expanded portion, 49.

91

Bloom, the whitish powder on some fruits, leaves, &c.

Boat-shaped, concave within and keeled without, in shape like a small boat.

Border of corolla, &c., 89.

Brachiate, with opposite branches at right angles to each other.

Brachy-, short, as *Brachycarpous*, short-fruited, &c.

Bract (*Bractea*), the leaf of an inflorescence. Specially, the bract is the small leaf or scale from the axil of which a flower or its pedicel proceeds, 73.

Bracteate, furnished with bracts.

Bracteolate, furnished with bractlets.

Bracteose, with numerous or conspicuous bracts.

Bractlet (*Bracteola*), or *Bracteole*, is a bract seated *on* the pedicel or flower-stalk, 73.

Branch, Branching, 27.

Breathing-pores, 144.

Bristles, stiff, sharp hairs, or any very slender bodies of similar appearance.

Bristly, beset with bristles. *Bristle-pointed*, 54.

Brunneous, brown.

Brush-shaped, see *aspergilliform*.

Bryology, that part of botany which relates to Mosses.

Bryophyta, Bryophytes, 163.

Bud, a branch in its earliest or undeveloped state, 27. *Bud-scales*, 63.

Bulb, a leaf-bud with fleshy scales, usually subterranean, 46.

Bulbils, diminutive bulbs.

Bulbiferous, bearing or producing bulbs. *Bulbose* or *bulbous*, bulb-like in shape, &c.

Bulblets, small bulbs, borne above ground, 46.

Bulb-scales, 46.

Bullate, appearing as if blistered or bladdery (from *bulla*, a bubble).

Byssaceous, composed of fine flax-like threads.

[Pg 198]

Caducous, dropping off very early, compared with other parts; as the calyx in the Poppy, falling when the flower opens.

Cæruleous, blue. *Cærulescent*, becoming bluish.

Cæspitose, or *Cespitose*, growing in turf-like patches or tufts.

Calathiform, cup-shaped.

Calcarate, furnished with a spur (*calcar*), 86, 87.

Calceolate or *Calceiform*, slipper-shaped, like one petal of the Lady's Slipper.

Callose, hardened; or furnished with callosities or thickened spots.

Calvous, bald or naked of hairs.

Calyciflorus, when petals and stamens are adnate to calyx.

Calycine, belonging to the calyx.

Calyculate, furnished with an outer accessory calyx (*calyculus*) or set of bracts looking like a calyx, as in true Pinks.

Calyptra, the hood or veil of the capsule of a Moss, 163.

Calyptrate, having a calyptra.

Calyptriform, shaped like a calyptra or candle-extinguisher.

Calyx, the outer set of the floral envelopes or leaves of the flower, 14, 79.

Cambium, Cambium-layer, 140.

Campanulate, bell-shaped, 90.

Campylotropous, or *Campylotropal*, curved ovules and seeds, 111. *Campylospermous*, applied to fruits of Umbelliferæ when the seed is curved in at the edges, forming a groove down the inner face; as in Sweet Cicely.

Canaliculate, channelled, or with a deep longitudinal groove.

Cancellate, latticed, resembling lattice-work.

Candidus, Latin for pure white.

Canescent, grayish-white; hoary, usually because the surface is covered with fine white hairs. *Incanous* is whiter still.

Canous, whitened with pubescence; see *incanous*.

Capillaceous, Capillary, hair-like in shape; as fine as hair or slender bristles.

Capitate, having a globular apex, like the head on a pin.

Capitellate, diminutive of capitate.

Capitulum, a close rounded dense cluster or *head* of sessile flowers, 74.

Capreolate, bearing tendrils (from *capreolus*, a tendril).

Capsule, a dry dehiscent seed-vessel of a compound pistil, 122.

Capsular, relating to, or like a capsule.

Capture of insects, 154.

Carina, a keel; the two anterior petals of a papilionaceous flower, 92.

Carinate, keeled, furnished with a sharp ridge or projection on the lower side.

Cariopsis, or *Caryopsis*, the one-seeded fruit or grain of Grasses, 121.

Carneous, flesh-colored; pale red. *Carnose*, fleshy in texture.

Carpel, or *Carpidium*, a simple pistil or a pistil-leaf, 106.

Carpellary, pertaining to a carpel.

Carpology, that department of botany which relates to fruits.

Carpophore, the stalk or support of a pistil extending between its carpels, 113.

Carpos, Greek for fruit.

Cartilaginous, or *Cartilagineous*, firm and tough in texture, like cartilage.

Caruncle, an excrescence at the scar of some seeds, 126.

Carunculate, furnished with a caruncle.

Caryophyllaceous, pink-like: applied to a corolla of 5 long-clawed petals.

Cassideous, helmet-shaped.

Cassus, empty and sterile.

Catenate, or *Catenulate*, end to end as in a chain.

Catkin, see Ament, 75.

Caudate, tailed, or tail-pointed.

Caudex, a sort of trunk, such as that of Palms; an upright rootstock, 39, 44.

Caudicle, the stalk of a pollen-mass, &c.

Caulescent, having an obvious stem, 36.

[Pg 199]

Caulicle, a little stem, or rudimentary stem (of a seedling), 11, 127.

Cauline, of or belonging to a stem, 36. *Caulis*, Latin name of stem.

Caulocarpic, equivalent to perennial.

Caulome, the cauline parts of a plant.

Cell (diminutive, *Cellule*), the cavity of an anther, ovary, &c.; one of the anatomical elements, 131.

Cellular Cryptogams, 162.

Cellular tissue, 131.

Cellulose, 131.

Cell-walls, 130.

Centrifugal (inflorescence), produced or expanding in succession from the centre outwards, 77.

Centripetal, the opposite of centrifugal, 74.

Cephala, Greek for head. In compounds, *Monocephalous*, with one head, *Microcephalous*, small-headed, &c.

Cereal, belonging to corn, or corn-plants.

Cernuous, nodding; the summit more or less inclining.

Chæta, Greek for bristle.

Chaff, small membranous scales or bracts on the receptacle of Compositæ; the glumes, &c., of grasses.

Chaffy, furnished with chaff, or of the texture of chaff.

Chalaza, that part of the ovule where all the parts grow together, 110, 126.

Channelled, hollowed out like a gutter; same as *canaliculate*.

Character, a phrase expressing the essential marks of a species, genus, &c., 181.

Chartaceous, of the texture of paper or parchment.

Chloros, Greek for green, whence *Chloranthous*, green-flowered; *Chlorocarpous*, green-fruited, &c.

Chlorophyll, leaf green, 136.

Chlorosis, a condition in which naturally colored parts turn green.

Choripetalous, same as polypetalous.

Chorisis, separation of the normally united parts, or where two or more parts take the place of one.

Chromule, coloring matter in plants, especially when not green, or when liquid.

Chrysos, Greek for golden yellow, whence *Chrysanthous*, yellow-flowered, &c.

Cicatrix, the scar left by the fall of a leaf or other organ.

Ciliate, beset on the margin with a fringe of *cilia*, i. e. of hairs or bristles, like the eyelashes fringing the eyelids, whence the name.

Cinereous, or *Cineraceous*, ash-grayish; of the color of ashes.

93

Circinate, rolled inwards from the top, 72.

Circumscissile, or *Circumcissile*, divided by a circular line round the sides, as the pods of Purslane, Plantain, &c., 124.

Circumscription, general outline.

Cirrhiferous, or *Cirrhose*, furnished with a tendril (Latin, *Cirrhus*); as the Grape-vine. *Cirrhose* also means resembling or coiling like tendrils, as the leaf-stalks of Virgin's-bower. More properly *Cirrus* and *Cirrose*.

Citreous, lemon-yellow.

Clados, Greek for branch. *Cladophylla*, 64.

Class, 178, 183.

Classification, 175, 183.

Clathrate, latticed; same as *cancellate*.

Clavate, club-shaped; slender below and thickened upwards.

Clavellate, diminutive of clavate.

Claviculate, having *Claviculæ*, or little tendrils or hooks.

Claw, the narrow or stalk-like base of some petals, as of Pinks, 91.

Cleistogamous (*Cleistogamy*), fertilized in closed bud, 115.

Cleft, cut into lobes, 55.

Close fertilization, 115.

Climbing, rising by clinging to other objects, 39, 151.

Club shaped, see *clavate*.

Clustered, leaves, flowers, &c., aggregated or collected into a bunch.

[Pg 200]

Clypeate, buckler-shaped.

Coadunate, same as *connate*, i. e. united.

Coalescent, growing together. *Coalescence*, 88.

Coarctate, contracted or brought close together.

Coated, having an integument, or covered in layers. Coated bulb, 46.

Cobwebby, same as *arachnoid*; bearing hairs like cobwebs or gossamer.

Coccineous, scarlet-red.

Coccus (plural *cocci*), anciently a berry; now mostly used to denote the separable carpels or nutlets of a dry fruit.

Cochleariform, spoon-shaped.

Cochleate, coiled or shaped like a snail-shell.

Cælospermous, applied to those fruits of Umbelliferæ which have the seed hollowed on the inner face, by incurving of top and bottom; as in Coriander.

Coherent, usually the same as *connate*.

Cohort, name sometimes used for groups between order and class, 178.

Coleorhiza, a root-sheath.

Collateral, side by side.

Collective fruits, 118.

Collum or *Collar*, the neck or junction of stem and root.

Colored, parts of a plant which are other-colored than green.

Columella, the axis to which the carpels of a compound pistil are often attached, as in Geranium (112), or which is left when a pod opens, as in Azalea.

Column, the united stamens, as in Mallow, or the stamens and pistils united into one body, as in the Orchis family.

Columnar, shaped like a column or pillar.

Coma, a tuft of any sort (literally, a head of hair), 125.

Comose, tufted; bearing a tuft of hairs, as the seeds of Milkweed, 126.

Commissure, the line of junction of two carpels, as in the fruit of Umbelliferæ.

Complanate, flattened.

Compound leaf, 54, 57. *Compound pistil*, 107. *Compound umbel*, 75, &c.

Complete (flower), 81.

Complicate, folded upon itself.

Compressed, flattened on opposite sides.

Conceptacle, 168.

Concinnous, neat.

Concolor, all of one color.

Conchiform, shell- or half-shell-shaped.

Conduplicate, folded upon itself lengthwise, 71.

Cone, the fruit of the Pine family, 124. *Coniferous*, cone-bearing.

Confertus, much crowded.

Conferruminate, stuck together, as the cotyledons in a horse-chestnut.

Confluent, blended together; or the same as *coherent*.

Conformed, similar to another thing it is associated with or compared to; or closely fitted to it, as the skin to the kernel of a seed.

Congested, Conglomerate, crowded together.

Conglomerate, crowded into a glomerule.

Conjugate, coupled; in single pairs. *Conjugation*, 170.

Connate, united or grown together from the first formation, 96.

Connate-perfoliate, when a pair of leaves are connate round a stem, 60.

Connective, Connectivum, the part of the anther connecting its two cells, 101.

Connivent, converging, or brought close together.

Consolidation (floral), 94.

Consolidated forms of vegetation, 47.

Contents of cells, 136.

Continuous, the reverse of interrupted or articulated.

Contorted, twisted together. *Contorted æstivation*, same as *convolute*, 97.

Contortuplicate, twisted back upon itself.

Contracted, either narrowed or shortened.

[Pg 201]

Contrary, turned in opposite direction to the ordinary.

Convolute, rolled up lengthwise, as the leaves of the Plum in vernation, 72. In æstivation, same as *contorted*, 97.

Cordate, heart-shaped, 53.

Coriaceous, resembling leather in texture.

Corky, of the texture of cork. *Corky layer* of bark, 141.

Corm, a solid bulb, like that of Crocus, 45.

Corneous, of the consistence or appearance of horn.

Corniculate, furnished with a small horn or spur.

Cornute, horned; bearing a horn-like projection or appendage.

Corolla, the leaves of the flower within the calyx, 14, 79.

Corollaceous, Corolline, like or belonging to a corolla.

Corona, a coronet or crown; an appendage at the top of the claw of some petals, 91.

Coronate, crowned; furnished with a crown.

Cortex, bark. *Cortical*, belonging to the bark (*cortex*).

Corticate, coated with bark or bark-like covering.

Corymb, a flat or convex indeterminate flower-cluster, 74.

Corymbiferous, bearing corymbs.

Corymbose, in corymbs, approaching the form of a corymb, or branched in that way.

Costa, a rib; the midrib of a leaf, &c. *Costate*, ribbed.

Cotyledons, the proper leaves of the embryo, 11, 127.

Crateriform, goblet-shaped or deep saucer-shaped.

Creeping (stems), growing flat on or beneath the ground and rooting, 39.

Cremocarp, a half-fruit, or one of the two carpels of Umbelliferæ, 121.

Crenate, or *Crenelled*, the edge scalloped into rounded teeth, 55.

Crenulate, minutely or slightly crenate.

Crested, or *Cristate*, bearing any elevated appendage like a crest.

Cretaceous, chalky or chalk-like.

Cribrose, or *cribriform*, pierced like a sieve with small apertures.

Crinite, bearing long hairs.

Crispate, curled or crispy.

Croceous, saffron-color, deep reddish-yellow.

Cross-breeds, the progeny of interbred varieties, 176.

Cross fertilization, 115.

Crown, see *corona*. *Crowned*, see *coronate*.

Cruciate, or *Cruciform*, cross-shaped. *Cruciform Corolla*, 86.

Crustaceous, hard and brittle in texture; crust-like.

Cryptogamous Plants, Cryptogams, 10, 156.

Cryptos, concealed, as *Cryptopetalous*, with concealed petals, &c.

Crystals in plants, 137.

Cucullate, hooded, or hood-shaped, rolled up like a cornet of paper, or a hood (*cucullus*), as the spathe of Indian Turnip, 75.

95

Culm, a straw; the stem of Grasses and Sedges, 39.

Cultrate, shaped like a trowel or broad knife.

Cuneate, Cuneiform, wedge-shaped, 53.

Cup-shaped, same as cyathiform or near it.

Cupule, a little cup; the cup to the acorn of the Oak, 122.

Cupular, or *Cupulate*, provided with a cupule.

Cupuliferous, cupule-bearing.

Curviveined, with curved ribs or veins.

Curviserial, in oblique or spiral ranks.

Cushion, the enlargement at the insertion or base of a petiole.

Cuspidate, tipped with a sharp and stiff point or *cusp*, 54.

Cut, same as incised, or applied generally to any sharp and deep division, 55.

Cuticle, the skin of plants, or more strictly its external pellicle.

Cyaneous, bright blue.

Cyathiform, in the shape of a cup, or particularly of a wine-glass.

Cycle, one complete turn of a spire, or a circle, 70.

[Pg 202]

Cyclical, rolled up circularly, or coiled into a complete circle.

Cyclosis, circulation in closed cells, 149.

Cylindraceous, approaching to the *Cylindrical* form, terete and not tapering.

Cymbæform, or *Cymbiform*, same as boat-shaped.

Cyme, a cluster of centrifugal inflorescence, 77.

Cymose, furnished with cymes, or like a cyme.

Cymule, a partial or diminutive cyme, 77.

Deca- (in words of Greek derivation), ten; as

Decagynous, with 10 pistils or styles, *Decamerous*, of 10 parts, *Decandrous*, with 10 stamens, &c.

Deciduous, falling off, or subject to fall; said of leaves which fall in autumn, and of a calyx and corolla which fall before the fruit forms.

Declinate, declined, turned to one side, or downwards.

Decompound, several times compounded or divided, 59.

Decumbent, reclined on the ground, the summit tending to rise, 39.

Decurrent (leaves), prolonged on the stem beneath the insertion, as in Thistles.

Decussate, arranged in pairs which successively cross each other, 71.

Deduplication, same as chorisis.

Definite, when of a uniform number, and not above twelve or so.

Definite Inflorescence, 72.

Deflexed, bent downwards.

Deflorate, past the flowering state, as an anther after it has discharged its pollen.

Dehiscence, the regular splitting open of capsule or anther, 103, 119.

Dehiscent, opening by regular dehiscence, 119, 123.

Deliquescent, branching off so that the stem is lost in the branches, 32.

Deltoid, of a triangular shape, like the Greek capital Δ.

Demersed, growing below the surface of water.

Dendroid, Dendritic, tree-like in form or appearance.

Dendron, Greek for tree.

Deni, ten together.

Dens, Latin for tooth.

Dentate, toothed, 55. *Denticulate*, furnished with denticulations, or little teeth.

Depauperate, impoverished or starved, and so below the natural size.

Depressed, flattened or as if pressed down from above.

Derma, Greek for skin.

Descending, tending gradually downwards. *Descending axis*, the root.

Desmos, Greek for things connected or bound together.

Determinate Inflorescence, 72.

Dextrorse, turned to the right hand.

Di- Dis (in Greek compounds) two, as

Diadelphous (stamens), united by their filaments in two sets, 99.

Diagnosis, a short distinguishing character or descriptive phrase.

Dialypetalous, same as polypetalous.

Diandrous, having two stamens, &c.

Diaphanous, transparent or translucent.

Dicarpellary, of two carpels.

Dichlamydeous (flower), having both calyx and corolla.

Dichogamous, Dichogamy, 116.

Dichotomous, two-forked.

Diclinous, having the stamens in one flower, the pistils in another, 85.

Dicoccous (fruit), splitting into two *cocci* or closed carpels.

Dicotyls, 23.

Dicotyledonous (embryo), having a pair of cotyledons, 23. *Dicotyledonous Plants*, 23, 182.

Didymous, twin.

Didynamous (stamens), having four stamens in two pairs, 100.

Diffuse, spreading widely and irregularly.

[Pg 203]

Digitate (fingered), where the leaflets of a compound leaf are all borne on the apex of the petiole, 58.

Digynous (flower), having two pistils or styles, 105.

Dimerous, made up of two parts, or its organs in twos.

Dimidiate, halved; as where a leaf or leaflet has only one side developed.

Dimorphism, 117. *Dimorphous, Dimorphic*, of two forms, 117.

Diœcious, or *Dioicous*, with stamens and pistils on different plants, 85.

Dipetalous, of two petals.

Diphyllous, two-leaved.

Dipterous, two-winged.

Diplo-, Greek for double, as *Diplostemonous*, with two sets of stamens.

Disciform or *Disk-shaped*, flat and circular, like a disk or quoit.

Discoidal, or *Discoid*, belonging to or like a disk.

Discolor, of two different colors or hues.

Discrete, separate, opposite of concrete.

Disepalous, of two sepals.

Disk, the face of any flat body; the central part of a head of flowers, like the Sunflower, or Coreopsis, as opposed to the ray or margin; a fleshy expansion of the receptacle of a flower, 113.

Disk-flowers, those of the disk in Compositæ.

Dissected, cut deeply into many lobes or divisions.

Dissepiments, the partitions of a compound ovary or a fruit, 108.

Dissilient, bursting in pieces.

Distichous, two-ranked.

Distinct, uncombined with each other, 95.

Dithecous, of two thecæ or anther-cells.

Divaricate, straddling; very widely divergent.

Divided (leaves, &c.), cut into divisions down to the base or midrib, 55.

Dodeca, Greek for twelve; as *Dodecagynous*, with twelve pistils or styles, *Dodecandrous*, with twelve stamens.

Dodrans, span-long.

Dolabriform, axe-shaped.

Dorsal, pertaining to the back (*dorsum*) of an organ. *Dorsal Suture*, 106.

Dotted Ducts, 148.

Double Flowers, where the petals are multiplied unduly, 79.

Downy, clothed with a coat of soft and short hairs.

Drupaceous, like or pertaining to a drupe.

Drupe, a stone-fruit, 120. *Drupelet* or *Drupel*, a little drupe.

Ducts, the so-called vessels of plants, 134.

Dumose, bushy, or relating to bushes.

Duramen, the heart-wood, 142.

Dwarf, remarkably low in stature.

E-, as a prefix of Latin compound words, means destitute of; as *ecostate*, without a rib or midrib; *exalbuminous*, without albumen, &c.

Eared, see *auriculate*, 53.

Ebracteate, destitute of bracts. *Ebracteolate*, destitute of bractlets.

Eburneous, ivory-white.

Echinate, armed with prickles (like a hedgehog). *Echinulate*, a diminutive of it.

Edentate, toothless.

Effete, past bearing, &c.; said of anthers which have discharged their pollen.

Effuse, very loosely branched and spreading.

Eglandulose, destitute of glands.

Elaters, threads mixed with the spores of Liverworts, 165.

Ellipsoidal, approaching an elliptical figure.

Elliptical, oval or oblong, with the ends regularly rounded, 52.

Emarginate, notched at the summit, 54.

Embryo, the rudimentary plantlet in a seed, 11, 127.

Embryonal, belonging or relating to the embryo.

Embryo-sac, 117.

[Pg 204]

Emersed, raised out of water.

Endecagynous, with eleven pistils or styles.

Endecandrous, with eleven stamens.

Endemic, peculiar to the country geographically.

Endocarp, the inner layer of a pericarp or fruit, 120.

Endochrome, the coloring matter of Algæ and the like.

Endogenous Stems, 138. *Endogenous plants*, an old name for monocotyledons.

Endopleura, inner seed-coat.

Endorhizal, radicle or root sheathed in germination.

Endosperm, the albumen of a seed, 21.

Endostome, the orifice in the inner coat of an ovule.

Ennea-, nine. *Enneagynous*, with nine petals or styles. *Enneandrous*, nine-stamened.

Ensate, *Ensiform*, sword-shaped.

Entire, the margins not at all toothed, notched, or divided, but even, 55.

Entomophilous, said of flowers frequented and fertilized by insects, 113.

Ephemeral, lasting for a day or less, as the corolla of Purslane, &c.

Epi-, Greek for upon.

Epicalyx, such an involucel as that of Malvaceæ.

Epicarp, the outermost layer of a fruit, 120.

Epidermal, relating to the *Epidermis*, or skin of a plant, 50, 141, 143.

Epigæous, growing on the earth, or close to the ground.

Epigynous, upon the ovary, 95, 99.

Epipetalous, borne on the petals or the corolla, 99.

Epiphyllous, borne on a leaf.

Epiphyte, a plant growing on another plant, but not nourished by it, 36.

Epiphytic or *Epiphytal*, relating to *Epiphytes*.

Epipterous, winged at top.

Episperm, the skin or coat of a seed, especially the outer coat.

Equal, alike in number or length.

Equally pinnate, same as abruptly pinnate, 57.

Equitant (riding straddle), 60.

Erion, Greek for wool. *Erianthous*, woolly-flowered. *Eriophorous*, wool-bearing, &c.

Erose, eroded, as if gnawed.

Erostrate, not beaked.

Erythros, Greek for red. *Erythrocarpous*, red-fruited, &c.

Essential Organs of the flower, 80.

Estivation, see *æstivation*.

Etiolated, blanched by excluding the light, as the stalks of Celery.

Eu, Greek prefix, meaning very, or much.

Evergreen, holding the leaves over winter and until new ones appear, or longer.

Ex, Latin prefix; privative in place of "e" when next letter is a vowel. So *Exalate*, wingless; *Exalbuminous* (seed), without albumen, 21.

Excurrent, running out, as when a midrib projects beyond the apex of a leaf, or a trunk is continued to the very top of a tree, 32.

Exiguous, puny.

Exilis, lank or meagre.

Eximius, distinguished for size or beauty.

Exo-, in Greek compounds, outward, as in

Exocarp, outer layer of a pericarp, 120.

Exogenous, outward growing. *Exogenous stems*, 139.

Exorhizal, radicle in germination not sheathed.

Exostome, the orifice in the outer coat of the ovule.

Explanate, spread or flattened out.

Exserted, protruding out of, as the stamens out of the corolla.

Exstipulate, destitute of stipules.

Extine, outer coat of a pollen-grain.

Extra-axillary, said of a branch or bud somewhat out of the axil, 31.

Extrorse, turned outwards; the anther is extrorse when fastened to the filament on the side next the pistil, and opening on the outer side, 101.

[Pg 205]

Falcate, scythe-shaped; a flat body curved, its edges parallel.

False Racemes, 78.

Family, in botany same as Order, 177.

Farina, meal or starchy matter, 136.

Farinaceous, mealy in texture. *Farinose*, covered with a mealy powder.

Fasciate, banded; also applied to monstrous stems which grow flat.

Fascicle, a close cluster, 77.

Fascicled, Fasciculated, growing in a bundle or tuft, as the leaves of Larch, 68, and roots of Peony, 35.

Fastigiate, close, parallel, and upright, as the branches of Lombardy Poplar.

Faux (plural, *fauces*), the throat of a calyx, corolla, &c., 89.

Faveolate, Favose, honeycombed; same as *alveolate*.

Feather-veined, with veins of a leaf all springing from the sides of a midrib, 51.

Fecula or *Fæcula*, starch, 136.

Female flower or *plant*, one bearing pistils only.

Fenestrate, pierced with one or more large holes, like windows.

Ferrugineous, or *Ferruginous*, resembling iron-rust; red-grayish.

Fertile, fruit-bearing, or capable of it; also said of anthers producing good pollen.

Fertilization, the process by which pollen causes the embryo to be formed, 114.

Fibre (woody), 133. *Fibrous*, containing much fibre, or composed of fibres.

Fibrillose, formed of small fibres, or *Fibrillæ*.

Fibro-vascular bundle or tissue, formed of fibres and vessels.

Fiddle-shaped, obovate with a deep recess on each side.

Fidus, Latin suffix for cleft, as *Bifid*, two-cleft.

Filament, the stalk of a stamen, 14, 80, 101; also any slender thread-shaped body.

Filamentose, or *Filamentous*, bearing or formed of slender threads.

Filiform, thread-shaped; long, slender, and cylindrical.

Fimbriate, fringed; furnished with fringes (*fimbriæ*).

Fimbrillate, Fimbrilliferous, bearing small *fimbriæ*, i. e. *fimbrillæ*.

Fissiparous, multiplying by division of one body into two.

Fissus, Latin for split or divided.

Fissular, or *Fistulose*, hollow and cylindrical, as the leaves of the Onion.

Flabelliform, or *Flabellate*, fan-shaped.

Flagellate, or *Flagelliform*, long, narrow, and flexible, like the thong of a whip; or like the runners (*flagellæ*) of the Strawberry.

Flavescent, yellowish, or turning yellow.

Flavus, Latin for yellow.

Fleshy, composed of firm pulp or flesh.

Flexuose, or *Flexuous*, bending in opposite directions, in a zigzag way.

Floating, swimming on the surface of water.

Floccose, composed of or bearing tufts of woolly or long and soft hairs.

Flora (the goddess of flowers), the plants of a country or district, taken together, or a work systematically describing them, 9.

Floral Envelopes, or *Flower-leaves*, 79.

Floret, a diminutive flower, one of a mass or cluster.

Floribund, abundantly floriferous.

Florula, the flora of a small district.

Flos, floris, Latin for flower.

Flosculus, diminutive, same as floret.

Flower, the whole organs of reproduction of Phænogamous plants, 14, 72.

Flower-bud, an unopened flower.

Flowering Plants, 10, 156. *Flowerless Plants*, 10, 156.

Fly-trap leaves, 65.

Fluitans, Latin for floating. *Fluviatile*, belonging to a river or stream.

Foliaceous, belonging to, or of the texture or nature of, a leaf (*folium*).

Foliate, provided with leaves. Latin prefixes denote the number of leaves, as *bifoliate*, *trifoliate*, &c. *Foliose*, leafy; abounding in leaves.

Foliolate, relating to or bearing leaflets (*foliola*); *trifoliolate*, with three leaflets, &c.

[Pg 206]

Folium (plural, *folia*), Latin for leaf.

Follicle, a simple pod, opening down the inner suture, 122.

Follicular, resembling or belonging to a follicle.

Food of Plants, 144.

Foot-stalk, either petiole or peduncle, 49.

Foramen, a hole or orifice, as that of the ovule, 110.

Foraminose, *Foraminulose*, pierced with holes.

Forked, branched in two or three or more.

Fornicate, bearing fornices.

Fornix, little arched scales in the throat of some corollas, as of Comfrey.

Foveate, deeply pitted. *Foveolate*, diminutive of *foveate*.

Free, not united with any other parts of a different sort, 95.

Fringed, the margin beset with slender appendages, bristles, &c.

Frond, what answers to leaves in Ferns, &c., 157; or to the stem and leaves fused into one, as in Liverwort.

Frondescence, the bursting into leaf.

Frondose, frond-bearing; like a frond, or sometimes used for leafy.

Fructification, the state or result of fruiting.

Fructus, Latin for fruit.

Fruit, the matured ovary and all it contains or is connected with, 117.

Fruit-dots in Ferns; see *Sorus*.

Frustulose, consisting of a chain of similar pieces, or *Frustules*.

Frutescent, somewhat shrubby; becoming a shrub (*Frutex*), 39.

Fruticulose, like a small shrub, or *Fruticulus*. *Fruticose*, shrubby, 39.

Fugacious, soon falling off or perishing.

Fulcrate, having accessory organs or *fulcra*, i. e. props.

Fulvous, tawny; dull yellow with gray.

Fungus, *Fungi*, 172.

Funicle, *Funiculus*, the stalk of a seed or ovule, 110.

Funnelform, or *funnel-shaped*, expanding gradually upwards into an open mouth, like a funnel or tunnel, 90.

Furcate, forked.

Furfuraceous, covered with bran-like fine scurf.

Furrowed, marked by longitudinal channels or grooves.

Fuscous, deep gray-brown.

Fusiform, spindle-shaped, 36.

Galbalus, the fleshy or at length woody cone of Juniper and Cypress.

Galea, a helmet-shaped body, as the upper sepal of the Monkshood, 87.

Galeate, shaped like a helmet.

Gamopetalous, of united petals, 89.

Gamophyllous, formed of united leaves.

Gamosepalous, formed of united sepals, 89.

Geminate, twin; in pairs.

Gemma, Latin for a bud.

Gemmation, the state of budding; budding growth.

Gemmule, a small bud; the plumule, 13.

Genera, plural of genus.

Geniculate, bent abruptly, like a knee (*genu*), as many stems.

Generic Names, 179.

Genus, a kind of a rank above species, 177.

Germ, a growing point; a young bud; sometimes the same as embryo, 127.

Germen, the old name for ovary.

Germination, the development of a plantlet from the seed, 12.

Gerontogæous, inhabiting the Old World.

Gibbous, more tumid at one place or on one side than the other.

Gilvous, dirty reddish-yellow.

Glabrate, becoming glabrous with age, or almost glabrous.

Glabrous, smooth, in the sense of having no hairs, bristles, or other pubescence.

100

Gladiate, sword-shaped, as the leaves of Iris.

Glands, small cellular organs which secrete oily or aromatic or other products; they are sometimes sunk in the leaves or rind, as in the Orange, Prickly Ash, &c.; sometimes on the surface as small projections; sometimes raised on hairs or bristles (*glandular hairs, &c.*), as in the Sweetbrier and Sundew. The name is also given to any small swellings, &c., whether they secrete anything or not; so that the word is loosely used.

Glandular, Glandulose, furnished with glands, or gland-like.

Glans (Gland), the acorn or mast of Oak and similar fruits.

Glareose, growing in gravel.

Glaucescent, slightly glaucous, or bluish-gray.

Glaucous, covered with a *bloom*, viz. with a fine white powder of wax that rubs off, like that on a fresh plum, or a cabbage-leaf.

Globose, spherical in form, or nearly so. *Globular*, nearly globose.

Glochidiate, or *Glochideous*, (bristles) barbed; tipped with barbs, or with a double hooked point.

Glomerate, closely aggregated into a dense cluster.

Glomerule, a dense head-like cluster, 77.

Glossology, the department of botany in which technical terms are explained.

Glumaceous, glume-like, or glume-bearing.

Glume, Glumes are the husks or floral coverings of Grasses, or, particularly, the outer husks or bracts of each spikelet.

Glumelles, the inner husks of Grasses.

Gonophore, a stipe below stamens, 113.

Gossypine, cottony, flocculent.

Gracilis, Latin for slender.

Grain, see *Caryopsis*, 121.

Gramineous, grass-like.

Granular, composed of grains. *Granule*, a small grain.

Graveolent, heavy-scented.

Griseous, gray or bluish-gray.

Growth, 129.

Grumous, or *Grumose*, formed of coarse clustered grains.

Guttate, spotted, as if by drops of something colored.

Gymnos, Greek for naked, as

Gymnocarpous, naked-fruited.

Gymnospermous, naked-seeded, 109.

Gymnospermous gynæcium, 109.

Gymnospermæ, or *Gymnospermous Plants*, 183.

Gynandrous, with stamens borne on, i. e. united with, the pistil, 99.

Gynæcium, a name for the pistils of a flower taken altogether, 105.

Gynobase, a depressed receptacle or support of the pistil or carpels, 114.

Gynophore, a stalk raising a pistil above the stamens, 113.

Gynostegium, a sheath around pistils, of whatever nature.

Gynostemium, name of the column in Orchids, &c., consisting of style and stigma with stamens combined.

Gyrate, coiled or moving circularly.

Gyrose, strongly bent to and fro.

Habit, the general aspect of a plant, or its mode of growth.

Habitat, the situation or country in which a plant grows in a wild state.

Hairs, hair-like growths on the surface of plants.

Hairy, beset with hairs, especially longish ones.

Halberd-shaped, see *hastate*, 53.

Halved, when appearing as if one half of the body were cut away.

Hamate, or *Hamose*, hooked; the end of a slender body bent round.

Hamulose, bearing a small hook; a diminutive of the last.

Haplo-, in Greek compounds, single; as *Haplostemonous*, having only one series of stamens.
Hastate, or *Hastile*, shaped like a halberd; furnished with a spreading lobe on each side at the base, 53.

Head, capitulum, a form of inflorescence, 74.

Heart-shaped, of the shape of a heart as painted on cards, 53.

Heart-wood, the older or matured wood of exogenous trees, 142.

Helicoid, coiled like a *helix* or snail-shell, 77.

Helmet, the upper sepal of Monkshood is so called.

Helvolous, grayish-yellow.

Hemi- in compounds from the Greek, half; e. g. *Hemispherical*, &c.

Hemicarp, half-fruit, one carpel of an Umbelliferous plant, 121.

Hemitropous (ovule or seed), nearly same as *amphitropous*, 123.

Hepta- (in words of Greek origin), seven; as *Heptagynous*, with seven pistils or styles. *Heptamerous*, its parts in sevens. *Heptandrous*, having seven stamens.

Herb, plant not woody, at least above ground.

Herbaceous, of the texture of an herb; not woody, 39.

Herbarium, the botanist's arranged collection of dried plants, 186.

Herborization, 184.

Hermaphrodite (flower), having stamens and pistils in the same blossom, 81.

Hesperidium, orange-fruit, a hard-rinded berry.

Hetero-, in Greek compounds, means of two or more sorts, as

Heterocarpous, bearing fruit of two kinds or shapes.

Heterogamous, bearing two or more sorts of flowers in one cluster.

Heterogony, *Heterogone*, or *Heterogonous*, with stamens and pistil reciprocally of two sorts, 116. *Heterostyled* is same.

Heteromorphous, of two or more shapes.

Heterophyllous, with two sorts of leaves.

Heterotropous (ovule), the same as *amphitropous*, 123.

Hexa- (in Greek compounds), six; as *Hexagonal*, six-angled. *Hexagynous*, with six pistils or styles. *Hexamerous*, its parts in sixes. *Hexandrous*, with six stamens.*Hexapterous*, six-winged.

Hibernaculum, a winter bud.

Hiemal, relating to winter.

Hilar, belonging to the hilum.

Hilum, the scar of the seed; its place of attachment, 110, 126.

Hippocrepiform, horseshoe-shaped.

Hirsute, clothed with stiffish or beard-like hairs.

Hirtellous, minutely hirsute.

Hispid, bristly, beset with stiff hairs. *Hispidulous*, diminutive of hispid.

Histology, 9.

Hoary, grayish-white; see *canescent*, &c.

Holosericeous, all over sericeous or silky.

Homo-, in Greek compounds, all alike or of one sort.

Homodromous, running in one direction.

Homogamous, a head or cluster with flowers all of one kind.

Homogeneous, uniform in nature; all of one kind.

Homogone, or *Homogonous*, counterpart of *Heterogone* or *Homostyled.*

Homologous, of same type; thus petals and sepals are the homologues of leaves.

Homomallous (leaves, &c.), originating all round an axis, but all bent or curved to one side.

Homomorphous, all of one shape.

Homotropous (embryo), curved with the seed; curved only one way.

Hood, same as *helmet* or *galea*. *Hooded*, hood-shaped; see *cucullate.*

Hooked, same as *hamate.*

Horn, a spur or some similar appendage. *Horny*, of the texture of horn.

Hortensis, pertaining to the garden.

Hortus Siccus, an herbarium, or collection of dried plants, 186.

Humifuse, *Humistrate*, spread over the surface of the ground.

Humilis, low in stature.

[Pg 209]

Hyaline, transparent, or partly so.

Hybrid, a cross-breed between two allied species, 176.

Hydrophytes, water-plants.

Hyemal, see *hiemal.*

Hymenium of a Mushroom, 172.

Hypanthium, a hollow flower-receptacle, such as that of Rose.

Hypo-, Greek prefix for under, or underneath.

Hypocotyle, or *Hypocotyl*, part of stem below the cotyledons, 11.

Hypocrateriform, properly *Hypocraterimorphous*, salver-shaped.

Hypogæan, or *Hypogæous,* produced under ground, 19.

Hypogynous, inserted under the pistil, 95, 99.

Hysteranthous, with the blossoms developed earlier than the leaves.

Icosandrous, having 20 (or 12 or more) stamens inserted on the calyx.

Imberbis, Latin for beardless.

Imbricate, Imbricated, Imbricative, overlapping one another, like tiles or shingles on a roof, as the bud-scales of Horse-chestnut and Hickory, 27. In æstivation, where some leaves of the calyx or corolla are overlapped on both sides by others, 98.

Immarginate, destitute of a rim or border.

Immersed, growing wholly under water.

Impari-pinnate, pinnate with a single leaflet at the apex, 57.

Imperfect flowers, wanting either stamens or pistils, 85.

Inæquilateral, unequal-sided, as the leaf of a Begonia.

Inane, empty, said of an anther which produces no pollen, &c.

Inappendiculate, not appendaged.

Incanous, Incanescent, hoary with soft white pubescence.

Incarnate, flesh-colored.

Incised, cut rather deeply and irregularly, 58.

Included, enclosed; when the part in question does not project beyond another.

Incomplete Flower, wanting calyx or corolla, 86.

Incrassated, thickened.

Incubous, with tip of one leaf lying flat over the base of the next above.

Incumbent, leaning or resting upon; the cotyledons are incumbent when the back of one of them lies against the radicle, 128; the anthers are incumbent when turned or looking inwards.

Incurved, gradually curving inwards.

Indefinite, not uniform in number, or too numerous to mention (over 12).

Indefinite or *Indeterminate Inflorescence,* 72.

Indehiscent, not splitting open; i. e. not dehiscent, 119.

Indigenous, native to the country.

Individuals, 175.

Indumentum, any hairy coating or pubescence.

Induplicate, with the edges turned inwards, 97.

Induviate, clothed with old and withered parts or *induviæ.*

Indusium, the shield or covering of a fruit-dot of a Fern, 159.

Inermis, Latin for unarmed, not prickly.

Inferior, growing below some other organ, 96.

Infertile, not producing seed, or pollen, as the case may be.

Inflated, turgid and bladdery.

Inflexed, bent inwards.

Inflorescence, the arrangement of flowers on the stem, 72.

Infra-axillary, situated beneath the axil.

Infundibuliform or *Infundibular,* funnel-shaped, 90.

Innate (anther), attached by its base to the very apex of the filament, 101.

Innovation, a young shoot, or new growth.

Insertion, the place or the mode of attachment of an organ to its support, 95, 99.

Integer, entire, not lobed. *Integerrimus,* quite entire, not serrate.

[Pg 210]

Intercellular Passages or *Spaces,* 131, 143.

Interfoliaceous, between the leaves of a pair or whorl.

Internode, the part of a stem between two nodes, 13.

Interpetiolar, between petioles.

Interruptedly pinnate, pinnate with small leaflets intermixed with larger.

Intine, inner coat of a pollen grain.

Intrafoliaceous (stipules, &c.), placed between the leaf or petiole and the stem.

Introrse, turned or facing inwards; i. e. towards the axis of the flower, 101.

Intruse, as it were pushed inwards.

Inversed or *Inverted,* where the apex is in the direction opposite to that of the organ it is compared with.

Involucel, a partial or small involucre, 76.

Involucellate, furnished with an involucel. *Involucrate,* furnished with an involucre.

Involucre, a whorl or set of bracts around a flower, umbel, or head, &c., 74, 75.

Involute, in vernation, 72; rolled inwards from the edges, 97.

Irregular Flowers, 86, 91.

Isos, Greek for equal in number. *Isomerous*, the same number in the successive circles or sets. *Isostemonous*, the stamens equal in number to the sepals or petals.

Jointed, separate or separable at one or more places into pieces, 64, &c.

Jugum (plural *Juga*), Latin for a pair, as of leaflets,—thus *Unijugate*, of a single pair; *Bijugate*, of two pairs, &c.

Julaceus, like a catkin or *Julus*.

Keel, a projecting ridge on a surface, like the keel of a boat; the two anterior petals of a papilionaceous corolla, 92.

Keeled, furnished with a keel or sharp longitudinal ridge.

Kermesine, Carmine-red.

Kernel of the ovule and seed, 110.

Key, or *Key-fruit*, a Samara, 122.

Kidney-shaped, resembling the outline of a kidney, 53.

Labellum, the odd petal in the Orchis Family.

Labiate, same as *bilabiate* or two-lipped, 92.

Labiatiflorous, having flowers with bilabiate corolla.

Labium (plural, *Labia*), Latin for lip.

Lacerate, with margin appearing as if torn.

Laciniate, slashed; cut into deep narrow lobes or *Laciniæ*.

Lactescent, producing milky juice, as does the Milkweed, &c.

Lacteus, Latin for milk-white.

Lacunose, full of holes or gaps.

Lacustrine, belonging to lakes.

Lævigate, smooth as if polished. Latin, *Lævis*, smooth, as opposed to rough.

Lageniform, gourd-shaped.

Lagopous, Latin, hare-footed; densely clothed with long soft hairs.

Lamellar or *Lamellate*, consisting of flat plates, *Lamellæ*.

Lamina, a plate or blade, the blade of a leaf, &c., 49.

Lanate, *Lanose*, woolly; clothed with long and soft entangled hairs.

Lanceolate, lance-shaped, 52.

Lanuginous, cottony or woolly.

Latent buds, concealed or undeveloped buds, 30.

Lateral, belonging to the side.

Latex, the milky juice, &c., of plants, 135.

Lax (*Laxus*), loose in texture, or sparse; the opposite of crowded.

Leaf, 49. *Leaf-buds*, 31.

Leaflet, one of the divisions or blades of a compound leaf, 57.

Leaf-like, same as *foliaceous*.

Leathery, of about the consistence of leather; coriaceous.

[Pg 211]

Legume, a simple pod which dehisces in two pieces, like that of the Pea, 122.

Leguminous, belonging to legumes, or to the Leguminous Family.

Lenticular, lens-shaped; i. e. flattish and convex on both sides.

Lappaceous, bur-like.

Lasio, Greek for woolly or hairy, as *Lasianthus*, woolly-flowered.

Lateritious, brick-colored.

Laticiferous, containing latex, 135.

Latus, Latin for broad, as *Latifolius*, broad-leaved.

Leaf-scar, *Leaf-stalk*, petiole.

Lenticels, lenticular dots on young bark.

Lentiginose, as if freckled.

Lepal, a made-up word for a staminode.

Lepis, Greek for a scale, whence *Lepidote*, leprous; covered with scurfy scales.

Leptos, Greek for slender; so *Leptophyllous*, slender-leaved.

Leukos, Greek for white; whence *Leucanthous*, white-flowered, &c.

Liber, the inner bark of Exogenous stems, 140.

Lid, see *operculum*.

Ligneous, or *Lignose*, woody in texture.

Ligulate, furnished with a ligule, 93.

Ligule, *Ligula*, the strap-shaped corolla in many Compositæ, 93; the membranous appendage at the summit of the leaf-sheaths of most Grasses, 67.

Limb, the border of a corolla, &c., 89.

Limbate, bordered (Latin, *Limbus*, a border).

Line, the twelfth of an inch; or French lines, the tenth.

Linear, narrow and flat, the margins parallel, 52.

Lineate, marked with parallel lines. *Lineolate*, marked with minute lines.

Lingulate, Linguiform, tongue-shaped.

Lip, the principal lobes of a bilabiate corolla or calyx, 92.

Litoral or *Littoral*, belonging to the shore.

Livid, pale lead-colored.

Lobe, any projection or division (especially a rounded one) of a leaf, &c.

Lobed or *Lobate*, cut into lobes, 55, 56; *Lobulate*, into small lobes.

Locellate, having *Locelli*, i. e. compartments in a cell: thus an anther-cell is often *bilocellate*.

Loculament, same as *loculus*.

Locular, relating to the cell or compartment (*Loculus*) of an ovary, &c.

Loculicidal (dehiscence), splitting down through the back of each cell, 123.

Locusta, a name for the spikelet of Grasses.

Lodicule, one of the scales answering to perianth-leaves in Grass-flowers.

Loment, a pod which separates transversely into joints, 122.

Lomentaceous, pertaining to or resembling a loment.

Lorate, thong-shaped.

Lunate, crescent-shaped. *Lunulate*, diminutive of *lunate*.

Lupuline, like hops.

Lusus, Latin for a sport or abnormal variation.

Luteolus, yellowish; diminutive of

Luteus, Latin for yellow. *Lutescent*, verging to yellow.

Lyrate, lyre-shaped; a pinnatifid leaf of an obovate or spatulate outline, the end-lobe large and roundish, and the lower lobes small, as in fig. 149.

Macros, Greek for long, sometimes also used for large: thus *Macrophyllous*, long or large-leaved, &c.

Macrospore, the large kind of spore, when there are two kinds, 160, 161.

Maculate, spotted or blotched.

Male (flowers or plants), having stamens but no pistil.

Mammose, breast-shaped.

Marcescent, withering without falling off.

Marginal, belonging to margin.

[Pg 212]

Marginate, margined with an edge different from the rest.

Marginicidal dehiscence, 123.

Maritime, belonging to sea-coasts.

Marmorate, marbled.

Mas., Masc., Masculine, male.

Masked, see *personate*.

Mealy, see *farinaceous*.

Median, Medial, belonging to the middle.

Medifixed, attached by the middle.

Medullary, belonging to, or of the nature of, pith (*Medulla*); pithy.

Medullary Rays, the silver-grain of wood, 140, 141.

Medullary Sheath, a set of ducts just around the pith, 140.

Meiostemonous, having fewer stamens than petals.

Membranaceous or *Membranous*, of the texture of membrane; thin and soft.

Meniscoid, crescent-shaped.

Mericarp, one carpel of the fruit of an Umbelliferous plant, 121.

Merismatic, separating into parts by the formation of partitions across.

Merous, from the Greek for part; used with numeral prefix to denote the number of pieces in a set or circle: as *Monomerous*, of only one, *Dimerous*, with two, *Trimerous*, with three parts (sepals, petals, stamens, &c.) in each circle.

Mesocarp, the middle part of a pericarp, when that is distinguishable into three layers, 120.

Mesophlœum, the middle or green bark.

Micropyle, the closed orifice of the seed, 110, 126.

Microspore, the smaller kind of spore when there are two kinds, 161.

Midrib, the middle or main rib of a leaf, 50.

Milk-vessels, 135.

Miniate, vermilion-colored.

Mitriform, mitre-shaped: in the form of a peaked cap, or one cleft at the top.

Moniliform, necklace-shaped; a cylindrical body contracted at intervals.

Monocarpic (duration), flowering and seeding but once, 38.

Monochlamydeous, having only one floral envelope.

Monocotyledonous (embryo), with only one cotyledon, 24.

Monocotyledonous Plants, 24. *Monocotyls*, 24.

Monœcious, or *Monoicous* (flower), having stamens or pistils only, 85.

Monogynous (flower), having only one pistil, or one style, 105.

Monopetalous (flower), with the corolla of one piece, 89.

Monophyllous, one-leaved, or of one piece.

Monos, Greek for solitary or only one; thus *Monadelphous*, stamens united by their filaments into one set, 99; *Monandrous* (flower), having only one stamen, 100.

Monosepalous, a calyx of one piece; i. e. with the sepals united into one body.

Monospermous, one-seeded.

Monstrosity, an unnatural deviation from the usual structure or form.

Morphology, *Morphological Botany*, 9; the department of botany which treats of the forms which an organ may assume.

Moschate, Musk-like in odor.

Movements, 149.

Mucronate, tipped with an abrupt short point (*Mucro*), 54.

Mucronulate, tipped with a minute abrupt point; a diminutive of the last.

Multi-, in composition, many; as *Multangular*, many-angled; *Multicipital*, many-headed, &c.; *Multifarious*, in many rows or ranks; *Multifid*, many-cleft;*Multilocular*, many-celled; *Multiserial*, in many rows.

Multiple Fruits, 118, 124.

Muricate, beset with short and hard or prickly points.

Muriform, wall-like; resembling courses of bricks in a wall.

Muticous, pointless, blunt, unarmed.

Mycelium, the spawn of Fungi; i. e. the filaments from which Mushrooms, &c., originate, 172.

[Pg 213]

Naked, wanting some usual covering, as achlamydeous flowers, 86; gymnospermous seeds, 109, 125, &c.

Names in botany, 179.

Nanus, Latin for dwarf.

Napiform, turnip-shaped, 35.

Natural System, 182.

Naturalized, introduced from a foreign country, and flourishing wild.

Navicular, boat-shaped, like the glumes of most Grasses.

Necklace-shaped, looking like a string of beads; see *moniliform*.

Nectar, the sweet secretion in flowers from which bees make honey, &c.

Nectariferous, honey-bearing; or having a nectary.

Nectary, the old name for petals and other parts of the flower when of unusual shape, especially when honey-bearing. So the hollow spur-shaped petals of Columbine were called nectaries; also the curious long-clawed petals of Monkshood, 87, &c.

Needle-shaped, long, slender, and rigid, like the leaves of Pines.

Nemorose or *Nemoral*, inhabiting groves.

Nerve, a name for the ribs or veins of leaves when simple and parallel, 50.

Nerved, furnished with nerves, or simple and parallel ribs or veins, 50.

Nervose, conspicuously nerved. *Nervulose*, minutely nervose.

Netted-veined, furnished with branching veins forming network, 50, 51.

Neuter, *Neutral*, sexless. *Neutral flower*, 79.

Niger, Latin for black. *Nigricans*, Latin for verging to black.

Nitid, shining.

Nival, living in or near snow. *Niveus*, snow-white.

Nodding, bending so that the summit hangs downward.

Node, a knot; the "joints" of a stem, or the part whence a leaf or a pair of leaves springs, 13.

Nodose, knotty or knobby. *Nodulose*, furnished with little knobs or knots.

Nomenclature, 175, 179.

Normal, according to rule, natural.

Notate, marked with spots or lines of a different color.

Nucamentaceous, relating to or resembling a small nut.

Nuciform, nut-shaped or nut-like.

Nucleus, the kernel of an ovule (110) or seed (127) of a cell.

Nucule, same as nutlet.

Nude, (Latin, *Nudus*), naked. So *Nudicaulis*, naked-stemmed, &c.

Nut, Latin *Nux*, a hard, mostly one-seeded indehiscent fruit; as a chestnut, butternut, acorn, 121.

Nutant, nodding.

Nutlet, a little nut; or the stone of a drupe.

Ob- (meaning over against), when prefixed to words signifies inversion; as, *Obcompressed*, flattened the opposite of the usual way; *Obcordate*, heart-shaped, with the broad and notched end at the apex instead of the base, 54; *Oblanceolate*, lance-shaped with the tapering point downwards, 52.

Oblique, applied to leaves, &c., means unequal-sided.

Oblong, from two to four times as long as broad, 52.

Obovate, inversely ovate, the broad end upward, 53. *Obovoid*, solid obovate.

Obtuse, blunt or round at the end, 54.

Obverse, same as *inverse*.

Obvolute (in the bud), when the margins of one piece or leaf alternately overlap those of the opposite one.

Ocellate, with a circular colored patch, like an eye.

Ochroleucous, yellowish-white; dull cream-color.

Ocreate, furnished with *Ocreæ* (boots), or stipules in the form of sheaths, 67.

Octo-, Latin for eight, enters into the composition of *Octagynous*, with eight pistils or styles; *Octamerous*, its parts in eights; *Octandrous*, with eight stamens, &c.

[Pg 214]

Oculate, with eye-shaped marking.

Officinal, used in medicine, therefore kept in the shops.

Offset, short branches next the ground which take root, 40.

Oides, termination, from the Greek, to denote likeness; so *Dianthoides*, Pink-like.

Oleraceous, esculent, as a pot-herb.

Oligos, Greek for few; thus *Oliganthous*, few-flowered, &c.

Olivaceous, olive-green.

Oophoridium, a name for spore-case containing macrospores.

Opaque, applied to a surface, means dull, not shining.

Operculate, furnished with a lid (*Operculum*), as the spore-case of Mosses, 163.

Opposite, said of leaves and branches when on opposite sides of the stem from each other (i. e. in pairs), 29, 68. Stamens are opposite the petals, &c., when they stand before them.

Oppositifolius, situated opposite a leaf.

Orbicular, *Orbiculate*, circular in outline, or nearly so, 52.

Order, group below class, 178. *Ordinal names*, 180.

Organ, any member of the plant, as a leaf, a stamen, &c.

Organography, study of organs, 9. *Organogenesis*, that of the development of organs.

Orgyalis, of the height of a man.

Orthos, Greek for straight; thus, *Orthocarpous*, with straight fruit; *Orthostichous*, straight-ranked.

Orthotropous (ovule or seed), 111.

Osseous, of a bony texture.

Outgrowths, growths from the surface of a leaf, petal, &c.

Oval, broadly elliptical, 52.

Ovary, that part of the pistil containing the ovules or future seeds, 14, 80, 105.

Ovate, shaped like an egg, with the broader end downwards; or, in plain surfaces, such as leaves, like the section of an egg lengthwise, 52.

Ovoid, ovate or oval in a solid form.

Ovule, the body which is destined to become a seed, 14, 80, 105, 110.

Ovuliferous, ovule-bearing.

Palate, a projection of the lower lip of a labiate corolla into the throat, as in Snapdragon, &c.

Palea (plural *paleæ*), chaff; the inner husks of Grasses; the chaff or bracts on the receptacle of many Compositæ, as Coreopsis, and Sunflower.

Paleaceous, furnished with chaff, or chaffy in texture.

Paleolate, having *Paleolæ* or paleæ of a second order, or narrow paleæ.

Palet, English term for palea.

Palmate, when leaflets or the divisions of a leaf all spread from the apex of the petiole, like the hand with the outspread fingers, 57, 58.

Palmately (veined, lobed, &c.), in a palmate manner, 51, 56.

Palmatifid, -lobed, -sect, palmately cleft, or lobed, or divided.

Paludose, inhabiting marshes. *Palustrine*, same.

Panduriform, or *Pandurate,* fiddle-shaped (which see).

Panicle, an open and branched cluster, 81.

Panicled, Paniculate, arranged in panicles, or like a panicle.

Pannose, covered with a felt of woolly hairs.

Papery, of about the consistence of letter-paper.

Papilionaceous, butterfly-shaped; applied to such a corolla as that of the Pea, 91.

Papilla (plural *papillæ*), little nipple-shaped protuberances.

Papillate, Papillose, covered with papillæ.

Pappus, thistle-down. The down crowning the achenium of the Thistle, Groundsel, &c., and whatever in Compositæ answers to calyx, whether hairs, teeth, or scales, 121.

Papyraceous, like parchment in texture.

Parallel-veined or *nerved* (leaves), 50.

[Pg 215]

Paraphyses, jointed filaments mixed with the antheridia of Mosses.

Parasitic, living as a parasite, i. e. on another plant or animal, 37.

Parenchymytous, composed of parenchyma.

Parenchyma, soft cellular tissue of plants, like the green pulp of leaves, 132.

Parietal (placentæ, &c.), attached to the walls (*parietes*) of the ovary.

Paripinnate, pinnate with an even number of leaflets.

Parted, separated or cleft into parts almost to the base, 55.

Parthenogenesis, producing seed without fertilization.

Partial involucre, same as an *involucel; partial petiole,* a division of a main leaf-stalk or the stalk of a leaflet; *partial peduncle,* a branch of a peduncle; *partial umbel,* an umbellet, 76.

Partition, a segment of a *parted* leaf; or an internal wall in an ovary, anther, &c.

Patelliform, disk-shaped, like the *patella* or kneepan.

Patent, spreading, open. *Patulous,* moderately spreading.

Pauci-, in composition, few; as *pauciflorous,* few-flowered, &c.

Pear-shaped, solid obovate, the shape of a pear.

Pectinate, pinnatifid or pinnately divided into narrow and close divisions, like the teeth of a comb.

Pedate, like a bird's foot; palmate or palmately cleft, with the side divisions again cleft, as in Viola pedata, &c.

Pedicel, the stalk of each particular flower of a cluster, 73.

Pedicellate, Pedicelled, borne on a pedicel.

Pedalis, Latin for a foot high or long.

Peduncle, a flower-stalk, whether of a single flower or of a flower-cluster, 73.

Peduncled, Pedunculate, furnished with a peduncle.

Peloria, an abnormal return to regularity and symmetry in an irregular flower; commonest in Snapdragon.

Peltate, shield-shaped; said of a leaf, whatever its shape, when the petiole is attached to the lower side, somewhere within the margin, 53.

Pelviform, basin-shaped.

Pendent, hanging. *Pendulous,* somewhat hanging or drooping.

Penicillate, Penicilliform, tipped with a tuft of fine hairs, like a painter's pencil; as the stigmas of some Grasses.

Pennate, same as pinnate. *Penninerved* and *Penniveined,* pinnately veined, 51.

Penta- (in words of Greek composition), five; as *Pentadelphous,* 99; *Pentagynous,* with five pistils or styles; *Pentamerous,* with its parts in fives, or on the plan of five; *Pentandrous,* having five stamens, 112; *Pentastichous,* in five ranks, &c.

Pepo, a fruit like the Melon and Cucumber, 119.

Perennial, lasting from year to year, 38.

Perfect (flower), having both stamens and pistils, 81.

Perfoliate, passing through the leaf, in appearance, 60.

Perforate, pierced with holes, or with transparent dots resembling holes, as an Orange-leaf.

Peri-, Greek for around; from which are such terms as

Perianth, the leaves of the flower collectively, 79.

Pericarp, the ripened ovary; the walls of the fruit, 117.

Pericarpic, belonging to the pericarp.

Perigonium, Perigone, same as *perianth*.

Perigynium, bodies around the pistil; applied to the closed cup or bottle-shaped body (of bracts) which encloses the ovary of Sedges, and to the bristles, little scales, &c., of the flowers of some other Cyperaceæ.

Perigynous, the petals and stamens borne on the calyx, 95, 99.

Peripheric, around the outside, or periphery, of any organ.

Perisperm, a name for the albumen of a seed.

Peristome, the fringe of teeth to the spore-case of Mosses, 163.

Persistent, remaining beyond the period when such parts commonly fall, as the leaves of evergreens, and the calyx of such flowers as persist during the growth of the fruit.

[Pg 216]

Personate, masked; a bilabiate corolla with a *palate* in the throat, 92.

Pertuse, perforated with a hole or slit.

Perulate, having scales (*Perulæ*), such as bud-scales.

Pes, pedis, Latin for the foot or support, whence *Longipes*, long-stalked, &c.

Petal, a leaf of the corolla, 14, 79.

Petalody, metamorphosis of stamens, &c., into petals.

Petaloid, Petaline, petal-like; resembling or colored like petals.

Petiole, a footstalk of a leaf; a leaf-stalk, 49.

Petioled, Petiolate, furnished with a petiole.

Petiolulate, said of a leaflet when raised on its own partial leaf-stalk.

Petræus, Latin for growing on rocks.

Phalanx, phalanges, bundles of stamens.

Phænogamous, or *Phanerogamous*, plants bearing flowers and producing seeds; same as Flowering Plants. *Phænogams, Phanerogams*, 10.

Phlæum, Greek name for bark, whence *Endophlæum*, inner bark, &c.

Phœniceous, deep red verging to scarlet.

Phycology, the botany of Algæ.

Phyllocladia, branches assuming the form and function of leaves.

Phyllodium (plural, *phyllodia*), a leaf where the seeming blade is a dilated petiole, as in New Holland Acacias, 61.

Phyllome, foliar parts, those answering to leaves in their nature.

Phyllon (plural, *phylla*), Greek for leaf and leaves; used in many compound terms and names.

Phyllotaxis, or *Phyllotaxy*, the arrangement of leaves on the stem, 67.

Physiological Botany, 9.

Phytography, relates to characterizing and describing plants.

Phyton, or *Phytomer*, a name used to designate the pieces which by their repetition make up a plant, theoretically, viz. a joint of stem with its leaf or pair of leaves.

Pileus of a mushroom, 172.

Piliferous, bearing a slender bristle or hair (*pilum*), or beset with hairs.

Pilose, hairy; clothed with soft slender hairs.

Pinna, a primary division with its leaflets of a bipinnate or tripinnate leaf.

Pinnule, a secondary division of a bipinnate or tripinnate leaf, 66.

Pinnate (leaf), when leaflets are arranged along the sides of a common petiole, 57.

Pinnately lobed, cleft, parted, divided, veined, 56.

Pinnatifid, Pinnatisect, same as pinnately cleft and pinnately parted, 56.

Pisiform, pea-shaped.

Pistil, the seed-bearing organ of the flower, 14, 80, 105.

Pistillate, having a pistil, 85.

Pistillidium, the body which in Mosses answers to the pistil, 159, 164.

Pitchers, 64.

Pith, the cellular centre of an exogenous stem, 138.

Placenta, the surface or part of the ovary to which the ovules are attached, 107.

Placentiform, nearly same as quoit-shaped.

Plaited (in the bud), or *Plicate*, folded, 72, 98.

Platy-, Greek for broad, in compounds, such as *Platyphyllous*, broad-leaved, &c.

Pleio-, Greek for full or abounding, used in compounds, such as *Pleiopetalous*, of many petals, &c.

Plumbeus, lead-colored.

Plumose, feathery; when any slender body (such as a bristle of a pappus or a style) is beset with hairs along its sides, like the plume of a feather.

Plumule, the bud or first shoot of a germinating plantlet above the cotyledons, 13.

Pluri-, in composition, many or several; as *Plurifoliolate*, with several leaflets.

Pod, specially a legume, 122; also may be applied to any sort of capsule.

Podium, a footstalk or stipe, used only in Greek compounds, as (suffixed) *Leptopodus*, slender-stalked, or (prefixed) *Podocephalus*, with a stalked head, and in*Podosperm*, a seed stalk or funiculus.

Pogon, Greek for beard, comes into various compounds.

[Pg 217]

Pointless, destitute of any pointed tip, such as a *mucro, awn, acumination*, &c.

Pollen, the fertilizing powder contained in the anther, 14, 80, 103.

Pollen-growth, 117. *Polleniferous*, pollen-bearing.

Pollen-mass, *Pollinium*, the united mass of pollen, 104, as in Milkweed and Orchis.

Pollicaris, Latin for an inch long.

Pollination, the application of pollen to the stigma, 114.

Poly-, in compound words of Greek origin, same as *multi-* in those of Latin origin viz. many, as

Polyadelphous, stamens united by their filaments into several bundles, 100.

Polyandrous, with numerous stamens (inserted on the receptacle), 100.

Polycarpic, term used by DeCandolle in the sense of perennial.

Polycotyledonous, having many (more than two) cotyledons, as Pines, 23.

Polygamous, having some perfect and some unisexual flowers, 85.

Polygonal, many-angled.

Polygynous, with many pistils or styles, 105.

Polymerous, formed of many parts of each set.

Polymorphous, of several or varying forms.

Polypetalous, when the petals are distinct or separate (whether few or many), 89.

Polyphyllous, many-leaved; formed of several distinct pieces.

Polysepalous, same as the last when applied to the calyx, 89.

Polyspermous, many-seeded.

Pome, the apple, pear, and similar fleshy fruits, 119.

Pomiferous, pome-bearing.

Porrect, outstretched.

Posterior side or portion of a flower (when axillary) is that toward the axis, 96.

Pouch, the silicle or short pod, as of Shepherd's Purse, 123.

Præcocious (Latin, *præcox*), unusually early in development.

Præfloration, same as *æstivation*, 97.

Præfoliation, same as *vernation*, 71.

Præmorse, ending abruptly, as if bitten off.

Pratensis, Latin for growing in meadows.

Prickles, sharp elevations of the bark, coming off with it, as of the Rose.

Prickly, bearing prickles, or sharp projections like them.

Primine, the outer coat of the covering of the ovule, 110.

Primordial, earliest formed; primordial leaves are the first after the cotyledons.

Prismatic, prism-shaped; having three or more angles bounding flat sides.

Procerous, tall, or tall and slim.

Process, any projection from the surface or edge of a body.

Procumbent, trailing on the ground, 39.

Procurrent, running through but not projecting.

Produced, extended or projecting; the upper sepal of a Larkspur is *produced* above into a spur, 87.

Proliferous (literally, bearing offspring), where a new branch rises from an older one, or one head or cluster of flowers out of another.

Propaculum or *Propagulum*, a shoot for propagation.

Prosenchyma, a tissue of wood-cells.

Prostrate, lying flat on the ground, 39.

Protandrous or *Proterandrous*, the anthers first maturing, 116.

Proteranthous, flowering before leafing.

Proterogynous or *Protogynous*, the stigmas first to mature, 116.

Prothallium or *Prothallus*, 160.

Protoplasm, the soft nitrogenous lining or contents, or living part, of cells, 129.

Protos, Greek for first; in various compounds.

Pruinose, Pruinate, frosted; covered with a powder like hoar-frost.

Pseudo-, Greek for false. *Pseudo-bulb,* the aerial corms of epiphytic Orchids, &c.

Psilos, Greek for bare or naked, used in many compounds.

Pteridophyta, Pteridophytes, 156.

Pteris, Greek for wing, and general name for Fern, enters into many compounds.

[Pg 218]

Puberulent, covered with fine and short or almost imperceptible down.

Pubescent, hairy or downy, especially with fine and soft hairs or *pubescence.*

Pulverulent or *Pulveraceous,* as if dusted with fine powder.

Pulvinate, cushioned, or shaped like a cushion.

Pumilus, low or little.

Punctate, dotted, either with minute holes or what look as such.

Puncticulate, minutely punctate.

Pungent, prickly-tipped.

Puniceous, carmine-red.

Purpureus, originally red or crimson, more used for duller or bluish-red.

Pusillus, weak and small, tiny.

Putamen, the stone of a drupe, or the shell of a nut, 120.

Pygmæus, Latin for dwarf.

Pyramidal, shaped like a pyramid.

Pyrene, Pyrena, a seed-like nutlet or stone of a small drupe.

Pyriform, pear-shaped.

Pyxidate, furnished with a lid.

Pyxis, Pyxidium, a pod opening round horizontally by a lid, 124.

Quadri-, in words of Latin origin, four; as *Quadrangular,* four-angled; *Quadrifoliate,* four-leaved; *Quadrifid,* four-cleft. *Quaternate* in fours.

Quinate, in fives. *Quinque,* five.

Quincuncial, in a quincunx; when the parts in æstivation are five, two of them outside, two inside, and one half out and half in.

Quintuple, five-fold.

Race, a marked variety which may be perpetuated from seed, 176.

Raceme, a flower-cluster, with one-flowered pedicels arranged along the sides of a general peduncle, 73.

Racemose, bearing racemes, or raceme-like.

Rachis, see *rhachis.*

Radial, belonging to the ray.

Radiate, or *Radiant,* furnished with ray-flowers, 94.

Radiate-veined, 52.

Radical, belonging to the root, or apparently coming from the root.

Radicant, rooting, taking root on or above the ground.

Radicels, little roots or rootlets.

Radicle, the stem part of the embryo, the lower end of which forms the root, 11, 127.

Rameal, belonging to a branch. *Ramose,* full of branches (*rami*).

Ramentaceous, beset with thin chaffy scales (*Ramenta*), as the stalks of many Ferns.

Ramification, branching, 27.

Ramulose, full of branchlets (*ramuli*).

Raphe, see *rhaphe.*

Ray, parts diverging from a centre, the marginal flowers of a head (as of Coreopsis, 94), or cluster, as of Hydrangea (78), when different from the rest, especially when ligulate and diverging (like rays or sunbeams); also the branches of an umbel, 74.

Ray-flowers, 94.

Receptacle, the axis or support of a flower, 81, 112; also the common axis or support of a head of flowers, 73.

Reclined, turned or curved downwards; nearly recumbent.

Rectinerved, with straight nerves or veins.

Recurved, curved outwards or backwards.

Reduplicate (in æstivation), valvate with the margins turned outwards, 97.

Reflexed, bent outwards or backwards.

Refracted, bent suddenly, so as to appear broken at the bend.

Regular, all the parts similar in shape, 82.

Reniform, kidney-shaped, 53.

[Pg 219]

Repand, wavy-margined, 55.

Repent, creeping, i. e. prostrate and rooting underneath.

Replum, the frame of some pods (as of Prickly Poppy and Cress), persistent after the valves fall away.

Reptant, same as repent.

Resupinate, inverted, or appearing as if upside down, or reversed.

Reticulated, the veins forming network, 50. *Retiform*, in network.

Retinerved, reticulate-veined.

Retroflexed, bent backwards; same as *reflexed*.

Retuse, blunted; the apex not only obtuse but somewhat indented, 54.

Revolute, rolled backwards, as the margins of many leaves, 72.

Rhachis (the backbone), the axis of a spike or other body, 73.

Rhaphe, the continuation of the seed-stalk along the side of an anatropous ovule or seed, 112, 126.

Rhaphides, crystals, especially needle-shaped ones, in the tissues of plants, 137.

Rhizanthous, flowering from the root.

Rhizoma, Rhizome, a rootstock, 42-44.

Rhombic, in the shape of a rhomb. *Rhomboidal*, approaching that shape.

Rib, the principal piece, or one of the principal pieces of the framework of a leaf, or any similar elevated line along a body, 49, 50.

Rimose, having chinks or cracks.

Ring, an elastic band on the spore-cases of Ferns, 159.

Ringent, grinning; gaping open, 92.

Riparious, on river-banks.

Rivalis, Latin for growing along brooks; or *Rivularis*, in rivulets.

Root, 33.

Root-hairs, 35.

Rootlets, small roots, or root-branches, 33.

Rootstock, root-like trunks or portions of stems on or under ground, 42.

Roridus, dewy.

Rosaceous, arranged like the petals of a rose.

Rostellate, bearing a small beak (*Rostellum*).

Rostrate, bearing a beak (*Rostrum*) or a prolonged appendage.

Rosulate, in a rosette or cluster of spreading leaves.

Rotate, wheel-shaped, 89.

Rotund, rounded or roundish in outline.

Ruber, Latin for red in general. *Rubescent, Rubicund*, reddish or blushing.

Rudimentary, imperfectly developed, or in an early state of development.

Rufous, Rufescent, brownish-red or reddish-brown.

Rugose, wrinkled; roughened with wrinkles.

Ruminated (albumen), penetrated with irregular channels or portions, as a nutmeg, looking as if chewed.

Runcinate, coarsely saw-toothed or cut, the pointed teeth turned towards the base of the leaf, as the leaf of a Dandelion.

Runner, a slender and prostrate branch, rooting at the end, or at the joints, 40.

Sabulose, growing in sand.

Sac, any closed membrane, or a deep purse-shaped cavity.

Saccate, sac-shaped.

Sagittate, arrowhead-shaped, 53.

Salsuginous, growing in brackish soil.

Salver-shaped, or *Salver-form*, with a border spreading at right angles to a slender tube, 89.

Samara, a wing-fruit, or key, 122.

Samaroid, like a samara or key-fruit.

Sap, the juices of plants generally, 136. *Sapwood*, 142.

Saprophytes, 37.

Sarcocarp, the fleshy part of a stone-fruit, 120.

[Pg 220]

Sarmentaceous, Sarmentose, bearing long and flexible twigs (*Sarments*), either spreading or procumbent.

Saw-toothed, see serrate, 55.

Scabrous, rough or harsh to the touch.

Scalariform, with cross-bands, resembling the steps of a ladder, 134.

Scales, of buds, 28; of bulbs, &c., 46.

Scalloped, same as *crenate*, 55.

Scaly, furnished with scales, or scale-like in texture.

Scandent, climbing, 39.

Scape, a peduncle rising from the ground or near it, as in many Violets.

Scapiform, scape-like.

Scapigerous, scape-bearing.

Scar of the seed, 126. *Leaf-scars*, 27, 28.

Scarious or *Scariose*, thin, dry, and membranous.

Scion, a shoot or slip used for grafting.

Scleros, Greek for hard, hence *Sclerocarpous*, hard-fruited.

Scobiform, resembling sawdust.

Scorpioid or *Scorpioidal*, curved or circinate at the end, 77.

Scrobiculate, pitted; excavated into shallow pits.

Scurf, Scurfiness, minute scales on the surface of many leaves, as of Goosefoot.

Scutate, Scutiform, buckler-shaped.

Scutellate, or *Scutelliform*, saucer-shaped or platter-shaped.

Secund, one-sided; i. e. where flowers, leaves, &c., are all turned to one side.

Secundine, the inner coat of the ovule, 110.

Seed, 125. *Seed-leaves*, see *cotyledons*. *Seed-vessel*, 127.

Segment, a subdivision or lobe of any cleft body.

Segregate, separated from each other.

Semi-, in compound words of Latin origin, half; as

Semi-adherent, as the calyx or ovary of Purslane; *Semicordate*, half-heart-shaped; *Semilunar*, like a half-moon; *Semiovate*, half-ovate, &c.

Seminal, relating to the seed (*Semen*). *Seminiferous*, seed-bearing.

Sempervirent, evergreen.

Sensitiveness in plants, 149, 152.

Senary, in sixes.

Sepal, a leaf or division of the calyx, 14, 79.

Sepaloid, sepal-like. *Sepaline*, relating to the sepals.

Separated Flowers, those having stamens or pistils only, 85.

Septate, divided by partitions.

Septenate, with parts in sevens.

Septicidal, where dehiscence is through the partitions, 123.

Septiferous, bearing the partition.

Septifragal, where the valves in dehiscence break away from the partitions, 123.

Septum (plural *septa*), a partition or dissepiment.

Serial, or *Seriate*, in rows; as *biserial*, in two rows, &c.

Sericeous, silky; clothed with satiny pubescence.

Serotinous, late in the season.

Serrate, the margin cut into teeth (*Serratures*) pointing forwards, 55.

Serrulate, same as the last, but with fine teeth.

Sessile, sitting; without any stalk.

Sesqui-, Latin for one and a half; so *Sesquipedalis*, a foot and a half long.

Seta, a bristle, or a slender body or appendage resembling a bristle.

Setaceous, bristle-like. *Setiform*, bristle-shaped.

Setigerous, bearing bristles. *Setose*, beset with bristles or bristly hairs.

Setula, a diminutive bristle. *Setulose*, provided with such.

Sex, six. *Sexangular*, six-angled. *Sexfarious*, six-faced.

Sheath, the base of such leaves as those of Grasses, which are

Sheathing, wrapped round the stem.

Shield-shaped, same as *scutate*, or as *peltate*, 53.

[Pg 221]

Shrub, Shrubby, 39.

Sieve-cells, 140.

Sigmoid, curved in two directions, like the letter S, or the Greek *sigma*.

Silicle, a pouch, or short pod of the Cress Family, 123.

Siliculose, bearing a silicle, or a fruit resembling it.

Silique, capsule of the Cress Family, 123.

Siliquose, bearing siliques or pods which resemble siliques.

Silky, glossy with a coat of fine and soft, close-pressed, straight hairs.

Silver-grain, the medullary rays of wood, 139.

Silvery, shining white or bluish-gray, usually from a silky pubescence.

Simple, of one piece; opposed to *compound*.

Sinistrorse, turned to the left.

Sinuate, with margin alternately bowed inwards and outwards, 55.

Sinus, a recess or bay; the re-entering angle between two lobes or projections.

Sleep of Plants (so called), 151.

Smooth, properly speaking not rough, but often used for glabrous, i. e. not pubescent.

Soboliferous, bearing shoots (*Soboles*) from near the ground.

Solitary, single; not associated with others.

Sordid, dull or dirty in hue.

Sorediate, bearing patches on the surface.

Sorosis, name of a multiple fruit, like a pine-apple.

Sorus, a fruit-dot of Ferns, 159.

Spadiceous, chestnut-colored. Also spadix-bearing.

Spadix, a fleshy spike of flowers, 75.

Span, the distance between the tip of the thumb and of little finger outstretched, six or seven inches.

Spathaceous, resembling or furnished with a

Spathe, a bract which inwraps an inflorescence, 75.

Spatulate, or *Spathulate*, shaped like a spatula, 52.

Species, 175.

Specific Names, 179.

Specimens, 184.

Spermaphore, or *Spermophore*, one of the names of the placenta.

Spermum, Latin form of Greek word for seed; much used in composition.

Spica, Latin for spike; hence *Spicate*, in a spike, *Spiciform*, in shape resembling a spike.

Spike, an inflorescence like a raceme, only the flowers are sessile, 74.

Spikelet, a small or a secondary spike; the inflorescence of Grasses.

Spine, 41, 64.

Spindle-shaped, tapering to each end, like a radish, 36.

Spinescent, tipped by or degenerating into a thorn.

Spinose, or *Spiniferous*, thorny.

Spiral Vessels or *ducts*, 135.

Spithameous, span-high.

Spora, Greek name for seed, used in compound words.

Sporadic, widely dispersed.

Sporangium, a spore-case in Ferns, &c., 158.

Spore, a body resulting from the fructification of Cryptogamous plants, in them the analogue of a seed.

Spore-case (*Sporangium*), 158.

Sporocarp, 162.

Sport, a newly appeared variation, 176.

Sporule, same as a spore, or a small spore.

Spumescent, appearing like froth.

Spur, any projecting appendage of the flower, looking like a spur but hollow, as that of Larkspur, fig. 239.

Squamate, Squamose, or *Squamaceous*, furnished with scales (*squamæ*).

[Pg 222]

Squamellate, or *Squamulose*, furnished with little scales (*Squamellæ*, or *Squamulæ*).

Squamiform, shaped like a scale.

Squarrose, where scales, leaves, or any appendages spread widely from the axis on which they are thickly set.

Squarrulose, diminutive of *squarrose*; slightly squarrose.

Stachys, Greek for spike.

Stalk, the stem, petiole, peduncle, &c., as the case may be.

Stamen, 14, 80, 98.

Staminate, furnished with stamens, 86. *Stamineal*, relating to the stamens.

Staminodium, an abortive stamen, or other body in place of a stamem.

Standard, the upper petal of a papilionaceous corolla, 92.

Starch, 136, 163.

Station, the particular kind of situation in which a plant naturally occurs.

Stellate, *Stellular*, starry or star-like; where several similar parts spread out from a common centre, like a star.

Stem, 39. *Stemlet*, diminutive stem.

Stemless, destitute or apparently destitute of stem.

Stenos, Greek for narrow; hence *Stenophyllous*, narrow-leaved, &c.

Sterile, barren or imperfect.

Stigma, the part of the pistil which receives the pollen, 14, 80, 105.

Stigmatic, or *Stigmatose*, belonging to the stigma.

Stipe (Latin *Stipes*), the stalk of a pistil, &c., when it has any, 112; also of a Fern, 158, and of a Mushroom, 172.

Stipel, a stipule of a leaflet, as of the Bean, &c.

Stipellate, furnished with stipels, as in the Bean tribe.

Stipitate, furnished with a stipe.

Stipulaceous, belonging to stipules. *Stipulate*, furnished with stipules.

Stipules, the appendages on each side of the base of certain leaves, 66.

Stirps (plural, *stirpes*), Latin for race.

Stock, used for race or source. Also for any root-like base from which the herb grows up.

Stole, or *Stolon*, a trailing or reclined and rooting shoot, 40.

Stoloniferous, producing stolons.

Stomate (Latin *Stoma*, plural *Stomata*), the breathing-pores of leaves, 144.

Stone-fruit, 119.

Storage-leaves, 62.

Stramineous, straw-like, or straw-colored.

Strap-shaped, long, flat, and narrow.

Striate, or *Striated*, marked with slender longitudinal grooves or stripes.

Strict, close and narrow; straight and narrow.

Strigillose, *Strigose*, beset with stout and appressed, stiff or rigid bristles.

Strobilaceous, relating to or resembling a

Strobile, a multiple fruit in the form of a cone or head, 124.

Strombuliform, twisted, like a spiral shell.

Strophiole, same as *caruncle*, 126. *Strophiolate*, furnished with a strophiole.

Struma, a wen; a swelling or protuberance of any organ.

Strumose, bearing a struma.

Stupose, like tow.

Style, a stalk between ovary and stigma, 14, 80, 105.

Styliferous, *Stylose*, bearing styles or conspicuous ones.

Stylopodium, an epigynous disk, or an enlargement at the base of the style.

Sub-, as a prefix, about, nearly, somewhat; as *Subcordate*, slightly cordate; *Subserrate*, slightly serrate; *Subaxillary*, just beneath the axil, &c.

Subclass, *Suborder*, *Subtribe*, 178.

Suberose, corky or cork-like in texture.

Subulate, awl-shaped; tapering from a broadish or thickish base to a sharp point.

Succise, as if cut off at lower end.

Succubous, when crowded leaves are each covered by base of next above.

[Pg 223]

Suckers, shoots from subterranean branches, 39.

Suffrutescent, slightly shrubby or woody at the base only, 39.

Suffruticose, rather more than suffrutescent, 37, 39.

Sulcate, grooved longitudinally with deep furrows.

Superior, above, 96; sometimes equivalent to posterior, 96.

Supernumerary Buds, 30, 31.

Supervolute, plaited and convolute in bud, 97.

Supine, lying flat, with face upward.

Supra-axillary, borne above the axil, as some buds, 31.

Supra-decompound, many times compounded or divided.

Surculose, producing suckers (*Surculi*) or shoots resembling them.

Suspended, hanging down. Suspended ovules or seeds hang from the very summit of the cell which contains them.

Sutural, belonging or relating to a suture.

Suture, the line of junction of contiguous parts grown together, 106.

Sword-shaped, applied to narrow leaves, with acute parallel edges, tapering above.

Syconium, the fig-fruit, 124.

Sylvestrine, growing in woods.

Symmetrical Flower, similar in the number of parts of each set, 82.

Sympetalous, same as gamopetalous.

Sympode, Sympodium, a stem composed of a series of superposed branches in such a way as to imitate a simple axis, as in Grape-vine.

Synantherous or *Syngenesious,* where stamens are united by their anthers, 100.

Syncarpous (fruit or pistil), composed of several carpels consolidated into one.

Synonym, an equivalent superseded name.

Synsepalous, same as gamosepalous.

System (artificial and natural), 182, 183.

Systematic Botany, the study of plants after their kinds, 9.

Tabescent, wasting or shrivelling.

Tail, any long and slender prolongation of an organ.

Taper-pointed, same as acuminate, 54.

Tap-root, a root with a stout tapering body, 32-35.

Tawny, dull yellowish, with a tinge of brown.

Taxonomy, the part of botany which treats of classification.

Tegmen, a name for the inner seed-coat.

Tendril, a thread-shaped organ used for climbing, 40.

Terete, long and round; same as *cylindrical,* only it may taper.

Terminal, borne at, or belonging to, the extremity or summit.

Terminology treats of technical terms; same as *Glossology,* 181.

Ternate, Ternately, in threes.

Tessellate, in checker-work.

Testa, the outer (and usually the harder) coat or shell of the seed, 125.

Testaceous, the color of unglazed pottery.

Tetra- (in words of Greek composition), four; as, *Tetracoccous,* of four cocci.

Tetradynamous, where a flower has six stamens, two shorter than the four, 101.

Tetragonal, four-angled. *Tetragynous,* with four pistils or styles. *Tetramerous,* with its parts or sets in fours. *Tetrandrous,* with four stamens, 100.

Tetraspore, a quadruple spore, 169.

Thalamaflorous, with petals and stamens inserted on the torus or *Thalamus.*

Thallophyta, Thallophytes, 165.

Thallus, a stratum, in place of stem and leaves, 165.

Theca, a case; the cells or lobes of the anther.

Thecaphore, the stipe of a carpel, 113.

Thorn, an indurated pointed branch, 41, 42.

Thread-shaped, slender and round or roundish, like a thread.

Throat, the opening or gorge of a monopetalous corolla, &c., where the border and the tube join, and a little below, 89.

[Pg 224]

Thyrse or *Thyrsus,* a compact and pyramidal panicle of cymes or cymules, 79.

Tomentose, clothed with matted woolly hairs (*tomentum*).

Tongue-shaped, long and flat, but thickish and blunt.

Toothed, furnished with teeth or short projections of any sort on the margin; used especially when these are sharp, like saw-teeth, and do not point forwards, 55.

Top-shaped, shaped like a top, or a cone with apex downwards.

Torose, Torulose, knobby; where a cylindrical body is swollen at intervals.

Torus, the receptacle of the flower, 81, 112.

Trachea, a spiral duct.

Trachys, Greek for rough; used in compounds, as, *Trachyspermous,* rough-seeded.

Transverse, across, standing right and left instead of fore and aft.

Tri- (in composition), three; as,

Triadelphous, stamens united by their filaments into three bundles, 99.

Triandrous, where the flower has three stamens, 112.

Tribe, 178.

Trichome, of the nature of hair or pubescence.

Trichotomous, three-forked.

Tricoccous, of three cocci or roundish carpels.

Tricolor, having three colors.

116

Tricostate, having three ribs.

Tricuspidate, three-pointed.

Tridentate, three-toothed.

Triennial, lasting for three years.

Trifarious, in three vertical rows; looking three ways.

Trifid, three-cleft, 56.

Trifoliate, three-leaved. *Trifoliolate*, of three leaflets.

Trifurcate, three-forked.

Trigonous, three-angled, or triangular.

Trigynous, with three pistils or styles, 116.

Trijugate, in three pairs (*jugi*).

Trilobed or *Trilobate*, three-lobed, 55.

Trilocular, three-celled, as the pistils or pods in fig. 328-330.

Trimerous, with its parts in threes.

Trimorphism, 117. *Trimorphic* or *Trimorphous*, in three forms.

Trinervate, three-nerved, or with three slender ribs.

Triœcious, where there are three sorts of flowers on the same or different individuals, as in Red Maple. A form of Polygamous.

Tripartible, separable into three pieces. *Tripartite*, three-parted, 55.

Tripetalous, having three petals.

Triphyllous, three-leaved; composed of three pieces.

Tripinnate, thrice pinnate, 59. *Tripinnatifid*, thrice pinnately cleft, 57.

Triple-ribbed, *Triple-nerved*, &c., where a midrib branches into three, near the base of the leaf.

Triquetrous, sharply three-angled; and especially with the sides concave, like a bayonet.

Triserial, or *Triseriate*, in three rows, under each other.

Tristichous, in three longitudinal or perpendicular ranks.

Tristigmatic, or *Tristigmatose*, having three stigmas.

Trisulcate, three-grooved.

Triternate, three times ternate, 59.

Trivial Name, the specific name.

Trochlear, pulley-shaped.

Trumpet-shaped, tubular; enlarged at or towards the summit.

Truncate, as if cut off at the top.

Trunk, the main stem or general body of a stem or tree.

Tube (of corolla, &c.), 89.

Tuber, a thickened portion of a subterranean stem or branch, provided with eyes (buds) on the sides, 44.

Tubercle, a small excrescence.

Tubercled, or *Tuberculate*, bearing excrescences or pimples.

Tubæform, trumpet-shaped.

Tuberous, resembling a tuber. *Tuberiferous*, bearing tubers.

Tubular, hollow and of an elongated form; hollowed like a pipe, 91.

[Pg 225]

Tubuliflorous, bearing only tubular flowers.

Tunicate, coated; invested with layers, as an onion, 46.

Turbinate, top-shaped.

Turio (plural *turiones*), strong young shoots or suckers springing out of the ground; as Asparagus-shoots.

Turnip-shaped, broader than high, abruptly narrowed below, 35.

Twining, ascending by coiling round a support, 39.

Type, the ideal pattern, 10.

Typical, well exemplifying the characteristics of a species, genus, &c.

Uliginose, growing in swamps.

Umbel, the umbrella-like form of inflorescence, 74.

Umbellate, in umbels. *Umbelliferous*, bearing umbels.

Umbellet (*umbellula*), a secondary or partial umbel, 76.

Umbilicate, depressed in the centre, like the ends of an apple; with a navel.

Umbonate, bossed; furnished with a low, rounded projection like a boss (*umbo*).

Umbraculiform, umbrella-shaped.

Unarmed, destitute of spines, prickles, and the like.

Uncial, an inch (*uncia*) in length.

Uncinate, or *Uncate*, hook-shaped; hooked over at the end.

Under-shrub, partially shrubby, or a very low shrub.

Undulate or *Undate*, wavy, or wavy-margined, 55.

Unequally pinnate, pinnate with an odd number of leaflets, 65.

Unguiculate, furnished with a claw (*unguis*), 91.

Uni-, in compound words, one; as *Unicellular*, one-celled.

Uniflorous, one-flowered.

Unifoliate, one-leaved. *Unifoliolate*, of one leaflet, 59.

Unijugate, of one pair.

Unilabiate, one-lipped.

Unilateral, one-sided.

Unilocular, one-celled.

Uniovulate, having only one ovule.

Uniserial, in one horizontal row.

Unisexual, having stamens or pistils only, 85.

Univalved, a pod of only one piece after dehiscence.

Unsymmetrical Flowers, 86.

Urceolate, urn-shaped.

Utricle, a small thin-walled, one-seeded fruit, as of Goosefoot, 121.

Utricular, like a small bladder.

Vaginate, sheathed, surrounded by a sheath (*vagina*).

Valve, one of the pieces (or doors) into which a dehiscent pod, or any similar body, splits, 122, 123.

Valvate, *Valvular*, opening by valves. *Valvate*, in æstivation, 97.

Variety, 176.

Vascular, containing vessels, or consisting of vessels or ducts, 134.

Vascular Cryptogams, 156.

Vaulted, arched; same as *fornicate*.

Vegetable Life, &c., 128. *Vegetable anatomy*, 129.

Veins, the small ribs or branches of the framework of leaves, &c., 49, 50.

Veined, *Veiny*, furnished with evident veins. *Veinless*, destitute of veins.

Veinlets, the smaller ramifications of veins, 50.

Velate, furnished with a veil.

Velutinous, velvety to the touch.

Venation, the veining of leaves, &c., 50.

Venenate, poisonous.

Venose, veiny; furnished with conspicuous veins.

Ventral, belonging to that side of a simple pistil, or other organ, which looks towards the axis or centre of the flower; the opposite of dorsal; as the *Ventral Suture*, 106.

Ventricose, inflated or swelled out on one side.

[Pg 226]

Venulose, furnished with veinlets.

Vermicular, worm-like, shaped like worms.

Vernal, belonging to spring.

Vernation, the arrangement of the leaves in the bud, 71.

Vernicose, the surface appearing as if varnished.

Verrucose, warty; beset with little projections like warts.

Versatile, attached by one point, so that it may swing to and fro, 101.

Vertex, same as *apex*.

Vertical, upright, perpendicular to the horizon, lengthwise.

Verticil, a whorl, 68. *Verticillate*, whorled, 68.

Verticillaster, a false whorl, formed of a pair of opposite cymes.

Vesicular, bladdery.

Vespertine, appearing or expanding at evening.

Vessels, ducts, &c., 134.

Vexillary, *Vexillar*, relating to the

Vexillum, the standard of a papilionaceous flower, 92.

Villose, shaggy with long and soft hairs (*Villosity*).

Vimineous, producing slender twigs, such as those used for wicker-work.

Vine, in the American use, any trailing or climbing stem; as a Grape-vine.

Virescent, *Viridescent*, greenish; turning green.

Virgate, wand-shape; as a long, straight, and slender twig.

Viscous, Viscid, having a glutinous surface.

Vitta (plural *vittæ*), the oil-tubes of the fruit of Umbelliferæ.

Vitelline, yellow, of the hue of yolk of egg.

Viviparous, sprouting or germinating while attached to the parent plant.

Voluble, twining; as the stem of Hops and Beans, 39.

Volute, rolled up in any way.

Wavy, the surface or margin alternately convex and concave, 55.

Waxy, resembling beeswax in texture or appearance.

Wedge-shaped, broad above, tapering by straight lines to a narrow base, 53.

Wheel-shaped, 89.

Whorl, an arrangement of leaves, &c., in circles around the stem.

Whorled, arranged in whorls, 68.

Wing, any membranous expansion. *Wings* of papilionaceous flowers, 92.

Winged, furnished with a wing; as the fruit of Ash and Elm, fig. 300, 301.

Wood, 133, 142. *Woody*, of the texture or consisting of wood.

Woody Fibre, or *Wood-Cells*, 134.

Woolly, clothed with long and entangled soft hairs.

Work in plants, 149, 155.

Xanthos, Greek for yellow, used in compounds; as *Xanthocarpus*, yellow-fruited.

Zygomorphous, said of a flower which can be bisected only in one plane into similar halves.